Altman on Altman

by the same author

in the same series

Altman on Altman

Edited by David Thompson

FARRAR, STRAUS AND GIROUX

NEW YORK

First published in 2006
by Faber and Faber Limited
120 Broadway, New York 10271

Published in the United States by
Farrar, Straus and Giroux

Typeset by RefineCatch Limited, Bungay, Suffolk

A CIP record for this book
is available from the British Library

ISBN 0-571-22089-4
978-0-571-22089-2

www.fsgbooks.com

Contents

Contents

List of Illustrations

List of Illustrations

Acknowledgements

This book originally arose from two desires. One was for Robert Altman to join the illustrious group of film directors – beginning with Martin Scorsese in 1989 – who have now given in print their own account of their careers in cinema. As ever, my warm gratitude is due to Walter Donohue for commissioning the series (to which I have previously contributed two books) and of course, this particular volume. I believe his patience has been rewarded. Thanks are also due to Richard T. Kelly for steering the book through its final stages.

The other was my own wish to continue my research and extend my contribution to celebrating the work of a great director about whom I was privileged to make a television documentary for the BBC's *Omnibus* series in 2002. It was called 'Robert Altman in England' and it covered his shooting of *Gosford Park*, as well as attempting a necessarily brief overview of his career. Two key people made this film possible, the *Omnibus* series editor, the ebullient Basil Comely, and the ever-patient producer of *Gosford Park*, David Levy, whose generous show of support and friendship towards me during the project far exceeded any expectations I had.

Next, my thanks are due to Robert Altman's wonderful team at the Sandcastle 5 office in New York; they have always made my visits there a pleasure. Wren Arthur has been extremely helpful and encouraging even while deluged with copious amounts of other work. Lowell Dubrinsky kept me supplied with videotapes of some of the harder-to-find Altmania, and Tim McDowell buried into the Altman archive to find some rare photographic treats. Josh Astrachan, who helped greatly on the *Omnibus* film, has also been very supportive to me.

Although the larger part of this book is based on Altman's conversations with me that took place in New York, it was supplemented by an interview filmed for *Omnibus*, as well as two on-stage events in London. My thanks are due to Robert Rider and Beverly Silverstone at the Barbican Centre and Iwona Blaswick at the Whitechapel Gallery for supplying me with audiotapes of these occasions and granting permission for their use. My gratitude is also due to Roger Crittenden of the National Film and Television School in Beaconsfield, where Altman's talk to students in June 2001 provided some extra material. That event was chaired by Gavin Millar, whose championship of Altman, especially on BBC's *Arena Cinema* series in the 1970s, was a great inspiration to me.

I cannot say enough in praise of the great work done by the Criterion Collection in their DVD releases of Altman films, which have not only been exceptional in quality but invaluable in providing commentaries by the director and supporting interviews. They have been very kind in allowing me to use some of this material from their releases of *3 Women*, *Secret Honor*, *The Player* and *Short Cuts*. Special thanks for this are due to Peter Becker and his team, including my great ally and friend Karen Stetler.

Altman has been fortunate in recent times in having his films released on DVD in fine transfers and in the correct screen ratio. I believe much of his work can now be properly appreciated even on the small screen, where it previously suffered from the dreaded 'pan and scan' of the Cinemascope (anamorphic) image so favoured by the director. I was also aided in the creation of this book by two recent major seasons of Altman's films, one in New York at Film Forum (where the ever-resourceful programmer Bruce Goldstein kindly gave me a private screening of *Images* in a beautiful new print), the other a complete retrospective at London's National Film Theatre, programmed by Geoff Andrew. Geoff is one of my oldest friends, and from the beginning of that friendship we have spent many occasions hunting out Altman films and debating their qualities. I am sure he is even unconsciously a large part of this book.

I must also thank my special friends in New York who have supported me on this journey. Kate Hirson, editor extraordinaire and a damn fine cook too, very generously allowed me to stay in her warm Chelsea apartment during my visits to New York. Orapin Tantimedh has made my life richer, Kent Jones has helped improve my brain, and Gavin Smith, editor of the wonderful *Film Comment*, has been a keen supporter, as well as helping me with photographic materials. Graham Fuller, who himself previously nurtured the idea of a book on Altman, graciously gave his support and has become a good friend and ally. Bruce Ricker kindly sent me a video cassette of *Jazz '34*, as distributed by his unique company Rhapsody Films. The irrepressible Jane Klein of the Museum of Television and Radio enabled me to see some rare examples of the Altman television output.

Help in all sorts of ways has also come from John Baxter, Gilbert Adair, Cathy Meade, Patrick McGilligan, Mike Hodges, Mike Kaplan, Denise Breton and Joe d'Morais. I owe a huge debt to that supreme authority on all things Altman, Richard Dacre, who has supplied me with videotapes and stills, not to mention regular doses of encouragement. His sterling work with Tise Vahimagi at the British Film Institute in tracking down every piece of television known to carry Robert Altman's name in the credits has proved invaluable in the creation of the TV-ography in this book. I also spent many hours of research in the British Film Institute Library and would like to thank the very helpful staff there – long may it remain in operation.

Finally, most thanks are, of course, due to Robert Altman himself, who gave up his time to wander back along the byways of the past and put up with my persistent questioning when I am sure he would rather not have to supply all the answers but let the films speak for themselves. It was a pleasure witnessing him at work on the set, it was an equally great pleasure subsequently meeting with him and his wife Kathryn more informally, and it was a very special pleasure to become part of his office and see one of his films unfold in the editing process.

David Thompson
April 2005

David Thompson

Foreword

By Paul Thomas Anderson

It feels home-grown and handmade. There have been a hundred who have tried to be Robert Altman – or Altman-esque – but they miss that certain ingredient: they aren't him. There's no-one like him. He can be imitated and he can influence, but he's impossible to catch up with or cage – he's unpredictable, and the river he follows is his own. He's stubborn and giving and petulant and comforting, and he has the best smile a movie director has ever had. A man from Kansas City who fought in wars, who tattooed dogs, who wrote songs and punched producers. He puffed out his chest and had the formula for chicken-shit plastered on his motorcycle helmet.

You can't call too many film directors artists. But Bob is. Directors can be a nasty, malevolent little group, but when Bob's name comes up – everybody stops and changes their tune. Everyone respects Bob. Everybody stands down and looks up.

Watching his films as a fan, then later as an observer on his sets, one thing holds true: it's impossible to see where the conversation ends and the scene begins. It all feels like a dress rehearsal, and before there's too much time to think or second-guess, he's moved on. Say something once, why say it again? As he likes to say, 'Let's get to the verb.'

I watched Bob shoot a scene and he had a big wide smile on his face – and as the scene went on and on and on and the actors strayed from the script and got better and better, he turned and said, 'This is the way. Good disintegration.'

What if Robert Altman had to fill out a form and list his credits? It would look funny. It would probably look fake. How could one person be responsible for so many good films? Add to that, how could one person be responsible for so many truly *great* films? The work and all that goes into it is food and drink to him. I once told him I was going to Hawaii for a vacation and he looked at me like I was crazy. I asked him why he was looking at me like that and he said, 'I could never do that. Too far from the action.'

I've stolen from Bob as best I can. When I first began to really digest movies as something I wanted to try – the work that spoke to me most was his. The films, and the man that he is, have put a soft boot-print in my mind's eye that I cherish.

From his work, I began to realise that I didn't need any of the things I'd learned in the 'How to Make Movies Book'. There didn't have to be lessons or a moral to the story; things could drift in and out and stories could ramble and be more effective in glimpsing moments of truth rather than going for the touchdown. They could be long, they could be musicals without people singing, and they could be dirty and smart at the same time. Beginnings, middles and ends could all flow delicately together in any order, and weren't even *needed* to be a great film. Things could just happen without explanation or too much fanfare, and the results would take care of themselves. This has been Bob's great contribution: it doesn't have to be spelled out. If it's there and an audience wants to take something, they are free to. And we are lucky audiences because of it. Bob lets his mind wander and allows us to enjoy it. He's nice to us because he's good to his instinct. It's hard to find heroes in Bob's movies. Most of his characters are just folks trying to move along without too much fuss. Bob's films taught me to trust that the most interesting thing – the *only* interesting thing on screen – is the people.

His movies were the first I saw that took away preciousness. I could feel that the hands that made these films were not too polite. Bob has always needed only some celluloid and some sound to get the action moving and send the actors on their way – because that's where the verb is. So it was okay to be rough and spit-shine it, there was no need to polish and admire, because that would be lame and it would all just get in the way of the good time that making films can be.

I'm so happy to introduce this book. I feel honoured to be near Bob's side from time to time. I got my eyes and ears opened to a new way with his work. We all did. The old saying that 'There's nothing that hasn't been done' is true – as long as we agree that Bob did it first.

Paul Thomas Anderson
November 2005

Introduction

1 Altman at the Lion's Gate multi-track soundboard while filming *Nashville*
(1975)

Whenever Robert Altman is asked about his philosophy of film-making, his answer is usually along these lines:

It's the doing that's the important thing. I equate film-making with sandcastles. You get a bunch of mates together and go down to the beach and build a great sandcastle. You sit back and have a beer, the tide comes in, and in twenty minutes it's just smooth sand. That structure you made is in everybody's memories, and that's it. You all start walking home, and someone says, 'Are you going to come back next Saturday and build another one?' And another guy says, 'Well, OK, but I'll do moats this time, not turrets!' But that, for me, is the real joy of it all, that it's just fun, and nothing else.

Altman's sandcastle analogy – which has provided the name of his production company and office – has remained consistent throughout his career, one of the most extensive and adventurous to be found in the history of American cinema. He didn't begin as a studio tea boy or a precocious student but learned his craft by making what would now be called corporate films in a wholly commercial world that explained the rules and techniques of a sport or the need for better road safety. From this, he graduated to television; not to the brow-beating, socially conscious live drama that spawned Sidney Lumet and John Frankenheimer but, rather, to inside the factory, churning out popular series based around simple concepts, likeable character actors and solid genre situations. Little of this prepared the world for the battered visuals, explosive humour and 'fuck 'em' attitude of *M*A*S*H*, which shocked the industry above all for being made not by a bearded 'movie brat' but a seasoned player of forty-five years of age.

Throughout the 1970s, now so often lauded as that great decade when American cinema had brains, sensitivity and an adult attitude, Altman seemed unstoppable, exploding myths and genres and creating the all-encompassing ensemble film *par excellence* in *Nashville*. These were films that revealed a truer American history, suggested life did not have happy endings and defied all expectations. Even while working with the major studios, Altman held to his independence and went his way no matter what. By the time he had delivered *Popeye*, a seriously inventive children's musical (and one that, contrary to popular misconception, made money), his maverick persona was regarded as too dangerous for a system dominated by power-hungry executives and agents only hot for the post-*Jaws* blockbuster. But Altman was, as the song in *Nashville* told it, determined to 'Keep a' Goin' and found himself an unexpected niche in filming challenging stage plays, as well as practically inventing a new form in television, the mockumentary, in *Tanner '88*.

Then, with *Vincent & Theo*, a biopic with a difference, and the smart reflexive games of *The Player*, Altman proved himself as protean as ever, leading to another string of multitextured features that led from an epic of small lives, *Short Cuts*, to a deliciously sly take on the British period mystery thriller, *Gosford Park*. Typically, the latter was not so much a 'whodunnit?' as a 'who gives a damn whodunnit?', exploring character and texture from an entirely fresh and personal viewpoint. And all through this extraordinary catalogue, he went into each project in the hope that if the pleasure taken in the process paid off, then that was far preferable to failing to translate the perfect script into a perfect film. Just like mucking about on the beach, really.

Putting aside the sheer volume of his work, it is Altman's turning upside down of movie conventions – the constant throwing out of the rule book – that has made him such a commanding presence. Surviving the constraints of little time and money in delivering hours and hours of generic television series clearly showed him exactly what needed to be done, just so that he could later undo it. Once liberated from the standard demands of master shot and close-ups to be handed over to an unseen editor, Altman began to allow himself to roam free, drifting around a scene like a bloodhound following the scent, zooming almost casually on to significant details or simply making surprising connections. By putting separate microphones on his actors, he found that not only could the camera be distant from the action, removing the performer's need to be aware of its position, but that he could also mix the sound to catch one conversation while filtering out another. All this contributed to Altman's determination to convey the fleeting nature of life as we experience it, with all the frustration of its lack of precision and the pleasure of happy accidents.

And what of Altman's actual preoccupations? These have always been harder to pin down, since by his own account so many of his projects have seemingly come about through serendipity. But often he has revealed his keen eye for the essence of the American character and has brilliantly undermined empty myths, be they of the glory of the Old West, the earnest homilies of country-and-western music or the splendour of wealth. Without any need for 'correctness', he has displayed a true liberal's hope for tolerance and honesty, and with *Tanner '88* provided one of the sharpest snapshots of the American political scene around. And it was his experience on that ground-breaking television series (where with consummate ease he blended fiction and reality) that led him on to a path which culminated in his impressionistic glide through the world of ballet, *The Company*. He feels sure – and he may well be right – that this element of his work may be what will eventually mark him out most of all.

Although Altman has rarely talked about the inheritance of cinema with the passion of, say, Martin Scorsese, two directors to whom he has often paid tribute are Federico Fellini and Ingmar Bergman. And something of the polar extremes found in the work of these esteemed European *auteurs* is reflected in Altman's own swing between the broad canvas of multi-character, multi-narrative extravaganzas (*M*A*S*H*, *Nashville*, *Gosford Park*) and intimate, troubled, metaphysical dramas, especially those focused on the female experience (*Images, 3 Women*). Altman has been attacked on occasion for his apparently cruel treatment of women in film. At the same time, it has been women who have come most strongly to his defence. Indeed, his exceptional work with actresses won him no less than a mentoring award from Women in Film, an occasion accompanied by speeches from, among others, Emily Watson and Sally Kellerman, as well as taped tributes by Jennifer Jason Leigh and Lily Tomlin. In return, Altman has always been unstinting in his appreciation of the actor's craft, insisting that they are the essence of a film. As a result, he has rarely had any problem in commanding impressive cast lists.

Above all, for him film really is a collaborative process, even if his embracing of the talent of others has led to some artistic partners moving enthusiastically in and uncomfortably out of his charmed circle. Famously, he has never been an easy director for screenwriters, who have found their carefully honed texts freely adapted and regarded as simply a blueprint to Altman's very personal sense of construction work. But he has never been less than open about his method, of the necessity of responding to the organic nature of film-making, the diverse personalities of his cast or even simply the climate on location. One of the analogies made most frequently is that Altman is like a supreme jazz composer, taking up solid riffs and tunes and guiding his virtuoso musicians through an entirely fresh set of variations and improvisations. If the result is not always as well tuned or satisfyingly constructed as a critic or an audience might demand, it is what it is (just as 'I yam what I yam') and there is always the chance it may provoke a deeper response in years to come. Altman has often said that the greatest films are the ones you leave not being able to explain but knowing that you have experienced something very special.

This book provides – as its subject would no doubt put it – only one version of the truth about Robert Altman and his cinema. Just like Cathryn in *Images*, he sees life as a series of reflecting mirrors, and where we find the real image is for us to decide. Partly for this reason Altman resisted being pinned down to giving a full account of his career until now. My opportunity came when I was able to observe and film Altman at work in England in 2001 on *Gosford Park* for the long-running (but now defunct) BBC arts series, *Omnibus*. Rarely have I witnessed a director more at ease on a set, thoroughly enjoying being surrounded by a stellar group of Britain's finest playing at being 1930s aristocrats and servants. Subsequently, we were reunited for a number of on-stage discussions, after which I casually pitched the idea of *Altman on Altman*. He agreed without giving it too much thought, and in December 2002 I spent two weeks in New York city, visiting him at his comfortable production office where he was editing *The Company*. Then, as in past interviews, he talked with great enthusiasm about the film-making process but remained guarded when it came to close analysis of his work. Even – or especially – when it comes to his most puzzling films, such as *Images* and *Quintet*, he sees little point in providing elucidation further than revealing his first instincts for creating the piece. Altman has generally declined to name his favourite films, suggesting instead that, like children, one cannot easily be favoured over another, although the tendency is to love the least accepted. And so it is for films like *Brewster McCloud*, *Images* and *Quintet*, which have never been embraced like, say, *Nashville* and *Gosford Park*, that he retains considerable affection. Do not look to the creator to damn his past creations.

Visiting the Altman office, the ambience of comfortable interchange and lack of ceremony reflects the attitude of his films. He was not at all precious about showing me, and others who passed through, more than a glimpse of his work in progress, and our excursions to the editing suite were frequent (the editor of eight of his features, Geri Peroni, was equally gracious; tragically, she took her own life in August 2004, a great blow to all at Sandcastle). On my first day there, Altman was in conversation with his musical collaborator Van Dyke Parks and he revealed that he was about to appear on television for the American Heart Association and 'come out' about a heart transplant that he received in 1996. When he wasn't engaged with me or other visitors or conducting telephone conversations, he would sit quietly playing patience with a park of tarot cards. When I was able to make a further brief visit to him in October 2004, he was sitting at his desk, still playing with the same pack. His determination to keep on working not diminished in the slightest by age or the vacillations of financiers, he was excited about his work on the *Tanner* sequel and looked forward to beginning rehearsals for the opera of *A Wedding* in Chicago. When I asked if he had enjoyed any recent movies, he insisted that he didn't have time to see them. He did concede, though, to having liked the Brazilian film *City of*

God. 'Don't know how they could have made it, a magnificent job,' he told me. 'Looked at closely, it's a little ragged and unbalanced, and you had to do the work to follow the story, but that was part of the mandate.' A fair assessment of an Altman film itself, I would say.

Early Years – The Calvin Company – First Features – Television

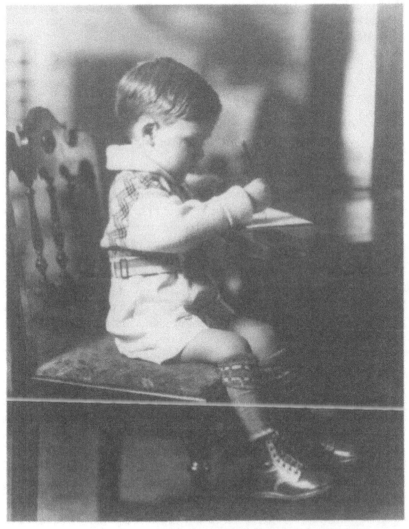

2 Altman as a young boy, already expressing himself with a pencil

Early Years

Robert Bernard Altman was born on 20 February 1925 in Kansas City, Missouri. His ancestors were German in origin; his great-grandfather Clement, born in Schleswig-Holstein (when the family name was 'Altmann'), emigrated to North America in the 1840s. Clement's son Frank Sr worked in the jewellery business and, in 1882, opened up a store in Kansas City. Its success led him to venture into real estate and construction, including 'The Altman Building' (demolished in 1978). He married Annetta (Nettie) Bolt, a concert pianist, in 1894, and they had six children, supplying the future Robert with four aunts and one uncle. The youngest son, Bernard – known as B.C. – became a successful life-insurance salesman and married Helen Matthews, from Nebraska, who converted to Catholicism for him. They had one son, Robert, and two daughters, Joan and Barbara.

DAVID THOMPSON: *Given your family background, it seems you grew up surrounded by women.*
ROBERT ALTMAN: I think that influenced me a lot. I had two sisters, both younger, and a first cousin, Louise, who often lived with us. I was the oldest of my generation, and for about five years until my first sister was born, I was the one baby of the family, so I got all the attention.

Were your family well-known in Kansas City?
Mezzo, mezzo . . . There was a building called the 'Altman Building', and the family was known in the city for a couple of generations – my father was born there and grew up there. His world was all about the country club and playing golf or gin rummy. It was a comfortable middle-class background, nothing out of the ordinary. My world was very small. I didn't go anywhere outside Kansas City until I went into the air force. That's when I learned there were places other than my home town.

Did culture and the arts play a part in your upbringing?
All of my aunts were artistically inclined in that *faux* manner: one of them was a painter, one of them played piano, one was a singer – they all toyed in the arts. The men were businessmen and carousers, that kind of thing. That was the culture there at that time.

Nothing really extraordinary has happened in my life, even if I've not taken the most conventional or comfortable path. Certainly not a terrible struggle. But I sensed from the very beginning of things that I had to make my own way, that I had to make myself known, that I had to create my own

3 Altman with his mother Helen and sisters Joan and, on the far right, Barbara

circumstances. And nothing has ever happened to me that I didn't instigate, but there's always a surprise here and there . . .

Were movies a passion for you as a child?
I loved movies, but they were *just* movies to me. In Kansas City there was a

theatre called the Plaza Theatre, and it was there all through my childhood. We had a way in through a manhole in the street, and we could crawl down it and go through the pipes and conduits and come into a door that led right into the men's room in the theatre. We'd chip in and one of us would buy a ticket and then come in and unlock the door so the rest of us could get in from the street. I remember once I had the mumps or chickenpox and had to stay home, and when my mother went out I climbed out of the window and went eight or ten blocks to the theatre and would sit through the movies all day. I remember I saw *King Kong* that way, and I saw *Viva Villa!*[1] with Wallace Beery as Pancho Villa, and I've never forgotten the scene in which they tied Joseph Schildkraut down and covered him with honey for the ants to eat him! But movies were just entertainment to me. Some were better than others, but I didn't think of them as I do now. It never occurred to me I would be involved with them, right up through the war.

I believe Brief Encounter *was a revelation to you?*
That was right after the war. I was in Los Angeles, and for some unknown reason I went into the Fairfax district by myself in the afternoon to see that movie. I thought, 'Here's Celia Johnson, an older woman with sensible shoes' – and she certainly wasn't a babe. And then suddenly I was in love with her. And when I walked out of that movie, it was a whole new thing in films for me – I'd never had a film affect me in any way, previously I always felt I'd been in my seat with a lot of other people just seeing something. I remember being very emotionally moved by it. It wasn't all tits and ass! I think that picture, that and *The Treasure of the Sierra Madre*, really impressed me most of all.

Later, films by Fellini and Bergman affected me very strongly. Bergman gave me the confidence to focus on a person's face and allow a character to have dignity. Fellini told me that anything's possible. And I know I've taken shots from Kurosawa's films and used them in mine . . .

The openness and variety of your films have often brought a comparison with the cinema of Jean Renoir. Is that something you recognize?
I very much like his work, but I don't know much about how any directors actually work, because I've never worked in any other position. I was never an assistant director, I was never an actor, I was never a prop man. I was never on a set other than as a director. And I've never seen another director working. I've produced films with quite a few directors, but I was more an enabler; I would never go on the set. Actually, I did spend about ten days on the set of Alan Rudolph's film *Trixie*, but that was mainly because I was so

4 Celia Johnson in 'sensible shoes' as Laura Jesson in David Lean's *Brief Encounter* (1945)

fascinated watching Emily Watson work. So I assume we mainly do the same thing, we have the same mandate.

Were you ever drawn to any of the other arts?
I was an artist and did a lot of drawings, and I had a little skill and talent for that.

What about the theatre?
When I was in the fifth or sixth grade I remember I took a book, a biography of Vasco da Gama[2] and I thought, 'This is really good and I'm going to make a play out of it and present it to the school to do it.' The book was really thick, so what I did was go through it and any time there were quotations, I wrote down the dialogue and who said it. Well, of course it made no sense whatsoever, which confounded me! So I abandoned that until I realized later how things weren't readily transferable.

Altman first attended St Peter's Catholic School and then, at the age of thirteen, graduated to Rockhurst High School, run by the Jesuits. In 1941 he went to Wentworth Military Academy in Lexington, Missouri, and followed this training by enlisting in the air force in 1945.

You said the air force was your first real taste of life outside Kansas City.
With the draft, I could have gone into service as an infantry officer, but doing an exam for the air force gave me a day off school in Kansas City. I really had no wish to be a pilot, but I passed and they sent me to St Louis for basic training, then back to Kansas City for about a month, which was great. Then I went to San Antonio in Texas for the flight training. Finally, I ended up in California, in Riverside. That was fine for me, because girls were what interested me at that time – girls, and how to get them. Then I was sent to the South Pacific.

Altman was stationed in Morotai in the Dutch East Indies, flying over forty bombing missions as the co-pilot of a B-24 in the 307th Bomb Group. He survived at least one crash.

Wasn't it while you were stationed overseas that the tedium you encountered led you to begin writing stories?
A second cousin of my father was the secretary to Myron Selznick, the brother of David O. Selznick,[3] and Myron was a big agent. I wrote her a

5 A Christmas drawing by Robert Altman, done while stationed in San
Antonio and unable to return home in 1943

letter from overseas. At that time I wouldn't write to my mother or father or
anybody because I didn't have the patience for that, but I could write to a
stranger what I thought was flowery, humorous stuff. I was writing to her
because she was exposed to all those movie stars, so I thought she would be
a good person to keep in contact with. She wrote me back saying, 'Oh, your
letter is so funny, you should be a writer.' And from that moment on I was a
writer, because she'd said it! I agreed with her, so I started writing. When I
got out of the service at nineteen years old, if anyone asked, 'What are
you?', I'd say I was a writer. And that's how it all started.

Son of B. C. Altman Receives Air Medal

Following is a letter from George C. Kenney, commanding general of the Far East air forces, to Bernard C. Altman of the Missouri—Kansas City agency, sent to Mr. Altman after his son, Flight Officer Robert B. Altman, was decorated with the Air Medal:

FLIGHT OFFICER ROBERT B. ALTMAN

Dear Mr. Altman:

Recently your son, Flight Officer Robert B. Altman, was decorated with the Air Medal. It was an award made in recognition of courageous service to his combat organization, his fellow American airmen, his country, his home and to you.

He was cited for meritorious achievement while participating in aerial flights in the Pacific Area from June 1, 1945 to June 26, 1945.

Your son took part in sustained operational flight missions during which hostile contact was probable and expected. These operations, consisting of bombing missions against enemy airdromes and installations as well as attacks on naval and cargo vessels, aided considerably in the recent successes in this theatre.

Almost every hour of every day your son, and the sons of other American fathers, are doing just such things as that here in the Pacific.

Theirs is a very real and very tangible contribution to victory and to peace.

I would like to tell you how genuinely proud I am to have men such as your son in my command, and how gratified I am to know that young Americans with such courage and resourcefulness are fighting our country's battle against the Japanese aggressors.

You, Mr. Altman, have every reason to share that pride and gratification.

Sincerely,
GEORGE C. KENNEY
General, USA,
Commanding.

6 A commendation for Altman's part in World War II

8

On his return to the US, Altman received his discharge and resisted going into the reserves. He married LaVonne Elmer, a model, in Kansas City, and the couple moved to Los Angeles in the summer of 1946. In 1947 they had a daughter, Christine. The couple were divorced in 1949.

How did you intend to break into movies?
My father had moved out to California and had a house in Malibu. The bottom apartment was rented to a guy named George W. George, who was the son of Rube Goldberg, the famous *New Yorker* cartoonist at the turn of the century who did crazy inventions and drew a famous strip. George had an uncle who was a film director.[4] George was going to be a film director too, and I was going to be a writer, so we just started working together. We wrote treatments and sold two of them, one to RKO, *Bodyguard*, with Lawrence Tierney, and *Christmas Eve*, with George Brent and Randolph Scott.[5] My first screen credit appears on *Bodyguard*: 'From an original story by Robert Altman and George W. George.' I was so keen I said I'd write the

7 Altman at a croquet game with his father B. C. and his mother Helen in California, 1947

screenplay and not charge them for it. Well, that's the dumbest thing anybody ever said. But they wouldn't let me even go on the set and watch the film being made.

Didn't you also manage to appear as an extra in The Secret Life of Walter Mitty?
Yes. My father once had a girlfriend named Bonny, and she had since married Norman McLeod,[6] who directed those famous Bob Hope and Danny Kaye pictures. My father was a very gregarious guy, so I met Norman through him. I told him I was interested in writing, and he said, 'If you're looking for a job, come on down to the Goldwyn studios and I'll put you in one of my pictures.' So I went and became an extra in *Walter Mitty* for three days, and I was paid something like $160 a day, which was a lot of money. I got in the make-up chair, and the make-up man made a serious pass at me, so I thought I'd really made the big time. But I never really considered becoming an actor. I went out to Fox and I read for *The Razor's Edge*, but I had no idea what it was about or what I was doing. So that didn't last.

Wasn't it around this time that you took up tattooing dogs as a business?
After the war I went to buy a dog, a bull terrier, and I discovered that there was something called Identi-Code, which meant tattooing dogs with their individual number, as well as the number of the state and the county, records all kept at the sheriff's office. I thought that was a terrific idea, and before I could get out of the shop, I'd become vice-president of the company, and I was the tattooer! We'd take the dog, and inside the groin of the right leg we'd shave the hair off, apply antiseptic oil, and with a tattooing machine, in block letters, I'd write the number. We thought we'd become millionaires, but all I got was just a few bites. We did Harry Truman's dog, because my dad knew him. I'd played poker with him, and we thought it was a great publicity stunt. I also tattooed a waiter who became curious about what we were doing. We were all a little drunk and I remember I wrote on the bottom of his foot his name – D. W. Stiles – and his army number. Eventually, we sold out to a dog-food company . . .

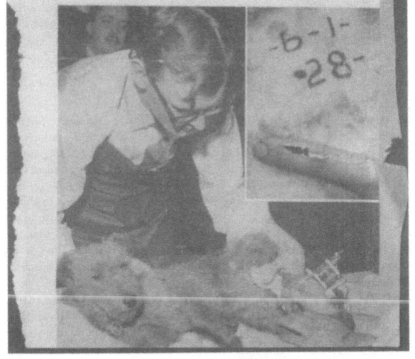

Poodle Tattoo is part of a program of the National Dog Record Bureau to mark city, state and personal code numbers inside right thigh of canines. The system, similar to one used by the Army K-9 Corps, will be employed as a nation-wide method of identification. Below, a conventional tattooing needle is used as "Ginger Snap" looks on. Inset reveals the way marks show up on the skin for easy recognition.

8 Tattooing dogs was one of Altman's less illustrious early occupations

The Calvin Company

When did your ambitions to be a director begin?
I never thought about being a director until later on. I wrote a play that was a dreadful rip-off of some popular kind of thing at the time, and as I couldn't get on a set in Hollywood, I decided my future lay on the stage in New York. So I got in an old car, and on the way there I stopped in Kansas City and spent three or four days carousing with old friends and family. I ran into a guy named Bob Woodburn, whose mother had been an art teacher of mine at grade school. He had been in *Junior Miss*, a Broadway play, and was also a stage manager. I lied quite a bit, telling him I was a writer on my way to New York to do my play. He was a generous guy and told me he was making movies over at the Calvin Company, this industrial film place. He said, 'Come over tomorrow and see it,' so I went over and saw the cameras and the sound stage, and I met the guys running the company. I lied quite a bit about my experience, and they hired me as a director of industrial films for $250 a month.

What kind of work did you do there?
We had to write our own scripts, so I wrote this particular script for the International Harvester Tractor Company, and they liked it. What I didn't know was that the people at the Calvin Company had no idea how to shoot it, so they said I could direct it. All the dialogue was between two men, one old man breaking in a young man. They'd be driving along and talking, and then they'd stop and see something. They couldn't figure out how to shoot dialogue in a car, as this was before tape was used – the sound went directly on to the film. So I 'invented' looping, which of course they had done in Hollywood, but I suspected that and just kind of made it up. The Calvin Company hated the word 'Hollywood'. They insisted they did business films, and though they had the 16mm equipment to do more stuff, they didn't use any of it.

I was there all in all for about six years. I learned all my technical craft there, as we had to shoot the film, edit it, score it and then resell it to the people who sponsored it in the first place.

It appears you made some sixty films at Calvin, with subjects ranging from road safety to basketball techniques. Did working at the Calvin Company give you opportunities for the kind of experimentation that came later?
I think that beginning probably helped me a great deal, because I approached

9 Altman directing an instructional film for the Calvin Company

everything from a different standpoint to the people there. As I'd never worked in any other film job, I'd not seen what other directors did, and I'm sure all that separated me in a funny way. It's like today when I see kids who go to film schools, and writers who say that by page 13 you have to have this happen, and by page 32 you have to have this happen, and by page 106 it has to be over, blah blah blah. Well, we didn't have all those rules, and it's not that we even broke them, because they didn't exist. Now I think these kids are hampered by rules – not that they can't think beyond them, just that they don't go beyond them, because they are axiomatic of what you do. I think there have been too many screenwriting schools and too many books, and people think that's what they must do. They treat it the same way they treat mathematics, and it's wrong.

You were now able to explore working with actors to some degree?
Yes, but I came in from a different place than everyone else. I didn't come from theatre – I learned theatre *after* I began working at Calvin. I was using local actors in Kansas City, which meant they were radio announcers,

10 Altman climbing a camera crane while filming *Better Football* (1954)

usually. Then I found through these actors that the only theatre in Kansas City was in the Jewish Community Centre, and they had an amateur theatre programme. So I went over there and I volunteered and I did stuff and made friends with many of the actors there, and they loved me because then when I used them in my films they got paid! So I kind of trained myself in the theatrical aspect of working with actors. All these things kept leading to a path . . .

I've seen a clip from one of the films, The Magic Bond, *in which you even had a realistic depiction of war, presumably shot in Kansas City!*
I did that for the VFW, the Veterans of Foreign Wars. I just went around Kansas City until I found some buildings they were tearing down, and we took our cameras, put our guys in uniform, got some mud and went in there among the destroyed buildings and just shot a couple of scenes as if they were among war rubble. That was all part of my evolution. I was always trying to take what I had seen in the cinema and use those dramatic ideas to get whatever message it was across.

So you always had making movies – by which I mean Hollywood, I suppose – in your sights?
Always. I left three times to go back there and each time I failed to get work, couldn't get arrested. I spent a frustrating year there once living on borrowed money, and when I returned to Kansas City they took me back at Calvin but with a salary cut. Then we started pushing these films more into what I would call 'entertainment' rather than nuts and bolts. I always carried a torch against this prejudice towards Hollywood. Forest Calvin ran the company, and Frank Barhydt was the main producer there. He was very generous with me, liked me a lot. Then I quit again, but I still couldn't score in Hollywood.

First Features

While in Kansas City, Altman made his first foray into television drama, producing an anthology series of fifteen-minute films called *Pulse of the City* in 1954. The same year he married Lotus Carelli, a television newscaster, and they had two sons, Michael and Stephen. They were divorced in 1957. Although he co-scripted a musical film, *Corn's-A-Poppin'*, in 1950, his first break as director of a feature came in 1955 with *The Delinquents*. It was filmed over two weeks in Kansas City, on a budget of around $60,000, employing mainly local talent, Calvin-trained cameraman Charles Paddock, friends and relations. It was eventually distributed by United Artists in 1957.

How did The Delinquents *happen?*
A guy in Kansas City named Elmer Rhoden Jr came to me and said, 'I want to make a movie.' His father owned the Midwest Fox chain of theatres. He said he wanted to make a movie about delinquents. So, with my sister taking dictation from me, I wrote this script in three or four days.

The Delinquents *dealt with teenage gangs, their wild parties and petty crimes. It now looks like a low-budget counterpart to the highly popular teen-gang movies released in 1955, such as* Rebel Without a Cause *and* Blackboard Jungle.

I don't know if I saw those pictures or not. I'd heard of James Dean, sure.[7] This kid Tommy Laughlin, who became *Billy Jack*,[8] was the star I hired for this picture, and he turned out to be a horror. He thought he *was* James Dean. I remember we were going to do one shot where he was coming up to this house, and he was supposed to be exhausted. I said, 'OK, we'll do this with you running into the house.' He said, 'No, I'm going to go three blocks down. Have your cameras ready and send me a signal, because I'm going to run for three blocks before I get there.' I said, 'OK.' But then he was late, or early, or we weren't ready, and we got into a kind of a fight. And someone told me that he was just doing the James Dean thing – doing what he'd read James Dean did on *East of Eden*.

11 *The Delinquents* (1957) in action in a Kansas City diner

James Dean would haunt you for quite a while . . .
After *The Delinquents* was finished and I was editing it out in California,
George W. George heard about Dean's death and said, 'Why don't we make
a documentary on James Dean?' And I said, 'Sure, great, I've just had
experience with the guy, I hate him!' So we did *The James Dean Story*
on our own, with George putting up the money. Lou Lombardo was the
cameraman, and Stewart Stern, who wrote *Rebel Without a Cause*, was
involved in the narration. I really wanted to deflate Dean, but it didn't turn
out that way. I began to realize how basically he was a good actor and
brought a whole new personality that kids responded to at that time. Making the documentary, I found myself more interested in him, and when we
reconstructed the traffic accident in which he was killed, I drove one of the
cars.

The James Dean Story, a rather solemn telling of Dean's life and death mainly
using location filming, stills, interviews and a portentous narration by Martin
Gabel, was released by Warner Brothers in 1957.

Television

How did you break into directing for television?
My agent at this time showed *The Delinquents* to Alfred Hitchcock. I went
and had a meeting with Hitchcock, who had liked the picture. He thought it
was different. He hired me to go to New York to produce on *Suspicion*, a
series of hour-long shows. This episode was directed by Robert Stevens.[9]
They wanted me because of my experience doing location shooting,
whereas everything they had done had been in studios. So I said, 'OK, I'll
do it, though I won't take any money or credit for it, because I'm a writer
and director, not a line producer.' I asked for two guys – the editor Lou
Lombardo and an art director who was also my brother-in-law, Chet Allen –
and my expenses. I shot some second-unit stuff, and on the basis of that, they
gave me two half hours to direct in the *Alfred Hitchcock Presents* series.[10]
I never spoke with Hitchcock during production.

Has Hitchcock been any kind of influence on you?
I've never been a big Hitchcock fan. His films are really too linear for me.
But I think *Rear Window* is his best film. I like that idea of removing one of
the senses, as he can't hear what's going on across the courtyard, and

12 James Dean as seen in *The James Dean Story* (1957)

confining the James Stewart character to a wheelchair, making him a voyeur.

You made two very interesting episodes of Alfred Hitchcock Presents – *'The Young One', with Carol Lynley as a teenage girl who frames a stranger for the murder of her guardian, and 'Together', with Joseph Cotten as a*

murderer locked in an office with the body of his victim after a party. Why didn't you do more?
After the second film I was offered another, but I read the script, thought it was no good and went into the office of the producer, a woman named Joan Harrison, and said, 'I think you're making a big mistake with this. I'm not going to direct this, and I advise you don't do it.' Well, that was a script she had personally developed, but I didn't know it at the time. And that ended my career at *Alfred Hitchcock Presents* . . .

Notes

1 *Viva Villa!* (1934), directed by Jack Conway and scripted by Ben Hecht, was a heavily mythologized version of the life of wild rebel and later president Pancho Villa, who led the struggle for the Mexican republic. Produced by MGM, the parts of the film shot in Mexico were directed, uncredited, by Howard Hawks.

2 Vasco da Gama was the famous Portuguese explorer who made history in 1497 by discovering a sea route to India via the Cape of Good Hope.

3 David O. Selznick (1902–65) was a hugely ambitious independent producer who, after working at MGM (he married Louis B. Mayer's daughter Irene) and other studios, founded his own company and made the highly successful epic *Gone with the Wind* (1939). His brother Myron (1898–1944) also began his career in cinema as a producer, but in 1928 abandoned this path to become Hollywood's leading talent agent and set up the trend of 'packaging' movies with his roster of directors, writers and stars.

4 Edwin L. Marin (1899–1951) began directing movies in the 1930s, spending much of his career at MGM and rarely rising above potboilers and second features.

5 *Bodyguard* (1948) was directed by Richard Fleischer and was a typical low-budget *film noir*, which RKO Pictures specialized in at the time. *Christmas Eve* (1947), also known as *Sinner's Holiday*, directed by Edwin L. Marin and made independently for producer Benedict Bogeaus, was a mix of comedy and drama with George Raft and Randolph Scott among the cast.

6 Directed by Norman McLeod, *The Secret Life of Walter Mitty* (1947) starred Danny Kaye as James Thurber's mild-mannered man who dreams of being brave and successful. Altman appears in a nightclub scene, smiling and smoking a cigarette.

7 Following his mother's death, James Dean (1931–55) was raised by relatives on an Iowa farm and then began acting in Los Angeles and New York, where he appeared on Broadway and attended classes at the Actors' Studio. Following bit parts in film and television, his break came with the lead roles in *East of*

Eden (1955), directed by Elia Kazan, and *Rebel Without a Cause* (1955), directed by Nicholas Ray, in both of which he epitomized the passionate, misunderstood young American of the post-war generation. After filming *Giant* (1956), directed by George Stevens, he was killed in a car crash on 30 September 1955, giving rise to a huge personality cult and numerous books and films about him.

8 Tom Laughlin (b. 1931), who claims to have been a 'greaser' in his school days, followed his lead role in *The Delinquents* by becoming an independent film-maker with *The Young Sinner* (1965), which he wrote, produced, directed, edited and starred in. His third film, *Billy Jack* (1971), in which he played a half Indian/half white former Green Beret vigilante, cost $800,000 and grossed over $80 million. He revived the character in subsequent films, but in 1992 decided to go into politics, recently running against Arnold Schwarzenegger for Governor of California.

9 Robert Stevens (1921–89) directed forty-two episodes of *Alfred Hitchcock Presents* from 1955 to 1960, including the celebrated 'The Magic Shop', as well as the premier segment of the original *Twilight Zone* series, 'Where Is Everybody?'

10 *Alfred Hitchcock Presents* made its début on American television on 2 October 1955. It was highly unusual at the time for a big name in cinema to work on the small screen, but Lew Wasserman, the head of MCA (which had become the parent company of Universal Pictures), persuaded Hitchcock to undertake a series in which he would personally introduce stories with a twist in their tail. Setting up Shamley Productions for this purpose, he directed only twenty out of over 300 shows himself, delegating most responsibilities to a team led by Joan Harrison, a long-time associate, and actor Norman Lloyd. The shows sold around the world and spawned the equally successful magazine series *Alfred Hitchcock Mystery Magazine*.

More Television – *Countdown* – *That Cold Day in the Park*

More Television

DAVID THOMPSON: *In spite of your dismissal from* Alfred Hitchcock Presents, *you went on to work solidly in television for ten years before breaking into feature films.*
ROBERT ALTMAN: I decided that television was the world I was shooting for. There were lots of opportunities during that time to do low-budget off-beat films, but they were always bad, and I always said I would keep doing television until I got a film that I really wanted to do. I didn't want to go out and make a feature just for the sake of it and then find out that was the end of it.

I don't know what the ratio is, but I bet if you look at film directors who only made one feature film, there's probably more of them than we think. You either do it through funding or you join the corporation, but there's always this autonomy thing, which has been referred to in different ways, such as *auteurism*. But basically the situation is, what is your job? Do you get hired to do what somebody tells you to do, or do you go into it and say, 'Ah, this is my art . . .'? You can't really go into those $100-million pictures and think you have control. If it's a low-budget film, yes, you do. Or if you have the element of the star, and he or she is 'yours' rather than 'theirs', that also gives you more power.

In 1956 you began working for Desilu, the television production company owned by Lucille Ball and Desi Arnaz, and there you made fourteen episodes of Whirlybirds, *described at the time as a 'western with helicopters'.*
It was great. It was a job and allowed me to make my car payments.

Did you have any creative freedom on those shows?
I never had anything to with casting anybody. They would give me a sheet, and it had me as the director, the names of the actors who were playing the characters and how much they were being paid. So I knew what the deal was and I could tell how important that actor was by how much he was

13 Filming *Whirlybirds* (1958–9). Altman directed eighteen episodes

being paid. I met my wife on *Whirlybirds*. She was an extra who came out one day with her own white stockings and played a nurse.

In 1960 Altman married Kathryn Reed, who was working as a movie and tele-vision extra after appearing in Earl Carroll's revues. She already had a daughter,

*Konni, from a previous marriage, and together she and Altman had one son,
Robert Jr, and adopted another, Matthew.*

Presumably you had little control over the scripts you were given.
I couldn't read those scripts, they were so bad. Tommy Thompson, who
was my assistant director even back then – one of my closest friends, he died
just when were finishing the shoot of *Dr T and the Women* – would pick me
up in his car about five o'clock and we'd drive to these locations, which
were usually out in the Valley, where they could fly the helicopters. I'd get in
the car, usually with a dreadful hangover, and he'd tell me what was happening in the script. He'd say, 'This is a murder mystery. The two guys get a
call, they're taking some baby chicks which have to be got to an incubator,
and halfway there they see a car stalled on the road and a motorist flags
them down. So they land, but the motorist produces a gun and comman-
deers the helicopter to take him some place, and they take him away. And in
the meantime they're afraid the chicks are going to die . . .' And I'd say,
'OK, I got it.' We shot those films over five days. Each half-hour was two
and a half days, so by lunch on Wednesday you'd finished one picture and
you were starting another. Usually we were inside for half a day and outside
for two days, so if we started outside on the Monday, on Wednesday we
were probably inside, so at noon we were through with that episode. And
that was it – if it wasn't finished, too bad, that's what they cut together.
After lunch you'd start the interiors for half a day of the next show and go
outside on Thursday and Friday.

One time we were doing a murder mystery, and on Wednesday Tommy
gave me a sheet detailing the actors and how much they're being paid. I
didn't know *any* of them, but there was this one guy who was getting, like,
$300 for the week, which was a lot of money then. So I looked at this guy
and I looked at the first scene, and he was down to be there with a group of
people, but he had nothing to say. Then we got to the next scene, and again
he had nothing to say. So I thought, 'Oh, either they're paying off some
friend of the producer or they're paying him off for some other show' –
because he had nothing to do with *our* show. The next day we were outside,
so I go out to the location, get a sandwich from the catering truck and I look
at the sheet – and there was that guy again, with nothing to do. So I had to
do some shots of feet going through the forest, and I said to Tommy, 'Get
that guy. I want to use him for that.' When we came back Friday, he was
still there! It just so happened that the last scene of that episode was the last
scene we were shooting. I'd been working with the other actors and I'd got
pretty friendly with them, so I told one of them, 'This is the last scene.

You're going to be up on that rock with a rifle, you'll be looking around, and the helicopter's going to come from behind that hill and come over. You're gonna go up to fire at the helicopter, but then you fall back over, off the rock, and you hit the ground.' He said, 'No, no.' I said, 'Don't worry. This isn't going to hurt you. You're not going to do the fall. The stunt man will do that.' He still said, 'No.' I said, 'Believe me, it'll be fine, what is the problem?' He said, 'Well, I don't think that's supposed to be me.' I said, 'What do you mean?' And I suddenly realized this actor wasn't the murderer – it was the guy they were paying the extra money. Now I realized he must have some kind of a reputation. But I'd shot this whole show, which was kind of a murder mystery, and all the time I had the wrong guy down for the murderer!

There was a terrific actor named Cecil Kellaway,[1] well known in the 1930s and 1940s, and he showed up on one of the shows. That was big news for me, and I liked him quite a bit. He came up to me at one point during the end of the shoot, when we were out near a Spanish church doing a scene with a priest, and he said, 'Mr Altman, I've been in this business for a long time, and I don't know what you're doing making these television shows, but you are a really talented director. I think you can do anything you want.' I said, 'Oh, thanks, that's very nice.' But he meant what he said, and I believed him. And it's that syndrome where you can walk down the street and see a kid with a baseball bat or cricket bat, whatever the culture is, and being a stranger you can say, 'Hey, I just saw the way you swing that bat, you've really got a good swing. Man, you could be big time.' And I think as a stranger you can change that kid's life, while as a parent you can't. Because you plant that seed, and it gives confidence. I think that little conversation sent me another way. I think almost anybody can do anything, but they have to have the chutzpah or the confidence to do it. And though I was thrilled to have money, because I was broke most of my life, I never felt so satisfied about the job as I did about having the opportunity to do these things with actors. As I've floated down this river, I think that kind of confidence – or maybe it's just ambition – has made the difference.

Making television films on such tight budgets and schedules must have taught you a great deal about the discipline needed on the job.
You have to make the choice. It's like cleaning the house – you have two hours to do it, so how thoroughly do you do it, and where do you start, and how do you manage to get it all done? And filming is always over-scheduled; there's always more work to do than you have time for. I got to the point with the *Whirlybird* shows where a couple of times we'd finish by

three o'clock and go back into the studio by four-thirty, and I was thrilled to be giving the crew a few hours off. But I found out that at this studio, Desilu, when those guys came in they were sent over to another stage to do grunt work. They didn't get off. So then I'd get to where we'd finish, and I would say, 'There's no point going in, because they'll put you guys to work somewhere else. Let's do some fun stuff.' So we'd do some very tricky helicopter shots to use the time up. But with those shows that were impossible to do in two and a half days, I should have done them in two, as far as the studio cared.

We were out on location one day. We had a prop truck, and there was a scene in which the two helicopter guys had been hijacked and they end up walking through the woods to get to civilization. We stopped at the side of the road, and I looked in the back of the prop truck, and there was a telephone booth. So I said, 'Bring that booth down and put it in the middle of the woods.' So we had these guys come along to this telephone booth, and I had one say to the other, 'Have you got a dime?' And the other would say, 'No', and he'd reply, 'Oh well', and they'd turn around and walk the other way. I shot that in such a way that you could take it out and the scene would just play with them continuing to walk. I thought it would be a laugh for the editor and the producer. That episode came on, and it was left in the picture. No one questioned it! The editor didn't read the scripts, and the producer never saw the goddamn things. So that taught me a lesson.

Many of the actors you worked with in television – I'm thinking of people like Keenan Wynn, Peggy Ann Garner, Michael Murphy, Robert Fortier, John Considine – would crop up on the cast lists of your films.
I've always been – loyal is not the word – keen to use people I'd used before, who liked me. So you're not coming in with ten actors on a project and having to worry about them, as they're all so insecure really – it's a tough job, it really is. As soon as I read a script, I'll say, 'Let's put so and so in that.' You get to develop a stock company that way. In television I realized that I couldn't take an extra and say, 'Now say this', because then they'd have to pay him as an actor – it just was not allowed. So by the time I got to do *The Troubleshooters*, which I produced as well, all those guys who were part of the regular crew of extras were all people whom I'd worked with before, and I moved them up to being actors.

And it was at this time you realized how important actors could be to the process?
I was working on *U.S. Marshal*, which was really one of the more dreadful

series I did. I mean, even the clothes were boring. Barbara Baxley, who was a terrific Broadway actress, was cast in an episode.[2] She came on the set, which was a farmhouse, and it took me about a minute and a half to realize, 'Hey, this girl has got all the credentials, she's good.' And we had an actor who was the guest star, and they had a scene together, and afterwards he said to me, 'We've got this great actress Barbara Baxley here. Can't we do something more with these scenes than making them just two-dimensional cut-outs?' And I said, 'Absolutely.' So I called Barbara, and we started working on the scenes – and the guy could not cut the mustard. It just destroyed him, because she delivered such a strong performance, she was so extraordinary and so powerful. From that point on, I started shooting for those kinds of actors, and the mandate was not just, 'Oh, this is the part, these are your words, walk over here.' Now I would say, 'Let's get *inside* of this thing.' And I think that was a big turning point.

Did you have any opportunities for technical experimentation? Or was it almost all by the book, shooting masters and close-ups?
I did that stuff. On the second Hitchcock show, 'Together', Curly Lindon[3] was the cameraman. He was a top Universal feature cameraman. This was the very beginning of television, and these guys were all under contract to the studios. They usually did major features, but they started getting assigned to television, and they didn't like doing that shit, they really didn't. They all had moustaches and they wore ascots. And Curly was a curmudgeon. So I come in as this novice director. I got along with Joe Cotten because we had mutual friends and he accepted me as a peer. We were in an office set, and I saw a desk and I said, 'Great, I want a close-up of the telephone and then to see so-and-so at the door as it opens, looking over the telephone.' And Curly says, 'Oh yeah? What kind of lens are you using?' And I was truly embarrassed. I said, 'We can't do that?' And he said, 'Not with any equipment I know!' It really scrambled me.

Shortly after that, I thought, 'I've got to learn what this stuff is about.' I got hold of Johnny Alonzo,[4] who was later a director of photography. He was a friend of mine, an actor at the time. He did a lot of stills photography, so I spent several weeks with him, learning how to develop and print, what you could do and what you couldn't do, because a lens is a lens. So when a guy now said to me, 'What lens are you using?' I could say, 'Well, I'm going to use a 50mm lens with a diopter.'[5] I did stills for quite a while and I got very good at it, taking photographs for probably five years. When I had all the equipment I wanted, I just gave it up, as it was very time consuming. But I think I did the right thing.

14 Roger Moore and Fay Spain in 'Bolt from the Blue' (1960), the episode of
Maverick written and directed by Altman

What about sound? Were you able to make any advances in that area?
I was always trying to figure out how to make these shows sound more real.
'Speak louder, louder' was all you heard from the sound mixer. 'Can't he
speak up?' And I'd say, 'Nobody's going to speak up. They're going to play
it the way they play it, and we're going to have to figure out a way to record

it.' Then I'd say, 'Why can't we do more channels so we can control it after the fact?'

Years later we built the first eight-track mixer. They were called Lion's Gate 8-Tracks, and the guy who mixed with them was Jim Webb. I think the first time we used this system was on *California Split*. Then we got to *Nashville*, with twenty-four characters, and then with *A Wedding* I arbitrarily doubled it to forty-eight characters. *Nashville* was a brand-new kind of thing for me, and because of the success of that I kept going for those big casts. I think you keep chasing whatever it is that you succeed at. If there's a squad of eight people and somebody cuts himself badly and there's no doctor, and one of them says, 'Oh I can fix that,' and takes care of it, sews it up or whatever – he's 'Doc' from then on, that's his job. And that happens with film, as I just kept pushing when people said, 'Oh, we can't do that, how are you going to do that?' Somebody would have an answer.

Radio drama was always fantastic to me, because you'd be listening and you'd hear a door squeak, and everybody in the audience saw a different door. Whatever kind of door it was, it was *your* door. And in my films I wanted to force the audience into a situation where they would be offering their own experience to the screen because they wouldn't necessarily hear everything that was said.

You've always preferred live sound, even if it's imperfect and not always clear, to recording dialogue after the shooting.
I was shooting at some big studio, Universal, I think. I finished with an actor at lunch time, said, 'Thank you' and 'Goodbye' and all that, then went to lunch. And during lunch I saw him walking across the lot, and I said, 'What are you doing here? I thought you'd been dismissed.' And he said, 'Oh, I had to go do looping.' I said, 'What do you mean?' He said, 'Well, as soon as we finished shooting, I had to go to loop all of my scenes.' I found out that when an actor had finished working, if there had been any outside stuff, they were automatically sent to looping. The director was never present, and they'd loop the actor that day so they didn't have to pay to bring him back. I said, 'Who was the director?' And he said, 'I don't know, some engineer.' I said, 'How can you do that without me there?' He said, 'They don't care *how* it's said, they just want it said.' So I raised hell and said to the actor, 'Don't you say one word of this stuff unless I'm in that room.' But that's they way they did it. They weren't concerned, because this was a manufacturing plant, and once the project left me, there wasn't anybody who cared.

I still despise looping or post-synching, though we have to do it occasionally, and though I tell actors I don't do it, we always have to change a word here or there, 'north' to 'south' or some such. I also don't care if the audience hears everything, and that's pretty hard to get across – that it's not important that they hear every word or that they know what that person is saying. I think that films became too closely connected with theatre, and theatre is about words and a way of presenting them to an audience in an unrealistic situation. If everybody projected like that at somebody's house, you'd leave the party.

I find that people always talk at the same time. In most conversations, by the time you get the first five words of your sentence out, the person you're talking to knows what it's going to be, has already formulated an answer and is starting that answer.

I was always trying to get away with this thing of actors talking at the same time. Lore has it that I started the fashion for overlapping dialogue, which simply isn't true at all. For my money, Howard Hawks did. The picture that impressed me the most in that way was *The Thing*, which was directed by his editor, Chris Nyby, but Howard Hawks was there every morning.[6] I saw that picture in New York in Times Square with a friend of mine who was a TWA pilot. We went in and sat up in the balcony, and I remember telling him – and he didn't know anything about the movies – 'That's what I'm talking about, that's the kind of thing I want to hear!' And oddly enough, Ken Tobey was in that picture – he was also the *Whirlybirds* star.

I was constantly hearing on sets, 'No, no, cut, that's no good', because I was allowing actors to overlap each other. I was told to leave that kind of thing to the editors. But putting individual mikes on actors finally allowed me to handle the whole thing the way I wanted.

Did you have any influence on the editing of your television work?
Oh, I never got near it. I never met half the editors! I never really dealt with an editor in an editing room until I was doing *The Roaring 20s* and *Maverick* at Warners.

On *The Roaring 20s*, normally we'd have ten set-ups in a morning, but I set up one scene in a dressing room with mirrors so I could do it all in one shot, and I didn't give them any coverage.[7] They came in the next day and say, 'You're fired. We cannot do this, we have to be able to edit!' I'd say, 'Why? I'm the editor.' It was always those kinds of confrontations. And I still do that today, only for myself. I did it many times in *Gosford Park*. I'd say, 'Great, I did it in one shot.' Just as long as I knew I had a cutaway so I could get back and truncate it.

15 Dorothy Provine as singer Pinky Pinkham in *The Roaring 20s* (1960–1)

I liked some of *The Roaring 20s*. They were anthology films really; the main characters had to be in them, but they weren't about them.

Many people are surprised to discover you directed on Bonanza.
I came in the second year of the show. That was the first time I dealt with colour, and it was one of the first television series to be shot in colour. I

introduced comedy into two or three of the scripts, which I preferred to the soppiness of most of them. But I became very good friends with Dan Blocker and all of those guys.

You had a chance to make something of a more adult nature at Fox with Bus Stop, *an anthology series spinning off from the William Inge play which had been filmed with Marilyn Monroe. Your first show in the series, 'The Covering Darkness', starred Robert Redford and Barbara Baxley, but then you caused great controversy with 'The Lion Walks Among Us', in which an attractive young drifter visits the fictional small town of Sunrise, commits a murder and persuades everyone he is innocent and almost gets off. Its themes of callous violence, sexual psychosis and alcoholism proved too much for prime-time television in 1961.*

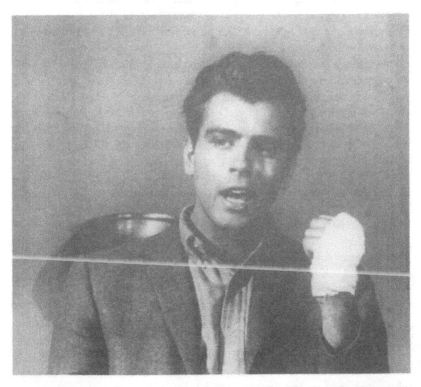

16 Fabian strikes a defiant pose in the dangerously violent episode Altman directed in the *Bus Stop* series, 'A Lion Walks Among Us' (1961)

It was adapted from a novel by Tom Wicker, a *New York Times* writer. Roy Huggins was the producer, and he and I were always at loggerheads. We cast Fabian[8] in it, and I remember he used to come to my house. My daughters were around twelve years old then, and they saved the Kleenex he blew his nose on! He was just a kid, not a good actor, and I worked with him, not trying to teach him how to act but just to loosen him up. Then we shot the film, and the sponsors, the Brown and Williamson Tobacco Company, said they wouldn't sponsor it. So it was taken off the air in places like Denver, for instance, and everywhere else it ran it did so without any of the usual commercials. The commercials that accompanied the film were by ABC; in other words, they were about their own programmes. Then the *New York Times* and *Newsweek*, I don't think they had seen it, but they talked about this film in which the violence was beyond tolerance.

Thomas J. Dodd, a senator from Connecticut, read those reviews and instigated an enquiry at the Congressional Committee on the Judiciary, where the network was told to behave. Did you think you were really pushing the envelope here?
I never thought about what the limits were. I knew there were certain things we couldn't do, but we just tried different ways to skin the cat. I felt that about everything. On one episode of *The Millionaire*[9] I had Adam Williams and Joanna Moore, who was in *Countdown*, and I said I wanted to do something really sexy, really beyond the censors. Every show was like that in some way – I was thinking they'd never get it, but the audience would. So we did a very erotic piece. It wasn't anything where they could say, 'Oh, I saw a nipple.' There was no way to pin it down. But we were always trying to beat the censors, whether they were our own producers or whether, in fact, they were a real censor or a sponsor censor. It was always a case of trying to get beyond the limits they imposed.

The one series you really had some artistic control over was Combat, *which still stands up as one of the most realistic depictions of war in a television series.*
I produced the series: I had control over scripts, casting and everything, wrote a few and directed every other episode for the first year. I went into it saying, 'OK, this is World War II, we've all seen this stuff before', and I started from the position that all the Germans should speak German, unless there's a real reason they should speak English. It was hard to find actors who could do that, and I'm sure if you look at those episodes today you'd find that this guy speaking German is really speaking Dutch or something

else. These actors all wanted a job and they were probably terrible. But at least we were able to approach the reality of the action a little. Shooting in black and white helped a lot too, as that's how we'd seen the war. Colour would have made things very difficult.

As we got into them, I realized I had this terrible problem: each story was

17 A taste of verisimilitude in the depiction of war in an episode of *Combat* (1962–3)

putting my heroes, the people who appeared in every episode every week, in jeopardy, but the audience knew they weren't really in jeopardy because they were the stars and they were going to come back next week. So the first thing I did was build a squad of ten or so guys who were running characters, and among them I would create a character who'd be in about three episodes and then in the fourth I'd say, 'OK, this is your last, because I want to kill you off.' And I would have him killed, not in a dramatic plot point way but just *en passant*. Suddenly a character would say, 'What happened? Riley's dead.' And they'd go, 'Riley, uh, Riley.' And this was one of the regular guys. It worked very well for us, whether or not the audience got it, as it made sense because of the way the other actors responded to the behaviour of this character.

It was a fairly popular series, in which Vic Morrow was the lead.[10] He was a real Method actor, and a good one, good at improvising and going to extremes, while Rick Jason, the other star, was more of a movie actor. Every time I did one of these episodes, I'd think, 'Ah, the next one. I can do this or this.' And I'd push it a little bit further. Each one used the set-up of a classic feature film. For example, this one would be my *Foreign Intrigue*,[11] and so on.

One episode, 'The Volunteer', was even shown out of competition at the Venice Film Festival.
I saw 'Cat and Mouse' again in Austin, Texas, when I was down there doing *Dr T.* and I must say I still thought it pretty good, well shot. We had a great cinematographer, Bob Hauser, and I learned a lot from him. We used a lot of smoke and netting, and worked a lot on creating depth to the image. Sometimes it was quite dangerous, with all those explosions going off. But the tougher you made it, the more the actors got into it.

With 'Cat and Mouse', I liked the idea of throwing together two guys who hated each other and having them trapped in a place where they needed each other. But I got into trouble because I was showing too harsh a view of war, and *Combat* was going out at 6.30 p.m. in the Midwest, when kids were watching. They said we were making them too grim, without enough jokes. I said, 'You mean there's a danger of kids not liking war?'

Probably the most memorable episode was 'Survival', in which Vic Morrow's character is separated from his men and wanders around a war-blasted terrain in a shell-shocked haze and is so delirious he surrenders to a dead German soldier.
I pushed so far on that one they locked me out of the MGM studios where

we filmed. The executive producer, Selig Seligman, had turned the script down, saying, 'Don't shoot this. I don't like it and I don't want it.' He thought there wasn't enough story to it, that it was too relentlessly grim. Then he left town, and I thought, 'Oh, fuck him, I'm just gonna do it.' And I did, and when he came back, he fired me, of course. I would sit in a bar next to the studios, and Vic Morrow would go to the editing room and then come over to the bar, and he'd say, 'They're doing this and this and this, what do you think?' And I'd say, 'No, no, have 'em do *this* and *this*.' Then he'd go back to the editing room. And that's the episode that got the Emmy nomination for Morrow!

You went on to make four films for the Kraft Suspense Theatre, *but you later told* Variety *their shows were 'as bland as its cheese'.*
That's true. They would keep turning scripts down because they wanted something less controversial. I was always trying to push those films further than they wanted, they were more interested in just putting a programme on the air and getting the ads. But I was doing little movies . . .

One of them, 'Once Upon a Savage Night', a story about a serial killer that ended with a multi-car pile-up, was expanded to make a TV movie, retitled Nightmare in Chicago *and reportedly given a theatrical release in the Midwest, Canada and Europe.*
'Once Upon a Savage Night' was shot on location in Chicago with high-speed colour stock, a 35mm positive stock with an ASA of about 800. We used every foot of raw stock we could find. In fact, we ended up shooting 100-ft rolls. I remember I had a scene with two actors and a truck. It was the last thing we were shooting. All we had left were just a few rolls, and they'd talk and I'd say, 'Cut! OK, reload and let's pick up from exactly where you left off.' I was always more comfortable doing location filming.

By this stage you must have been itching to make feature films.
I left *Kraft Suspense Theatre* with this guy Ray Wagner, and we formed a company. That's when I got my space over in Westwood Boulevard, which we called Westwood Productions. We bought *Me and the Archkook Petulia*, which I wanted Barbara Turner to script. I also asked Roald Dahl to write a screenplay from an original idea by myself and Brian McKay, *Death, Where is Thy Sting-a-ling-ling?*, which was also known as *The Chicken and the Hawk*, about World War I pilots.

18 Altman sporting a fez while directing a scene in *Once Upon a Savage Night*, later known as *Nightmare in Chicago* (1964)

Both those films eventually went into the hands of others. *Petulia*, with a screenplay credited to Lawrence B. Marcus, was filmed by Richard Lester with Julie Christie and George C. Scott in 1968. *Death* was begun by David Miller with Gregory Peck but never finished. Through a deal made by his new agent,

George Litto, Altman directed a film pilot, 'Chicago, Chicago', for a television series called *Nightwatch,* but it was not picked up.

While you were waiting for your break into features, you made some comic short films, three of which you've occasionally allowed people to see: The Kathryn Reed Story, *a birthday present for your wife;* The Party, *with Robert Fortier as a hapless guest at a very 1960s party, one of a projected series of juke-box movies called ColorSonics; and* Pot au feu, *a parody of a TV cookery programme explaining the recipe for the perfect marijuana joint.*

I did those just for myself. They were unfinanced, just bringing together a few friends, borrowing a camera and so on. But because of one of those films I got hired to do *M*A*S*H:* Ingo Preminger looked at *Pot au feu* and loved it, so it served its purpose.

You've always had a very liberal attitude towards smoking pot.
To me it's no different to having a drink at the end of the evening, except that's legal. Marijuana should be, because it's never killed anybody. It's

19 Altman and his sons in the mid-1960s – from left to right, Stephen, Robert Jr (or Bobby) and Michael

been my drug of choice. I find it relaxing, but I don't think it really does anything for you on a creative level. I never drank when I was working, it never affected my work, and the same is true of grass.

I had photos taken of me in the 1960s on the beach with a joint in my hand and placed in the press, but for me to try to hide that would make me as duplicitous as they are. So I don't hide it or make an issue of it. In a generation or two, those things are usually no longer an issue.

Has that rebellious image worked against you?
It's not really served me well at all. My career has been hurt by it, but then so has everyone's, the further away from the norm they get. What's the loss? I can only judge loss from my personal level – that I didn't get to go through the machinations of making films from the start, which is what I really wanted to do. But that's just a personal loss; it doesn't affect anybody else. Maybe if I had gone on to do work without certain of my attributes involved in it, then the work wouldn't have been so compelling to so many people. What it really boils down to is, it doesn't make any difference.

Countdown

How did your first studio movie, Countdown, *happen?*
There was a book I tried to buy called *The Pilgrim Project* by Hank Searle, which I thought was terrific. It was about sending a guy to the Moon on *Gemini*, and then he had to wait there until they could develop *Apollo* to come and pick him up. It was all about beating the Russians. It was owned by someone else; then Warner Brothers got it, and they had a low-budget film programme. They offered it to me, and I took it without hesitation. That was *Countdown*. I thought it a pretty good little film. I tried to show astronauts as human beings with problems, and I had scenes with over-lapping dialogue, in which I made sure that every word wasn't being heard. There was quite a bit of excitement over my work at the studio.

When I was finishing the film, Jack Warner, who had been in Europe, came back, although when he came on the set I wasn't there. Then over the weekend he watched the dailies. On Sunday I got a call at home – I was going to start editing the next day – and it was Bill Conrad,[12] who was then an executive producer at the studio. He told me, 'Don't come to the studio, they won't let you through the gates.' I said, 'What do you mean?' 'Well, Jack Warner saw your dailies and he said, "That fool has actors talking at the same time."' And I had to drive up to the gate, and there was a

20 Lee Stegler (James Caan) and 'Chiz' Stewart (Robert Duvall) prepare for
take-off in *Countdown* (1968)

cardboard box with all this stuff from my desk, which the guard handed to
me. I was not allowed in the studio. And they cut the picture for kids.
Meanwhile, I went off to Spain for a film that never happened.

Actually, being fired from *Countdown* was great for me, because each
time something like that happens, you get a battle scar and you know how
to protect yourself in that situation again. It was the choice I had to make at
that time in my career. Was I going to try to keep going in television? Why
was I staying inside this bubble? Am I the artist here? And I made the only
choice that was really available to me, because I would never have survived
inside the system. I would have been chewed up and spat out. So since then
I've been underground all my life, and I have no complaints.

How did the studio's version of Countdown *differ from yours?*
They rewrote the ending we shot. I left it ambiguous – the guy was probably
going to die on the moon. When he landed there, he was supposed to find a
shelter with a beacon on it. But he only had so much life support, and he
landed prematurely and hadn't seen the beacon. He was saying, 'I think I

see it, I'm going towards it.' He goes off in one direction, and the camera pans back and reveals the beacon is in the opposite direction. That was how I ended it. They had him taking a toy mouse, spinning it and going off in the direction it pointed – and finding the beacon.

In the US, *Countdown* was released as a supporting feature to *The Green Berets*, John Wayne's patriotic Vietnam War film. It was severely cut for its UK release.

That Cold Day in the Park

Your next film, That Cold Day in the Park, *based on a novel by Richard Miles, told the story of a woman who keeps a younger man prisoner in her house and was an independent production set up with Commonwealth United in Canada.*
I read that book and said, 'Let's buy it.' I had a friend named Don Factor, who was part of the Max Factor family, and we bought the book. We went to London and got Gillian Freeman,[13] who's still a friend of mine, to write it. We spent a long time trying to raise the finance, and I think in the end Don put up most of the money himself. I think we did it for about half a million dollars.

I understand the original idea was to cast Elizabeth Taylor and set the film in London. How did it come to be filmed in Vancouver?
Originally I'd gone up there to see whether I could make *Images*. I had Sandy Dennis in mind for it, as I had previously offered her *Petulia*, but she was really interested in doing *That Cold Day in the Park*.
There was no film industry up in Vancouver, and we built an enormous set in an old warehouse. The whole apartment must have been 3,000 square feet, and that's where the action mostly took place. Leon Ericksen designed that, and it was my first experience with him. He's a genius. He had done *The Rain People* for Francis Ford Coppola, and in that were Jimmy Caan and Bob Duvall, whom I'd worked with on *Countdown*, so it was all very incestuous.

Although the film isn't as extreme in style as what was to come, there is a lot of play with reflecting surfaces and objects, and a tantalizing scene in a doctor's clinic when you eavesdrop on the women talking about sex and contraception.

21 Frances Austen (Sandy Dennis) and The Boy (Michael Burns) in *That Cold Day in the Park* (1969)

I shot that from outside, looking through windows into a semi-basement room. You couldn't really hear what they were saying. There was very little location work.

Laszlo Kovacs was the cinematographer, and it was really a first film in a funny way, very pretentious and stylized. At the time I could have been attracted to anything I could make, but somehow when I read it I thought this would be a terrific film. I went to a number of actresses, including Ingrid Bergman. Bergman fired back an answer, saying she thought it was a disgusting film and it made her wonder why anyone would think of her. The idea of the woman getting a whore for this guy in order to keep him inside was pretty strong, I guess.

After I was hired on *M*A*S*H*, Dick Zanuck saw *That Cold Day in the Park* and said, 'If I'd seen that picture before, I'd never have let that guy get near!'

Notes

1 Cecil Kellaway (1893–1973) was born in South Africa and arrived in Hollywood in the early 1930s, where he made his mark as a character actor – notably in *Wuthering Heights* (1939) – and was twice nominated for an Academy Award: for *Luck of the Irish* (1948) and *Guess Who's Coming to Dinner?* (1967). He appeared in two episodes of *Whirlybirds*, 'Shoot Out' and 'Buy Me a Miracle'.

2 The episode of *U.S. Marshal* featuring Barbara Baxley was 'Kill or Be Killed' and was syndicated on 22 February 1960. The male guest star was Paul Richards.

3 Lionel Lindon (1905–71) began his career as a director of photography in Hollywood in the 1940s, and among his many credits are *The Blue Dahlia* (1946), *Alias Nick Beal* (1949), *The Manchurian Candidate* (1962) and *Grand Prix* (1966). He also worked a great deal in television, on such seminal series as *Alfred Hitchcock Presents*, *Johnny Staccato*, *The Munsters*, *Ironside* and *Night Gallery*.

4 John A. Alonzo (1934–2001) began his career as a TV actor, appearing in one episode of *Combat*, 'The Prisoner', and in *Once Upon a Savage Night*. In 1964 he turned to cinematography and his credits included *Vanishing Point* (1971), *Harold and Maude* (1971), *Farewell, My Lovely* (1975), *Norma Rae* (1979), *Scarface* (1983) and *Internal Affairs* (1990).

5 A 50mm lens is close to the human eye in terms of perspective and range. A diopter is the measuring unit of the magnifying power of a lens, and a diopter lens magnifies the image, making extreme close-ups possible. Often a split diopter is used to divide the image and keep both the foreground and the background in sharp focus. A diopter lens may also be used in the eyepiece of a camera to adapt it to the sight of the operator.

6 *The Thing . . . From Another World* (1951) was produced for RKO Pictures by Howard Hawks, written by the ace team of Howard Hecht and Charles Lederer, and officially directed by Hawks's former editor, Christian Nyby. According to the testimony of many of the cast, though, Hawks himself directed most of the film. Hawks's trademark technique of having the actors overlap their dialogue was evident from his screwball comedy *Twentieth Century* (1934) onwards.

7 It is usual practice in filming scenes for cinema or television to offer the editor a variety of angles and different-sized shots of the same action and/or dialogue, so that something can be cut out or the scene shortened or lengthened. Filming in one shot leaves no room for any flexibility of this kind.

8 Fabian Forte (b. 1943) was a teen singing sensation in the mid-1950s, discovered at the age of fifteen, whose hit singles included 'Turn Me Loose' and 'Tiger'. In 1959 he made his movie début in *Hound-Dog Man* and went on to

act in over thirty films. He still performs on television and in concert with other singers of his generation.

9 The episode of *The Millionaire* featuring Joanna Moore was called 'Millionaire Jackson Greene', or 'Beatnik', and was first transmitted on 23 December 1959.

10 Vic Morrow (1932–82) appeared in films from the 1950s, including *The Blackboard Jungle* (1955) and *Men in War* (1957), but after directing two features his career was tragically ended in a helicopter accident during the shooting of *Twilight Zone – The Movie* (1983). He was married to actress Barbara Turner, who appeared in Altman's TV drama *Nightmare in Chicago*. Following their divorce in 1964, she married Altman's former associate turned successful television director Reza Badiyi and became a scriptwriter. Among her credits are *Georgia* (1995), *Pollock* (2000) and *The Company* (2003). Jennifer Jason Leigh (b. 1962), Morrow and Turner's daughter, has appeared in two of Altman's films, *Short Cuts* and *Kansas City*.

11 *Foreign Intrigue* (1956), directed by Sheldon Reynolds, starred Robert Mitchum travelling through Europe investigating the cause of his millionaire employer's death. It was based on a TV series of the same title which ran from 1951–5.

12 William Conrad (1920–1994) was a character actor in movies from the 1940s, usually playing heavies, who turned to producing and directing in the 1950s. In the 1960s he narrated the popular TV cartoon series *The Bullwinkle Show* and then became famous as the overweight private eye in the series *Cannon* (1971–6).

13 Gillian Freeman had previously scripted *The Leather Boys* (1965), adapted from her own novel.

3

M*A*S*H – Brewster McCloud –
McCabe & Mrs Miller

M*A*S*H

When blacklisted screenwriter Ring Lardner Jr[1] read the novel M*A*S*H (standing for Mobile Army Surgical Hospital, an army unit three miles from the front during the Korean War) by a pseudonymous Richard Hooker – it was still in galley form before publication, and he'd been asked to write a commendation for the cover – he called his friend and former agent, producer Ingo Preminger (brother of Otto), suggesting it would be great material for a film. Preminger approached Richard Zanuck and David Brown, then running 20th Century Fox, who were interested. However, between ten and fifteen directors turned it down, including Stanley Kubrick, Sidney Lumet, Sydney Pollack, Gene Kelly and George Roy Hill. Then Altman was sent the script by his agent George Litto, who pitched him as director to Preminger.

DAVID THOMPSON: *What interested you in doing* M*A*S*H?
ROBERT ALTMAN: To me the fun of all of these movies I've made has been taking your mates and creating something like a stock company. The first people I think of for a film are people I've worked with before, usually most recently. And rarely have I had a film where somebody hands me a script and then I go and do exactly that script – even the ones that seemed to happen that way, like M*A*S*H. I had worked for five years on a project called *The Chicken and the Hawk*, a World War I flying film, and the whole idea of making a farcical film with all these characters, filling the screen with people, started there. But I had no credentials at that time, and it was too expensive. When I was given the script for M*A*S*H, I thought it was dreadful, and on the face of it, I felt it wasn't going to work. There were no peripheral characters; it was just about five people and a bunch of extras. But I thought, 'I can make this picture by doing the same thing that I was going to do in *The Chicken and the Hawk* and fill it with all this life.'

I went up to San Francisco, where there was a lot of Theatre of the Absurd going on and you could see twenty-five people interacting on stage. I hired about twenty actors for M*A*S*H, many of whom had never been in a movie before.[2] But to get them into the film, there had to be a corresponding name like Charlie in the script, otherwise the studio wouldn't hire

44

them. So I went through the script and gave names to all these characters I wanted and put one or two lines in for each of them. Then, when it came to casting parts, the studio said, 'OK, we've got to hire somebody for this role.' And I said, 'Well, he's got to be in every scene.' I'd done this in television before, when I would give six people one line each in order to have extras whom I could talk to.[3] And that's how that philosophy started, and how I was able to get into the system of the studios. When I began making movies, I was in no position to attract star names, and I think that also got me headed towards this sort of ensemble work that I like a lot.

When you began shooting on 14 April 1969 on the Fox backlot in the Santa Monica mountains, what were the studio's expectations?
It was a cheap picture that Fox thought would just play in drive-ins, and they didn't care too much about it. Fox had two other war movies going on: *Patton: Lust for Glory* and *Tora! Tora! Tora!*, both big-budget pictures.[4] I knew that and decided that the way to keep out of trouble was to stay out of their sightline – and the best way to do *that* was not to go over budget or over schedule. The picture was budgeted at $3.5 million, and I think I brought it in half a million under budget, which was a lot. But I said right off the bat to all my artists, 'Don't raise our heads, and don't draw attention to ourselves. Let's not go into the commissary to eat, let's not talk about the picture, because they're diverted. We can sneak this one through . . .'

What finally made you feel you could work with Lardner's script?
The original book was terrible, racist and filled with jokes for the sake of jokes. But Ring Lardner had added in operations, and I thought if I could make them vivid and real, these terrible jokes could work because that's how those guys kept sane. Nobody was fighting any idealistic war.
   Lardner didn't like the movie. He said I'd destroyed his script and that I'd double-crossed him, and he was very upset about it. But when he won the Academy Award, he didn't say anything about me. He had also told me he thought I was going to win the directing award for sure, and so there was no point in me saying anything either . . .

Although the film is supposed to be taking place in the 1950s, it feels much more contemporary than that, from the haircuts on.
I had hidden the fact it was set in the Korean War, but the studio forced me to put the legend on the front saying, 'And then there was . . . Korea.' Although the book and script were set in Korea, to me it was Vietnam. I wanted to mix it up and have people thinking of it as a contemporary story

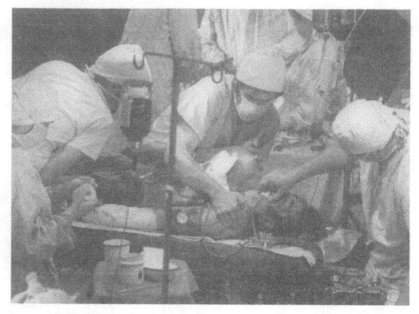

22 An unsparing view of surgeons at work in the operating theatre in
M*A*S*H (1970)

– that is, 1969, 1970. All the political attitudes in the film were about Nixon and the Vietnam War.

Did the behaviour of the men in service reflect any of your own wartime experiences?
Mainly the silliness that went on. We were on an island with an Australian hospital, and that was great, as there were nurses and we would steal jeeps, smuggle whisky in and have parties. Planes were commandeered for flying beer from Australia . . . all that stuff was the routine of the day.

The scene of Hot Lips' humiliation in the shower has a flavour of that.
Sally Kellerman was very nervous about it. I don't think she'd been naked in a film before. I said to her, 'Just go in and take your shower, and when the curtain flies up, protect yourself at all times. It's no big deal.' I thought it was her modesty, that she didn't want to be seen naked for the usual reasons, but afterwards she said she didn't care about showing her body, it was just she felt her hips were too big. So it was her vanity, not her modesty. The first take, Sally hit the ground so fast that we couldn't tell what she was

23 Having a 'sMASHing' time in Manila in 1945. Altman is third from the left, holding a glass

doing. So when we did the second take, Gary Burghoff, who played Radar, and I stood on either side of the camera with our pants down, so when the tent went up she saw the two of us standing there naked. That's why she froze before falling, and how we got the shot we wanted. She's a great actress, and I think the whole scene is one of the high points of the film.

What do you have to say about the treatment of women in the film? They certainly seem at the mercy of the jokes and whims and sexual needs of the men.
I remember once, in front of about five thousand students, I was accused of being a misogynist. They were asking how could I treat women in this way? I said, 'I *don't* treat women that way. I'm showing you the way I observed women were treated, and still are treated, in the army.' The same was true for gays and blacks. Of course, the film's humour level was very crude and loaded with sexist jokes, but our attitude was that nothing was as obscene as the destruction of the young men sent in to fight a war that was only a political situation, a terror set up by the right wing of America.

24 Party time in *M*A*S*H* (1970) – centre frame, Hawkeye (Donald
Sutherland), below him in the Uncle Sam hat, Trapper John McIntyre (Elliott
Gould), and in front, Duke Forrest (Tom Skerritt)

So it was all in the attitude of the characters?
Well, these were doctors, not soldiers. They didn't have guns or take part in
combat; they just had to repair or bury an endless line of casualties, so it
was hard for them at the time to take any army regulations seriously. It
made no difference to them whether they were promoted or demoted
because they were needed as surgeons. And they couldn't have kept their
sanity without that kind of behaviour.

The operating scenes still seem very graphic.
Those were what really interested me, and I wanted them to be absolutely
real and outrageous, with blood everywhere, and yet have everybody carrying on as if they were mechanics repairing an automobile. The actual scenes
were medically accurate. We put a real surgeon, our technical advisor, in
there, and all the actors knew what operations they were doing. We went to
a lot of trouble to get the colour of the blood right.

The grimy, unflattering camerawork on M*A*S*H was immediately distinctive. Was that hard to achieve?
The first cinematographer I hired was just shooting a different film to me. I knew there was something wrong, because I hired him over the objections of the studio, and they were telling him he had to be sure to do this and this and *this*, and I couldn't figure out why he wasn't shooting what *I* wanted the way I wanted it. Finally, I fired him and I got Hal Stine, then an old guy of about sixty-five years old, whom I'd worked with at Warner Brothers on *The Roaring 20's*. I brought him out of retirement, and he did a great job – he was used to working fast.

M*A*S*H already has your trademark use of slow zooms.
I did that a lot as soon as the zoom lens appeared. It was a tool, and I got a lot of criticism for it. 'Oh, you should never move that camera, those zooms are false and they change the whole perspective.' I said, 'I know what they do, but this is the way I'm telling this story.' And I did a lot of that, a lot of arbitrary moves with the zoom lens. Now everybody's doing it.

How did you get the rough-hewn look of the film?
Except for the football game, we put number three fog filters on the camera, always trying to destroy that colour image, making it dirty rather than crisp and bright. When we did *Combat* we were shooting in black and white, and it was easier to evoke those kind of things. Colour was a different issue. But when it comes to these choices, you say these things in interviews to justify what you've done, and from that point on, that's what I think. So there's probably 60 per cent truth and 40 per cent fiction in it! I still do the same thing today. I say to myself, 'Why have I done that? Oh, I know . . .'

So these choices were always instinctive?
I don't know if anything in film can be completely instinctual for me, as I've done so much. Every one of these things I do, whatever they are, these little techniques or idiosyncrasies, have been done for some reason. Nobody's the inventor of anything.

How much of your distinctive visual style then is in the pre-planning with cinematographers?
My head is full of smoke and fog – I don't see anything, I just know that if you blow it away, we'll see it. I don't know how I'm going to shoot a film at first. I'll talk about things with a cinematographer, but we never resolve

anything. We're still talking right up until the time we have to shoot. Suddenly, then, the visual style of the film is set. But the minute you make a rule, you break it. And if you don't break it, you're a fool.

My marriages with cinematographers normally last about three pictures, because if you work with the same people you begin to know what each other is going to do. There comes a natural time to go and seek out other partners – at least on a weekend . . .

Everyone remembers the PA announcements of M*A*S*H *as a high point.* The film was too jumpy: I needed a form of punctuation. We were already into the editing, and I remember coming up with the idea one day just as I was turning into my driveway. Danny Greene, my editor, went out and made a lot of shots of loudspeakers, and we used them like chapter headings, taking stuff from an official army manual from 1951. All the films mentioned were old Fox titles. One announcement came from a memo from the head of the editorial department at the studio. We'd had photographs up on the wall in the editing room, and a memo had come around: 'Take down all pictures of naked girls!' They wanted rooms to be clean and pristine. We'd get David Arkin, who played the sergeant, and have him record the announcements for the film. The last one, describing the film you've just seen, actually came from the studio newsletter.

Wasn't this the first time the word 'fuck' was heard in a mainstream picture? It was the first time it was ever used outside of an X-rated picture. It was the actor John Schuck who decided to say it during the football game, and he did it as a joke. It certainly wasn't written, and I didn't tell him to do it. But in the dailies, there it was. The reason it was eventually allowed in an R-rated picture was that it wasn't used in a sexual context; it was just profanity.

Your son shares a credit for the title song, 'Suicide Is Painless'. We needed a song, and I came up with this title. My son Michael, who was thirteen or so then, was writing songs, so I suggested he did it, because I didn't think it would be any more than a song to accompany the *faux* funeral. Michael wrote the lyrics and Johnny Mandel reworked it, and we liked it so much we used it as the title music. It could have become a hit then, as it did later with the TV series, but none of the record companies wanted to promote a lyric about suicide.

25 The Last Supper scene in *M*A*S*H* (1970)

Where did you get the idea of parodying Leonardo da Vinci's The Last Supper *for the funeral of Painless?*

We shot that scene in the studio one morning. I didn't know what I was going to do. I looked at this set with the table and I said, 'Get them all in their white hospital stuff and find me a picture of the Last Supper.' We had them all in those positions, and I thought that was a little arch, as did many other people, but then, so what? This is not so serious. What difference does it make if it works or not? This isn't the end-all of anything. These movies, they're just caprices.

It's just like with any artists, they don't know what you're talking about when you say, 'Oh my God, you're such an inspiration.' They shut up, because all they're doing is drawing and painting something which has occurred to them. They don't see that genius – and it isn't genius; it just happens to strike a nerve at that time. If you took the middle part of Picasso's work and started with that, Picasso wouldn't be Picasso, because all of it has to be seen in the time that it's in. If *M*A*S*H* had been two years earlier or two years later, it probably would have been a turkey.

Did your Catholic background have anything to do with the Last Supper inspiration?
I was brought up a Catholic – that was my childhood and my schooling – but I never bought it. On Sundays when the family would go to Mass, I would do anything to duck out. I went to school at the same place, so I knew the escape routes. My mother kept saying, 'Oh, Bobby, when you get into the war, you'll need to turn to your religion.' And when I went into the army, that was the last year I went to church in my life. Other than a marriage, I never went to a church service as a parishioner of any kind. And it was no big deal with me; it simply didn't compute. Yet I'm *simpático* with it. I was indoctrinated, even though it never registered. And I think with these strong, organized religions, it's a way to polarize people into a condition. And now it's coming down to choosing between the Christians and the Muslims, and the Jews are kind of stuck in the middle.

Religion appears to be becoming more and more of an influence on American politics.
Yet politics have to leave it alone in order to succeed. If the Democrats came out and said, 'We're not taking any Catholics,' then all the Catholics would be Republican. It's the same thing when politicians talk about black Republicans, because they're so identifiable it's hard to avoid it, but they have to go back to the black population because it's on the increase, and the Latin population is really on the increase, and the white people still want it their way.

Who cast Elliott Gould and Donald Sutherland in the lead roles?
Ingo hired them, and I agreed, though I didn't know either of them. I brought in Tom Skerritt, who had been in *Combat*, and everyone else. Elliott and Donald became a tight twosome, and they were the stars in their minds. They didn't get my direction at *all*, though it was a natural way for Elliott to work. Don tried but he was less successful than Elliott. They complained that I was spending all my time with the extras. And it's true. I figured those two had lines written for them and they knew what they were doing . . . So, three or four weeks into the film they complained to the producer and tried to have me fired. They said, 'This guy is going to ruin our careers.' I didn't know about it until about a year later, when Elliott told me. But had I found out then, I would have quit. Or I would have been so wounded it would have been a very different film. But if you don't know something, you're just stupid and go your own way. I don't give directions anyway, but they felt I was devoting too much time on other people and the background extras and not enough on them.

So what you're after is behaviour rather than a performance?
Yes, but I don't know very much about performance anyway. I don't understand acting, by which I mean I don't understand how they do it. I don't understand what anybody's technique is. I've learned through the years that actors are really the ones who are *doing* the thing. I can't tell them how to act, like saying be meaner or this or that. I can't do it. I've had lots of complaints from actors. Burt Lancaster in *Buffalo Bill* said afterwards, 'Altman didn't give me any directions. He's not a good director.' That's not what I do. I try to create an atmosphere where these actors can stretch into it. But mostly they're all pretty conservative anyway. They have a safety net, too. After all, it's their faces up there as long as the picture's still alive. And they don't really have control over films – an actor can go in and give a perfectly terrific performance and it can end up being for nought. I think most films are overacted, because people are afraid that if they don't do something extreme then it's not worth it. It's difficult for anybody – actors, writers, directors – to say, 'Oh, we're shooting this scene. Just sit in this chair and do nothing.' That's hard to do, because you don't see it in the context of anything else – you don't hear the music, you don't know what's happened before or what's going to happen afterwards.

I learned something on *The Company*. When I shot scenes with Neve Campbell and James Franco, I just left out all the obligatory dialogue, because the audience knows all that. But I was very worried about it. I thought, 'Why isn't this done more often? Maybe the audience *have* to be told.' I made kind of an intellectual decision: 'I'm going to do it this way and see if that works.' But having done it, what if it doesn't work? I think it does, but again, I don't know for sure. Most films are concerned with doing what has already been done better, rather than doing what may not have been done.

Doesn't improvisation play a large part in your work with the actors?
The main artists for me are the actors, because they take this sketchy script and put three-dimensional life into it. Now I get accused a lot of using improvisation, but that's a misunderstanding. For me improvisation is a rehearsal tool. Once we go to shoot the film, everyone pretty much knows what's going to happen, unless it's some scene with three hundred people, and we say, 'OK, fire! Everybody run!', then that's usually improvised. Most of all, I just encourage actors to feel comfortable.

*What was the initial reaction to M*A*S*H?*
The first reviewer was a guy from *Variety*, and it was his first assignment.

He'd come down from San Francisco or somewhere, and when he went out to see the film at Fox, the head of publicity said to him, 'Don't worry about this picture, this is going right to the drive-ins, this is shit.' And the man from *Variety* wrote a bad review. Afterwards, he got in touch with me and said, 'Listen, I want to tell you something.' I said, 'You're the first reviewer who saw it and you very nearly fucked my film up!' He said, 'I loved it, but I was so new on the job, and this guy said it was a bad picture.' And although his review had said such-and-such a scene was so funny that people would fall out into the aisles, he went on to criticize it. I said, 'I'm the injured party. Don't tell me your problems, I've got my own.'

But didn't the studio's attitude change after a crucial screening in San Francisco?
Darryl Zanuck[5] was in Europe at the time, and his son Dick and David Brown were running the studio. He came back just as the film was finished and we screened it to him. His cronies said, 'All these operating scenes have to come out,' and they reported that he also wanted us to get rid of all that operating shit. But there were two French girls he had brought with him, and they said, 'No, we love this picture, don't do it, that's the best part.' And because of those two dames, he allowed the scenes to stay in. I said, 'Let me preview it,' and we went to San Francisco, where at a big, 3,000-seat house they showed *M*A*S*H* before *Butch Cassidy and the Sundance Kid*. Dick Zanuck was there because he'd flown up in the company jet to see a Stanford football game, as that was his *alma mater*. The crowd went nuts; they really, really loved it. And I remember grabbing him by the shoulders and I said, 'Dick, you have got to listen to these people and you've got to let the picture go out the way it is.' And he did. But that was just a series of accidents. And everything turns on that. Somebody makes a judgement, 'Oh, we'll cancel that picture', and they probably had a stomach ache or gas or they had a bad day or they're pissed off . . . Another day they would approve anything. So it just happens to be the luck of the draw. It's how you hit people, especially when they're told they have the power of judgement. 'What do you think?' When you ask someone that, it's terrible, because you're forcing them to form an opinion, which they do not want to do.

M*A*S*H opened in New York on 25 January 1970, which I guess was a critical day for you.
I remember there was a blizzard, it was about 15 degrees below zero, and no one was on the streets. But when I went to check out the theatre on Third

Avenue, the line was around one block after another. It was a thrilling sight. The word was out about the film, and it was immediately a hit.

I understand even the US forces were eventually allowed to see the film, such was the excitement surrounding it. It won the Palme d'Or at the 1970 Cannes Film Festival, and it went on to be one of the three top-grossing Hollywood films of the year. According to Variety, *it grossed over $70 million in the US. Ingo Preminger and Fox did very well out of the film's success – what did you make out of it?*
I got $75,000 dollars for doing M*A*S*H, and they were supposed to give me a percentage of the profits, but they never did. If you consider the spin-off of the TV series,[6] that picture made a billion dollars for Fox. They didn't approach me about the series, and I wouldn't have done it anyway.

What were your objections to the television series?
Every Sunday night an Asian war was in our living rooms, and no matter what platitudes they came out with, still the bad guys were the dark-skinned, narrow-eyed people. I just thought that was obscene at the time, when we were still in Vietnam. It was the opposite message to what we felt we were making in the film.

I remember at my mother's funeral, this friend of hers told me, 'Oh, Mr Altman, your mother was so proud of you. We see that M*A*S*H every week!'

Brewster McCloud

After working at Fox, you went to MGM for what you described as your 'adult fairy tale', Brewster McCloud, *about a young man, played by Bud Cort, who dreams of flying and commits a series of bizarre murders.*
I was forty-four when I made M*A*S*H, so I had no illusions about the business. Fox didn't want me at all. *Brewster McCloud* came about thanks to M*A*S*H. Lou Adler,[7] the record producer who had the Mamas and the Papas, had this script called *Brewster McCloud* and he came to me. I said, 'Yeah, I'll do this, it'll be good.' I saw in it something I'd never seen before, a mix of fairy tale and fantasy, and I sat down and rewrote it, making it very farcical and broad. Really I began by thinking about bird shit! My kids were quite young then and would come in and say, 'Dad, there's bird shit on the car.' And when you start looking around, it's amazing, there's bird shit everywhere. It's one thing we really can't control.

Wasn't it originally meant to be set in New York?
Yes, at the TWA terminal at New York's JFK airport, which had a very modern look, and at the end of the original script that's where Brewster took off from. I guess the Houston Astrodome was new then, and it was an indoor arena of a size nobody had experienced. I can't remember who brought it up, but the idea fascinated me and I went down to look at it. It was all in such bad taste. It was quite an accomplishment to make it happen there, but I thought, 'How else can you show that this guy flies unless he's trapped, as if in a cage?' That became his freedom, that he'll never be free!

How did you cast the film?
I put Bud Cort in it as he had a small part in M*A*S*H, and Sally Keller-man, Rene Auberjonois, Michael Murphy, John Schuck, who'd all been in it, too. But then I've always had a tendency to do this, to take the people I'm working with and say, 'Let's do *this* now.'

Shelley Duvall we found down there in Houston. I had gone away for a week, and the guys I was working with, Tommy Thompson and Brian McKay, said, 'Oh, we went to a party, found a girl, and you've got to meet her. She is special!' I said, 'Oh, shit, these guys probably got drunk . . .' When they'd seen her, she was trying to sell paintings by her boyfriend. So I had her come in to see me, and she didn't know that we were looking at her for a part. But I didn't believe her. I thought it was an act. She had these eyelashes painted on her face, weighed about four pounds, and if she had any tits they were on her back. 'Hi, what do want me to do?' I said, 'Oh, you'll want to read for this part.' 'What's that mean?' I said, 'What does it *mean*? You know how to read?' I decided to shoot a test, so I took her out in the park and put a camera on her and just asked her questions. I was really quite mean to her, as I thought she was an actress. But she wasn't kidding; that was her. She was an untrained, truthful person. She was very raw in *Brewster* but quite magic. Then I put her in *McCabe* and told her she'd really have to act now. Julie Christie took her under her wing and helped her a lot. And of course, for *Popeye*, nobody could have played Olive Oyl like Shelley. Nobody else looks like that. And she was great in all the films.

Michael Murphy's character, the San Francisco cop Frank Shaft, looked like a joke at the expense of the slick cop played by Steve McQueen in Bullitt.
Yes, and I parodied the car chase. I felt that was a really irresponsible scene, because you weren't supposed to care about any of the people who got killed as a result of his driving. I had my cop commit suicide.

26 Shelley Duvall as Suzanne and Bud Cort as Brewster in *Brewster McCloud*
(1970)

*Where did the idea of Rene Auberjonois doing his ornithological lecture
come from?*
Like the loudspeakers in *M*A*S*H*, I wanted a form of punctuation in the
film, and I had the idea of a guy giving a lecture on birds and then gradually
becoming one himself. The part wasn't written. Rene arrived on a Sunday
and we shot for eleven hours the next day, with everything coming from a
manual, except the opening speech, which I wrote the night before.

So the script was changed a great deal during the shoot?
I rewrote it entirely. The guy who wrote the original script, Doran William
Cannon,[8] had in his contract with Lou Adler that no one could share credits
with him or rewrite it. So it came out with his name on it. He wrote an
article in the *LA Times*, I believe, about how I had fucked up his work.
But the majority of writers will not understand that they are part of a
collaboration in films. The word 'writer' means you write and then you are
one on one with your audience. Well, in films you're not one on one with
your audience.

27 Brewster (Bud Cort) finally takes flight in the Houston Astrodome in
Brewster McCloud (1970)

I have a bad reputation with writers, developed over the years: 'Oh, he
doesn't do what you write, blah blah blah.' On the other hand, I had a very
hard-nosed writer on *The Company*, Barbara Turner, who wanted everything just the way she conceived it. She's notorious for that. I said, 'Barbara,
I'm going to do this picture but I'm not going to do that.' She just suffered.
She'd come in and say, 'They should say *this*,' and I said, 'Barbara, I can't
work that way.' But I had her there every minute of the time, just as I did
with Julian Fellowes on *Gosford Park*. I love to have someone to help
writing scenes, but they have to be a collaborator. It's probably one of the
reasons why in the 1980s I filmed a lot of plays where I didn't even have a
screenplay. With *Come Back to the Five and Dime, Streamers, Secret
Honor* and *Fool for Love* I just had the Samuel French text in my pocket.
That was the guide. But they're all *just* guides.

Ring Lardner was very pissed off with me because I didn't have my
guys in *M*A*S*H* speak with a New England accent, because they were
supposed to be from Maine. Sutherland was from Nova Scotia and has a
Canadian accent. I said, 'These are not dialect experts. I can't take them in

and teach them accents, and what the hell does that have to do with them anyway? Suppose I had another guy in the part?' 'Well, that's the way I wrote it.' 'Then *you* go and direct the motherfucker, if that's what you want.' That's what they all want, and I understand it – they wrote it, they have imagined it, so it's there. And it's very hard to take that away from them.

What kind of release did Brewster McCloud *have?*
At the time, I think it was a very original kind of film. *M*A*S*H* was released in the first week of January 1970 and was still running when I shot *Brewster McCloud* in June. Then this guy who was known as 'the smiling cobra', Jim Aubrey, took over MGM. He was just stripping the place in a corporate fashion, and he disliked the film. It was released around Christmas time and soon pulled. Judith Crist, who was a leading critic then, said she and her son flipped coins and they put *M*A*S*H* as their number-one film and *Brewster* as their number-two film of the year. But *Brewster* just didn't have a chance. Had they released it in the spring of 1971 when they should have done, it might have had a chance. But I doubt whether it would have succeeded in a big way – it had no movie stars in it, it was too cute.

You said in an interview in Playboy *magazine in 1976 that* Brewster McCloud *was your favourite among your films at the time.*
I think it's probably among the most creative and original films I've done. *Nashville* is another. But every one I feel that way about has things that I think no one had ever envisaged. And how they got done, I don't know . . .

McCabe & Mrs Miller

McCabe was a novel by Edmund Naughton published in 1959. Producer David Foster owned the rights and brought the project to Altman, who assigned his sometime associate Brian McKay to write a script. Altman's suggestion for the title was The Presbyterian Church Wager, but everyone else felt it was too confusing a description of the film.

McCabe & Mrs Miller *was described at the time of its release by John Wayne as 'corrupt'. It looks like no Western made before and few since.*
With every film, it's like, 'Come look through my window, the way it looks from here is the way it looks to me. And this may not be any more the truth than the truth from over here. But just look through my window . . .'

That was my plan with *McCabe*. I certainly didn't do the film for the story. I thought this was great – 'This story, everyone knows it, I don't have to deal with it.' The hero was a blustering kind of second banana, a gambler who was a loser. There was the whore with the heart of gold, and the heavies were the giant, the half-breed and the kid. So everybody knows the movie, those characters and the plot, which means they're comfortable with it and gives them an anchor. And I can really deal with the background.

Something was in my mind then that I've never been able to find out about, but I saw a Western picture either when I was a kid or later, maybe on television. It's like the way certain memories persist – it was a cowboy picture with these streets and tall buildings with flat-board fronts. It didn't look like any Western town I'd seen, there weren't a lot of horses around. I remember a guy walking across and entering a doorway, and it was just different, somehow very real. That really impressed me. It could have been a dream, it could have been anything.

Vilmos Zsigmond's photography has an unusual, yellowish tone to it. Wasn't that achieved by flashing the film – exposing it to light before it was developed?
Yes. It was a big risk, probably silly. But it was the only way you could get that effect, as they didn't have the post-treatment of film you have now so it can be done after the fact. And by doing it on the negative, the studio would have no choice but to accept it. My main reason for doing that, which I also did in *The Long Goodbye*, was I was doing everything to destroy the clarity of the film, including using a heavy number three fog filter. I wanted it to have that antique, historical look, which you could do with black and white, but I asked, 'Why was that more effective?' Because if you're dealing with the truth, which is colour, since no one sees in black and white, why is that not as real? So I really set out to make it look like those old photographs do.

That look was also there in the town you created specifically for the film.
The whole film was shot about forty miles from Vancouver. There was already a dilapidated town there, with a rooming house for the people who worked in the saw mills. We continued to build up the town as we were shooting. We started with the saloon on the bridge, and as the picture opens you see the mines and other buildings going up – the bathhouse, the whore-house and the church.

Leon Ericksen is just the most brilliant designer I've ever worked with. I work very closely with the production designer. I don't want part of a set;

I want an arena in which whatever we're going to do can take place. So only on rare occasions when there are budget problems will I accept the request, 'Can we build this room with just three walls?' Usually I'll say, 'I don't think so. I want the whole environment, because when I arrive there and the actors arrive there, I don't know how I'll want to shoot it. And I may just want to turn around and shoot the other way.' So I always prefer to have the complete atmosphere you get from a complete set, a room with walls on all sides and a ceiling and a floor, windows, and so on.

The costumes in McCabe *are not what you usually expect in a Western.*
I told Warner Brothers to send up a truckload of period Western clothes, because I wanted it to be as if I were making an immigration film. It had occurred to me that cowboys didn't wear those hats we're familiar with from so many pictures. Almost nobody who conquered the west was American; they were first-generation immigrants from Italy, Ireland, France, England, Holland, most of the northern countries. They spoke with Swedish

28 John McCabe (Warren Beatty) rides into town with the Bear Paw whores in *McCabe & Mrs Miller* (1971)

accents, Irish accents, Italian accents. They certainly didn't all sound like George Bush from Texas – I mean, that came years later. And they came with their silverware, their knife, fork and spoon, items of clothing and watches, all from Europe and finely crafted there. And the clothes were the same as they wore in Europe. So the only cowboy hat I put on anybody was the one on Keith Carradine's character.

I'm convinced that the reason people made Westerns with everybody wearing those cowboy hats was because that's what they saw from the photographs of the time. But we found out that a photographic plate at the time was so expensive that you would have a photographer in his shop, and when he hears that some guy's just ridden into town wearing the funniest hat you've ever seen, he just had to take a picture of him. And that's the record of the time that's passed down.

There's no question that the actors look very authentic in their clothes.
I got all the actors out one morning on location and told them all to pick out their wardrobe. I said, 'You all get one pair of pants, a pair of boots, two shirts, one jacket, a vest or a sweater, and one hat. Then you go to the prop department and there's stuff to pick up there like silverware.' You could tell a lot about the actor by the character of the clothes they selected. The more experienced the actors, the more they went for the character clothes. I remember Rene Auberjonois picked the most torn, ratty kind of stuff, so he looked like a ragman. Then I told them, 'Now, over there are needles and thread and patches, because you're living here during the winter, these are the only clothes you have and you wouldn't last twenty minutes with a hole in your sleeve. You'd freeze. So sew them up!' For two days everybody was sitting there repairing their wardrobe. But the message came through that there was a reality to what it was; it wasn't just a wrapping. It gave them a focus and a unity emerged from that.

Apart from Warren and Julie, most of the actors were people I'd used in *M*A*S*H* and *Brewster McCloud* or they were local. The three girls who played the Bear Paw whores were local girls, and many of the guys working as carpenters on the set were put in wardrobe and became extras.

The whole film has a real feeling for the period, with all its cruelty and desperation.
The whole idea was that in 1901, in the north-west territory, you would find in the law books that the maximum fine for first-degree murder of a Chinaman was $50! If you were tried and convicted, of course. It was considered the same as if you were shooting a dog. And I was really

interested in the truth about opium. The Canadians brought the Chinese in
to build their railroads. They wouldn't let any women come in; they had a
head tax on women. So these guys were working like mules for fifteen years
to earn enough money to go back and buy a bride. Instead of allowing them
women, they imported and kept them supplied with opium. The opium,
although it was illegal in Canada and the US, was taxed at $150 a barrel by
the Canadian government. But it was made available to the Chinese,
because it kept their libido down. It's on record that when there was a
particularly tough mine face – and we included this in the movie – they sent
the dynamite down with the Chinese workers and it would go boom, the
tunnel opened, and you had ten dead Chinks.

We planned the film along these lines, and that's why I dealt so much with
all the people in that town. Which pissed Warren off.

*It's been widely reported that Warren Beatty didn't really enjoy your
methods.*
I don't think Warren would be happy with *anybody*'s methods. That's him.
He wasn't happy with *McCabe*: he didn't like the way I mixed it, that you
couldn't hear every word, with a lot of things. It was scary for him, because
he hadn't done that before and he wasn't used to it. Yet he was the one who
sought me out for the film. He chased the picture; I didn't go after him to do
it. He was great in *McCabe* – the film would not be what it is without him –
and he contributed a lot of dialogue, and he's the one that put the gold
tooth in. But he just isn't much fun to work with. He's kind of a control
freak and he can't let go because he's a director, a producer and was the last
movie star of an era. The best thing he did was to bring Julie Christie in.
These affairs of the heart help. Sometimes they're better than the film, you
know – 'I got to do the picture, but I had to use the girl.' But this girl was
better than *he* was.

For the first take, Warren simply wouldn't act. He was cautiously putting
himself through it, because he knew he was going to do it eighteen, twenty
times. I'll always do a scene twice, just because it takes so long to set the
goddamn thing up! Because you don't know yourself how it's going to be.
But after three or four takes, I've seen what it is and I will say, 'I'm happy
with this, unless you think you can do better.' 'Oh yeah, give me another
one.' It's in their heads often. And I'll always give them another one or two,
but if nothing happens, I'll stop there. I won't shoot many, many takes
unless there's some technical thing wrong. I usually end up using one of the
first two or three. Julie is one of those intuitive actresses and was good right
away, while Warren wouldn't be doing it until at least take four. He

29 Lovers on and off screen – Warren Beatty as John Q. McCabe and Julie
Christie as Mrs Constance Miller in *McCabe & Mrs Miller* (1971)

seriously got progressively better. But as he was getting better, she was
diminishing. So you cut it in the middle, but you don't have the best of
either of their performances.

In the scene where Warren has a soliloquy while loading his gun, we went
to take seven. I remember it was about 10 o'clock at night and I said,

'That's great, Warren, we've got this really good.' And he said, 'I don't think so. I'll do another one.' Then we got up to take nine, and Warren said, 'Which one do you like?' I said, 'I don't know, I've got take three circled, and take five, and take seven.' 'Well, which one do you like?' I said, 'I can't remember, Warren. I've seen it so many times nothing's surprising me, so I'm not a good judge.' So he wanted another, and then another. And then I turned to my assistant director, Tommy Thompson, and said, 'I'm going to go to bed. Stay with Warren, let him shoot as many takes as he wants, and I'll see you guys tomorrow.' I thought that would shame him, but no, he went on and did another seven more takes. And I think we used take three or five!

In *McCabe* particularly I shot individual close-ups of everybody, and a lot of the cutting is forced by that. In *Gosford Park* and *The Company*, I don't think I shot a close-up of *anybody*, unless it was just the only thing to do. But we're all imitating something we've seen before – even if it's done a little bit differently, the basis of it is still there. I don't think anything is really original. Veins coming off of arteries are different, that's all. Everything I've done has been drawn from something else, even if it's just an impression. What other references do we have except for what we've seen? I'm just not original enough; I don't have an original mind that way. I'm more of an adaptor. If I see something, I think, 'Oh, we can do it this way. Once I've got set on my track I'll follow it.'

The final scene in the snow is beautifully sustained, and I've heard that most of the flakes we see falling are the real thing.
We had shot everything else, and we were shooting the scene where Julie crosses the bridge at night. Then these big snow flakes, the size of breakfast cereal, started to fall and it turned really cold. I found out it was something like 28 degrees F. So we stayed up all night and ran the hosepipes we used to create rain so that we could freeze everything. The next morning, everything looked beautiful, with icicles everywhere, like fairyland. But Warren didn't want to come out of his trailer. He wouldn't get into his costume. He said, 'What are we going to do? We're going to go out in the snow and shoot some stuff, and then it's going to melt and it'll be gone, and then we're going to have to start over again.' I said, 'What *else* are we going to do? We have nothing left to shoot. Let's go and try and work fast, and if we get busted out, we do.' And finally he agreed. And it continued to snow for eight days . . .

The other thing was, it wasn't just that it snowed; it was really deep. If you walked twenty yards and looked around, there would be no footprints. We were able to move equipment around, go into places, and we still had that 'virgin snow' look. So we went right up to the limit, and the minute we finished that final chase, when Warren died and they went to put the fire out in the church, the snow just started to melt. And in two days it was gone. So that was really good fortune.

The soundtrack of McCabe & Mrs Miller *daringly used just three songs from the Canadian poet and songwriter Leonard Cohen's first album,* Songs of Leonard Cohen *– 'Winter Lady', 'Sisters of Mercy' and 'The Stranger Song'. They fit the mood of the film so beautifully, it's as if they were written for the film.*

I knew when I was shooting the movie that I didn't want a conventional western movie score. So I had those old songs on the player-piano in the whorehouse, and that furnished some music. One of the characters who hung around the saloon was a violinist, so I used him at times to score things. Then I had an Indian guy with a flute, but I don't think I used him in the end ... I never knew exactly what the music should be, but I knew I didn't want strings and horns in a background score. When I finished the movie, I went to Paris for about ten days with Tommy Thompson. During that time we went to a party at somebody's apartment. I didn't know anybody there, everybody was speaking French, and on the hi-fi was the first Leonard Cohen album.

Let me cut back to Vancouver several years before when I was shooting *That Cold Day in the Park*. I lived in a house with my editor Danny Greene and Brian McKay, who was then one of my assistants. That first Leonard Cohen album had come out, and I was just crazy about it. We'd come home in the rain to eat dinner, and we'd put that record on so often we wore out two copies! We'd just get stoned and play that stuff. Then I forgot all about it through the next movies. When I walked into that apartment and heard that music, I said, 'Shit, that's my movie!' So I called the editor, Lou Lombardo, and said, 'Get hold of the Leonard Cohen album, transfer all those songs, and I'll be back in a couple of days.'

I literally left Paris within two days, and back in the cutting room we put those songs on the picture and they fitted like a glove. I think the reason they worked was because those lyrics were etched in my subconscious, so when I shot the scenes I fitted them to the songs, as if they were written for them. But it had never occurred to me to use them, because this was not the kind of music you would put to a picture like that. I put in about ten of them at first – of course, we way overdid it – and then we ended up with the three songs that were finally used, and I thought they were just wonderful. I think that's a pretty accurate and truthful story.

I didn't know Leonard then, and when I told Warners what I wanted to do, they said, 'No, he's with Columbia, so we can't get those, but we have guys who do the same kind of thing.' So I got on the telephone to Leonard Cohen – I found him in Nashville – and I said, 'Hi, my name is Robert Altman,' and he said, 'Oh my God, just a minute!' Then he turned to whoever he was with and said, 'Honey, I've got Robert Altman on the phone, can you believe it?' He said he was a great fan of mine, and I told him that I was a great fan of his. He said he didn't like *M*A*S*H* so much, but *Brewster McCloud* was the best picture ever. I told him what I wanted to do, and he said it was not a problem. He not only arranged it for me – for next to nothing, minimal rates – but he made the record company do a deal with Warners that the day the picture was released, if there were any profits from his album after that date, some of it went to us. That's just unheard of, but it's the way things should be.

What was Cohen's reaction to the film?
I had an assembly of the movie in New York, and I got Leonard and his new manager to come to a screening room to show it to him, as I needed him to play some guitar transitions for me. We ran the picture and there wasn't a great deal of enthusiasm for it, which was kind of funny. But he went into the studio and called me that night and said, 'I've just finished those guitar pieces. They've been sent to you, but I do have to tell you I don't like this picture very much.' I said, 'I'm really disappointed.' He said, 'I'm not for the picture, though I agreed for my music to be used.' And that broke my heart, it just sent me down to the bottom floor.

A year later I was doing *Images*. I was living in a house in London which Johnny Williams had rented when he was doing *Fiddler on the Roof*. We were preparing to go to Ireland, and the phone rang, and it was Leonard Cohen. He said, 'Bob, I just saw *McCabe & Mrs Miller*, and I just think it's absolutely fantastic. I love it.' And that took the weight of the world off my shoulders! I said, 'I can't tell you what this means to me.' He said, 'I don't know what was wrong with me. I was being pressured by my new management, blah blah blah.' But it made me feel better.

As I understand it, the first prints shown of McCabe & Mrs Miller *had to be done in Canada, and they muddied the picture and sound too much.*
McCabe was not a success when it opened – people said they couldn't understand the dialogue and they didn't get the tone of it. Ten years later, it suddenly popped up and became a minor classic, or what they call a 'cult movie'. But for me, a cult is not enough people to make up a minority!

Notes

1 Ring Lardner Jr (1915–2000) began his career as a scriptwriter in the 1940s, sharing an Academy Award with Michael Kanin for *Woman of the Year* (1942). As a member of the Hollywood Ten, accused of being a communist sympathizer and refusing to co-operate with the House Un-American Activities Committee, he was sentenced to a year's imprisonment and as a blacklisted writer was forced afterwards to work under pseudonyms, not receiving an official credit until *The Cincinnati Kid* (1965).

2 Many of the actors came from the American Theatre Ensemble, run by husband and wife William and Scott Bushnell, who would later figure large in Altman productions. John Schuck, G. Wood and Rene Auberjonois were all performing in Jules Feiffer's play *Little Murders* at the American Conservatory Theatre in San Francisco when 'discovered' by Altman.

3 Normally only an assistant director can address extras on a movie set.

4 *Patton: Lust for Glory* (1970), an intelligent portrait of the World War II General George Patton, directed by Franklin J. Schaffner and with George C. Scott in the title role, cost $18 million. *Tora! Tora! Tora!* (1970), about the events leading up to the Japanese attack on Pearl Harbor, was co-directed by Richard Fleischer, Toshio Masuda and Kinji Fukasuku, and cost around $20 million.

5 Darryl F. Zanuck (1902–79) joined Warner Brothers as a screenwriter in 1923. Ten years later he had formed his own company, 20th Century Pictures, which a year later merged with Fox. He was chief of production at 20th Century Fox until 1956, when he became an independent producer but continued in a special relationship with his old studio. After the debacle over *Cleopatra* (1963), Zanuck became president of 20th Century Fox and appointed his son, Richard Zanuck, as vice-president in charge of production. Then in 1969 they became, respectively, chairman and chief executive of the studio. In December 1970 the father fired the son, but he only retained control of 20th Century Fox for another year. Richard Zanuck returned briefly but then formed his own company with David Brown (who would later produce *The Player*), and they had two huge hits with *The Sting* (1973) and *Jaws* (1975).

6 *M*A*S*H* the television series, starring Alan Alda as Hawkeye and Wayne Rogers as Trapper, was conceived and written by Larry Gelbart. It first aired in 1972 and ran for fourteen seasons.

7 Lou Adler (b. 1933) was a prominent popular music entrepreneur from the late 1950s, managing Jan & Dean and writing songs. He started Dunhill Productions, whose acts included Barry McGuire and the Mamas and the Papas, and produced Carole King's first songs. He branched into cinema by producing *Monterey Pop* (1967), and produced and directed *Cheech and Chong's Up in*

Smoke (1978). He was also a producer on *The Rocky Horror Picture Show* (1975) and its sequel, *Shock Treatment* (1978).

8 Doran William Cannon's previous screen credit was as writer of Otto Preminger's *Skidoo* (1968).

4
Images – The Long Goodbye – Thieves Like Us – California Split – Nashville

DAVID THOMPSON: *The early 1970s were clearly a good time for you, when your movies connected with an audience willing to be challenged and stimulated by films with a personal voice.*
ROBERT ALTMAN: I think it was the time . . . It's like, 'When did you step into the river? When did you get into this current?' It's when you did it. I don't think you have a lot of control over that. At that time critics like Pauline Kael[1] had a lot of influence, film started opening up more as an art form, and this was then closed off in the 1980s. Now, of course, everything is driven not by who makes the film but who's in it, will it make $100 million, will it work for fourteen-year-olds? The films I made didn't cost that much, the competition wasn't so heavy and the audiences were there. I survived, and to keep surviving I had to follow this river. And it really didn't have anything to do with my resolve or my fortitude or my great vision. Once I had learned to survive on a certain path it was very difficult for me to cross over on to another path – where I probably would not have survived.

Would you defend cinema as an art form?
I think film is an art form because there's nothing else exactly like it. People have asked me through the years, 'What film-maker has influenced you the most?' And I say, 'I don't know their names, but when I see a film that's really bad, I think, "Hmm, I'm never going to do *that* . . ." ' The film-makers I like I'm also very jealous of, because it's a very competitive business, so it's hard for me to say. We all copy from ourselves or somebody else. No minds came from scratch, nor do any painters – they have to start some place, and it has to refer to other work.

Do you see a connection between what you do in films and painting?
I compare myself more to a muralist. The first thing I have to know is how big is the wall I have to paint? Is it a little wall or is it seventy feet high? And what is the subject? Even Diego Rivera had to be told that, although he wouldn't do it the way they wanted. I always have to have a boundary or an

edge, to know where there's a stopping place, otherwise you go into an abyss.

And that's where a script comes in?
My films are not about the words that people say, though that doesn't mean I'm not following the author's story. But writing for films is a very different thing from books. When you write a novel, you are one on one with your audience. If you sell a hundred million copies, one person at a time reads that text. They set their own tempo. They read the book and they go along and say, 'Oh, she's going to do that?' So they put it down: 'I'll go back to it tomorrow. I want this to last; I don't want to read the last page.' With a film, if it's two hours and ten minutes, it's two hours and ten minutes *every time* it runs. And if you get a hundred people in a movie theatre, everyone sits down in a different frame of mind. Some people have come in because there's such tragedy in their lives that they want to forget something; other people want to feel good. Suddenly you have to bring that whole audience together into the tempo that the film has. And it's impossible. If I made a film and everybody liked it, it would be mush, it would be nothing.

Images

I've read that you wrote the original script for Images – *in which a woman living in an isolated house experiences fantasies of interchangeable male lovers and murder – in* 1968 *in a hotel on the beach in Santa Monica, Los Angeles.*
The script actually began when I had an office in Los Angeles and went across the street one day for some lunch. As I was sitting there by myself, this scene came to me: a husband and wife are having an argument, and he is going in and out of the bathroom. And at one point she looks up, and it's someone she's never seen before. And that to me is a very frightening idea.

You've suggested in the past that Ingmar Bergman's Persona *was a key influence on the film.*
It impressed me a lot. I'm sure that film was largely responsible for *Images* and *3 Women*. There was a power in *Persona*, and I think that came from the fact that one woman talked and the other didn't, more than anything else. We know the situation, and if we know all these situations, then we have a certain expectation of what these situations are going to bring. The trick, to me, is not to bring that expectation.

30 Susannah York – as Cathryn – sees reflections of herself in mirrors and in
the younger Cathryn Harrison – as Susannah – in *Images* (1972)

You originally planned to make Images *in Vancouver with Sandy Dennis,
but* That Cold Day in the Park *took its place. Then you wanted to make it
with Julie Christie.*
I started it several times . . . I even came close to doing it in Milan with
Sophia Loren.

It's said that you saw Susannah York in Jane Eyre[2] *on an Aer Lingus flight to
Europe but that you had some trouble persuading her to take the part.*
I flew from London to Corfu, where she was vacationing, as I'd never met
her. I remember standing on a beach and drinking a lot of yoghurt . . . She
was reluctant to commit at the beginning, but then she agreed. She came
back to London, and we began pre-production. At that time she'd been
married for some years, but she'd had no children. Then just as we were
ready to set off for Ireland, she called me to say she had to see me. She was in
tears. She said, 'I can't do the movie, I'm pregnant.' I said, 'Well, so what?
We'll play it pregnant.' So we did.

We had one total nude shot, and she wasn't sure about that, but I said,
'That's the fun of it, to see that Rubens body. I'll shoot, I'll show it to you
before anyone else, and if you don't want me to use it, I won't.'

Images was dealing with a woman without children who had a certain wealth but no particular activities. I really made Susannah use what she knew about this kind of woman and had her improvise her scenes with Cathryn Harrison at the end.

Wasn't the children's story York reads in the film her own creation?
The story, 'In Search of Unicorns', was something she was already writing and in the process of finishing at that time. So I said, 'Let's just use this.' And we made it part of the narrative. I believe it was published: it was a kind of kindergarten *Lord of the Rings*. And that story became a large part of the picture. It fitted because we were going into a world that was frightening, which she was attempting to trivialize with children's images of unreality. And it also played the role of a musical accompaniment.

The music score by John Williams is very rich and strange, quite unlike what he mainly composes today.
John Williams[3] had scored a lot of the television work I did at Universal, and he'd become a personal friend. I let him read the script and suggested to him that he record his music and then I'd shoot the film and use his score. We didn't *completely* do that, but it's a method I've employed since. I'm not much interested in music that just goes along with the action. John came up with Stomu Yamash'ta, a percussionist who would do an act creating all sorts of sounds, like throwing a rock on to the strings of the piano. In his score, John would write descriptions of sounds that he would then perform.

You filmed from October to December 1971 in County Wicklow and in the Ardmore Studios in Ireland. How did that suit you?
I wanted a non-real, English-speaking atmosphere, and Ireland in the winter-time gave me those vistas that you wouldn't immediately recognize. Ireland was backward then; it was hard to make phone calls. And I remember that if you flew there and you were carrying, for instance, a *Playboy* magazine, they took it away from you.

So it suited your purposes, that she's living in such a secluded world?
It's entirely her world, and we made a lot of the details real but at the same time suggesting her fantasy, such as all the blood you see on the carpet and the tomato ketchup bottle on the table. We kept mixing all those things up.

Vilmos Zsigmond's photography is both ravishing and constantly surprising.

I'm always attracted to reflections and images through glass, anything that destroys the actual image and puts different layers of reality on it. And the camera played a key role in the film. The actors even played to it. The husband has his own camera, which he uses to look at her, after which she'd look at *our* camera.

You said in the film's promotion booklet that 'The story is not in any sense autobiographical . . . I have never known a woman like the one in the script.' Yet you do seem to have specialized in creating female characters who tend to be 'unstable', to put it mildly.

Well, I've probably dealt with more female characters than most people, although I've done a few films with no women at all. But I grew up in a household of women, and as a kid I had two sisters and a cousin around me, and my dad was not around a lot. And I was taught by nuns. Women were in a position to wield authority over me when I was young. I suppose I'm more comfortable with women because of growing up that way, and I certainly learned how to manipulate them, or how to manipulate myself through their world. I don't pretend to know the working of the female mind, but I think, on balance, women are more interesting than men.

Did you do special research into schizophrenia?

No. I had a few basic ideas about schizophrenia, like anybody. After making *Images* I was asked to speak at an international convention of psychologists and psychiatrists, which I refused to do. I said, 'Anything in the film comes from myself, and I don't know where it comes from. I trust instinct more than any study or logical conclusions.' There were some rather serious pieces written about the film, and psychiatrists liked it, as I recall. And I do think of it as a psychological story, not a ghost story, because we were inside the woman's head, and the men were made up by her, really. My way of dealing with schizophrenia was to cut between scenes as they are and as they *appear* to her, and mixing them together without making a definite reality. All the symbols in the film, the chimes, the camera, all fed into her psychosis.

Susannah York won the Best Actress prize at the Cannes Film Festival in 1972, but the film was poorly distributed and had very little success with the public.

I still like the film. It's a little heavy-handed, but I wouldn't change it. I thought when I made *Images*, 'It's over, everyone is just going to flip over this film. It's going to be the greatest discovery since hash!' And nobody liked it much.

The Long Goodbye

The Long Goodbye, based on Raymond Chandler's novel featuring his private detective Philip Marlowe investigating the aftermath of a friend's supposed suicide, was originally going to be directed by Peter Bogdanovich, and a screenplay had been commissioned from Leigh Brackett, who'd written the 1946 version of *The Big Sleep*, starring Humphrey Bogart and Lauren Bacall and directed by Howard Hawks.

Wasn't this an instance when you actually felt enthused by the script?
Originally I didn't want to do that picture. I'd enjoyed reading Chandler,[4] though I never did finish *The Long Goodbye*, and I'd liked those 1940s movies, but I just didn't want to play around with them. I was in Ireland shooting *Images*, and Elliott Kastner and Jerry Bick[5] sent me the script. At first I said, 'I don't want to do Raymond Chandler. If you say "Philip Marlowe", people just think of Humphrey Bogart.' Robert Mitchum was being proposed for it. But I just didn't want to do another Philip Marlowe film and have it wrap up the same way all the other films did. I think it was David Picker, the production chief at United Artists, who suggested Elliott Gould for Marlowe – and *then* I was interested. So I read Leigh Brackett's script, and in her version, in the last scene, Marlowe pulled out his gun and killed his best friend, Terry Lennox. It was so out of character for Marlowe, I said, 'I'll do the picture, but you cannot change that ending! It must be in the contract.' They all agreed, which was very surprising. If she hadn't written that ending, I guarantee I wouldn't have done it. It said, 'This is just a movie.' After that, we had him do his funny little dance down the road and you hear 'Hooray for Hollywood', and that's what it's really about – 'Hooray for Hollywood'. It even looked like a road made in a Hollywood studio. And with Eileen Wade driving past, it's *The Third Man*!
I remember at the première I had a publicist named Regina Gruss, and she had an older sister, probably in her fifties. When the film was over and everybody was saying they loved everybody, I was going down the aisle, and she came up to me and said, 'Mr Altman, isn't he going to get in trouble for that . . .?' She just couldn't believe that we could have such an ending.

Was the idea of Marlowe's cat in the original script?
No, that came from a story a friend told me about his cat only eating one type of cat food. It serves as a comment on friendship, and it tied in with the ending, because Marlowe thought Terry Lennox was his great friend, and he

31 Altman directs Nina van Pallandt as Eileen Wade and Elliott Gould as
Philip Marlowe in *The Long Goodbye* (1973)

had gone missing. His cat was around only when he got fed, and when he
didn't, the cat was gone too . . .

The film makes amusing play between this character from a novel written in
1953 and the Los Angeles of 1973.
I decided we were going to call him Rip Van Marlowe, as if he'd been asleep
for twenty years, had woken up and was wandering through this landscape
of the early 1970s but trying to invoke the morals of a previous era. I put
him in that dark suit, white shirt and tie, while everyone else was smelling
incense and smoking pot and going topless; everything was health food and
exercise and cool. So we just satirized that whole time. And that's why that
line of Elliott's – 'It's OK with me' – became his key line throughout the film.
    Many years later I got a letter from a guy who had been in prison in
Ecuador for about twelve years, and he was getting out. He had written a
book while there, a *faux* Chandler story. So he wrote about Marlowe at
a later date. And he had seen *The Long Goodbye* in prison, where they'd run

76

it a number of times. He said to me that since he had no way of knowing of what Los Angeles was like, he hoped I would forgive him that in his book he'd taken the film and described all the places that Marlowe went to as if that was it. So he used my conceit to create his own conceit.

We never leave Marlowe's side throughout the film.
Marlowe was in every scene in the film, because it was his viewpoint. And when he was at the beach house, where Nina Van Pallandt and Sterling Hayden had some scenes on their own, I didn't know what to do. So I had Sterling say, 'Marlowe, go down and count the waves, my wife and I are going to talk.' And they sent him down to the beach, but I kept his reflection in the window so that he was always present in a way.

How did the extraordinary way you used the camera, as if it was another character constantly stalking the action, evolve?
I decided that the camera should never stop moving. It was arbitrary. We would just put the camera on a dolly and everything would move or pan, but it didn't match the action; usually it was counter to it. It gave me that feeling that when the audience see the film, they're kind of a voyeur. You're looking at something you shouldn't be looking at. Not that what you're seeing is off limits; just that you're not supposed to be there. You had to see over someone's shoulder or peer round someone's back. I just think that in so many films everything's so beautiful, the lighting is gorgeous and with each shot everything is relit. My method also means you don't have to light for close-ups; you only have to accommodate what may happen, so you just light the scene and it saves a lot of time. The rougher it looked, the better it served my purpose.

I was worried about the harsh light of southern California and I wanted to give the film the soft, pastel look you see on old postcards from the 1940s. So we post-flashed the film even further than we did on *McCabe*, almost 100 per cent, I believe.

Did these artistic choices worry anybody?
No one gave me any trouble, but then nobody knew what I was talking about . . . The people I had to be responsible to, they didn't know what I was doing. If I had made the film ten years earlier under the studio system, the head of the camera department would have come to me and complained. In fact, the head of editing at Fox said to me about *M*A*S*H*, 'We can't show this film. It's out of focus, it's soft.' They were shooting *Patton* at the same time, and after a period of time seeing the dailies from that film and our

dailies, they were sending messages to the director Frank Schaffner in Spain saying, 'This doesn't look dirty or real enough!'

How were your relations with Elliott Gould after M*A*S*H?
I actually offered him the lead in *McCabe & Mrs Miller*, but he turned it down. After *M*A*S*H* he came to me and said that at first Donald and he didn't think I knew what I was doing, but now he realized that he'd made a dreadful mistake.

Casting Nina Van Pallandt, who was best known as one half of that Scandinavian singing duo Nina and Frederik, must have caused a few jaws to drop.
United Artists didn't want me to use her. I'd only seen her on *The Johnny Carson Show*, when she was mixed up with the Clifford Irving scandal,[6] and I thought she was just Chandler's blonde. But they let me do a test. Laszlo Kovacs shot it with her and Elliott, and then they saw it and said, 'Great, go ahead.' But later David Picker told me they were going to say I couldn't use her. Other than that, I had control of all the casting.

Sterling Hayden,[7] who many thought was washed up and in decline after his naming names to HUAC, was also quite a risk.
I originally wanted Dan Blocker[8] for the role, but he died just before shooting began, and I was persuaded to meet Sterling, who was just perfect. He improvised a lot of his dialogue, and he was pretty well whacked out all the time. He was an alcoholic, and when he smoked grass and had the booze in him he was something else. But he was wonderful. I loved him.

In the Chandler novel, Roger Wade is actually murdered, but you changed that to a suicide.
I gave everyone on the film a copy of *Raymond Chandler Speaking* to read, because I wanted them to know about his fascination with suicide. For me, Wade was Chandler, someone who didn't want to struggle any more. He's also like Irwin Shaw, James Jones or Ernest Hemingway – very macho, a heavy drinker, out of his time.

The director Mark Rydell[9] made a great impression as Marty Augustine, especially in the scene where he threatens Marlowe by callously smashing a Coke bottle in the face of his pretty girlfriend.

32 A Malibu Beach party in *The Long Goodbye* (1973) – from left to right,
Roger Wade (Sterling Hayden), Philip Marlowe (Elliott Gould), Eileen Wade
(Nina Van Pallandt) and Dr Verringer (Henry Gibson)

He had done *The Cowboys* with John Wayne, and we were all in London
together at the same time with Johnny Williams, working on *Images*. When I
got back to Los Angeles I asked him if he wanted to play Marty Augustine.

I was living at that same house in Malibu that we shot as the Wades'
house. Elliott, Mark, me, my wife and four or five others were in that house
all day and we were drunk, ripped and stoned. We planned to go for dinner,
but before we left, I came up with this scene with the Coke bottle, and we
thought that was great. Then we went up to a beach restaurant, four of us,
and there was this waitress who was looking after us. I said, 'Look at her
face, that's the kind of girl who should be Marty Augustine's girl, the one he
should hit with the Coke bottle.' So I talked to her and said, 'I know this
sounds silly, but you know who these guys are, Elliott Gould and so on, and
we think you'd be perfect for our movie.' Then, when we were about to leave
not one of us had any money or credit cards at all, so I said, 'You'll have to
trust us with this cheque. I'll come back tonight with a credit card.' And she
went, 'Oh God, don't try that one!'

Anyway, we shot the bottle scene, and in the next scene she had her jaw
wired up and her nose bandaged up. After the movie was over she got an

agent, went to MGM and had a couple of small roles. She played a nurse in the *Dr Kildare* series or something. Then that petered out and she ended up back on the bar circuit, living down in Malibu. Seven years later, she's living in a house with four other girls, and she comes home about two-thirty in the morning and these people were all crazy on drugs. She went into her bedroom, closed the door, and one of these guys at this party suddenly opened the door and jumped on her. She started screaming, and he literally bit her nose off. Then he jumped out of the window and killed himself on the rocks below. So seven years later she ended up looking exactly like she had as Marty Augustine's girlfriend. Now that's spooky . . .

For an audience today, the strangest member of the cast has to be one Arnold Schwarzenegger.
His name was Arnold Strong at the time. David Arkin, who was playing one of the sidekicks, said to me, 'I've got a friend, he's just terrific, he's got the damnedest muscles you've ever seen.' I said, 'Fine, bring him along, we'll use him as one of the guys.' Arnold doesn't talk about it now though – he doesn't remember the film.

The use of music is very witty and original, with the same theme turning up in different styles and orchestrations appropriate to the scene.
I went to Johnny Williams, and he wrote this song with Johnny Mercer, 'The Long Goodbye', and I came up with the idea of using it *everywhere*. And Johnny started paraphrasing it in all these different versions, even down to a doorbell and the band in Mexico. I've always said at the beginning of conceiving a film, 'I'd love the music to be indigenous, so that there's not going to be any violins that you can't see, that it won't come from nowhere.' I've never completely achieved that, though in *The Long Goodbye* the music became a character in itself.

The reason we have to have music in films is to put a cocoon around it, so the audience doesn't become conscious of other people or embarrassed by being there. The music is a kind of tunnel to help keep your focus. I don't understand music, but it's something that can be so visceral and inside you, and I try not to lead what the action is going to be – I mean, we don't hit those chords so you think, 'Oh, I'm going to get scared.' One day I'll do a film without any music. I almost did it with *The Gingerbread Man*, but then . . .

How was the movie received?
When the picture opened, it was a big, big flop. It opened in Los Angeles and

Chicago and a few other cities, and the ad campaign was Elliott with a cat on his shoulder, a smoking .45 and a cigarette in his mouth, with Nina as a slick blonde beside him. And it just failed. I went to David Picker and said, 'You can't do this. No wonder the fucking picture is failing. It's giving the wrong impression. You make it look like a thriller and it's not, it's a satire.' So they pulled the film, and we got Jack Davis from *Mad* magazine to do a new poster with all the characters, and we opened it in New York and it was a smash hit. By the time that happened, it was too late for Los Angeles and those other cities. If New York had been our first opening, we would have had a successful film. But the film has stood up over the years, in a strange way. Some British critics didn't like Elliott Gould playing Philip Marlowe, and I was confused about that, because I had read a lot of the books, and what Chandler wrote was really a bunch of thumbnail sketches or thematic essays, all about Los Angeles, and Marlowe was just a device to unite them, and I felt we were very close to that. Everyone said Elliott's not Philip Marlowe and I wasn't being true to the author, but what they were really saying was that Elliott Gould wasn't Humphrey Bogart. In fact, I believe we were closer to Chandler's character than any of the other renditions, where they made him a kind of movie superhero.

Thieves Like Us

The script for your next film was initiated by you and written by Joan Tewkesbury,[10] a former child actress, dancer, choreographer and theatre director who was keen to break into film-making.

I had hired Joan Tewkesbury as script supervisor on *McCabe*, and it was during that time that I read this book – I don't know who gave it to me – called *Thieves Like Us*. I just loved it. I didn't know it had been made into a movie by Nick Ray, *They Live By Night*,[11] and I was well into production when I found out. I never looked at the film, and I've only ever seen pieces of it since. I hired Joan to write it, but I said, 'Don't be an original writer, I want exactly what's in this book. Don't help it, just translate it.' That's why it's such a linear film.

I knew exactly the guys I wanted in the picture, and I never deviated from that. I cast it with Shelley Duvall and Keith Carradine,[12] whom I'd found for *McCabe & Mrs Miller*, John Schuck and Bert Remsen, all people I was working with at the time. I never thought of anybody else. Calder Willingham had done a screenplay before which I rejected, though he ended up getting a credit on the screen. Nobody was interested in the film, as none of

33 The young lovers in *Thieves Like Us* (1974) – Keith Carradine as Bowie and Shelley Duvall as Keechie

these actors were anybody. United Artists didn't like the idea; they didn't see any future in it. But the budget was low, only about $1.25 million. And at the time they wanted me to make *Nashville*.

The novel was written by Edward Anderson in 1937 and was a pretty desolate depiction of the Depression in the Deep South through a gang of amateurish bank robbers, the youngest of whom, Bowie, forms a romantic partnership with a girl, Keechie, and makes her pregnant.

In the novel, she dies in the shoot-out at the cabin. The only change I made was that I had her live and put that little coda in the railway station, saying that she survived and went off, pregnant, into the world. It just seemed to me that to kill them both was too brutal an ending, and I wanted the sense that something from these people continued on.

While all the guys were murderers, we didn't treat them that way. They were simply the kind of people they were. It was during the Depression and everyone was poor, and they just got into trouble. They only believed stealing was bad if you got caught. But as the picture develops, they lose their joyous spirit and become what they are.

A key feature of the film was your continual use of old radio programmes on the soundtrack.
Once again, I was looking not to have a conventional movie score. At that time in the 1930s that's all I did as a kid, listen to the radio for two hours when I got home from school. Radio was everywhere, filled with commercials – it's what created the consumer society. I went to a journalist in Denver called John Dunning, who had a collection of old recordings that we went through. We got all the clearances sorted out, and I decided to score the film with these old radio programmes. They were all equivalents to *The Archers* in Britain – soap operas like *Merton Marge* and *Our Gal Sunday*.

You used Gangbusters *and* The Shadow *to underscore the actual scenes of crime.*
We were really trying to get the audience to think about the atmosphere of crime and how it was represented in those Depression years. With the first bank robbery, we didn't go in and show the guns – this was not an action film but more about the attitude of the characters. The framing of them in the car, using a long lens, was close to cartoon proportions or like the ads and illustrations you'd see in detective novels and magazines. And that matched the radio programmes you hear.

And for the young lovers we heard The Radio School of the Air Presents Romeo and Juliet.
The love-making scene was particularly good, I think. We underlined the playfulness of their falling in love, the first sex experience and all those Lucky Strikes she smokes, all while bringing up the *Romeo and Juliet* theme. Their naïve attitudes really seemed to fit the period.

Keith Carradine and Shelley Duvall were very tender and natural in those scenes.
Their scenes together were scripted, but when we came to do them, we'd improvise in rehearsal. But you really have to know what's going on. The actors and crew have to know where they're going; you have to set the perimeter of it. I'm not so concerned about rehearsing too much; it's all up to the actors, what they want to do and how they feel it works the best. In the first place, you're dealing with the location and the space, what I want the audience to see from these things and what I am heading towards. We'd

rehearse the whole scene the way the actors were comfortable with it, and then we'd say, 'This is the way we'll shoot it.' Normally these intimate scenes are done complete – four or five minutes, as long as it takes, we'll play it all the way through. I won't talk to the actors off screen, unless it's an action scene and they're prepared, so they know I'm going to give them certain cues. Otherwise it's a big shock to them to have someone saying to them, 'Do this now.'

For the bed scene, I did a lot of the operating myself on the close-ups.

It's interesting that there's no nudity during the love-making, only afterwards when Keechie takes a bath.

I love nudity in films, because I think it shows the characters are actually in a very private moment. It's not how you usually see them, and it gives the audience a sense of voyeurism. Especially in the case of someone like Shelley, who's not one of those glamour girls with big breasts. None of it was done in a sexual way; it was just showing the innocence of those characters.

Why did you use a French cameraman on this film?

Any time I mentioned Mississippi to anybody, they went, 'Oh shit, that's the asshole of America, God but it's ugly down there!' Mississippi is in fact a very lush, green state, although a lot of it is poor. I wanted a European cameraman who would not have a prejudice when I said 'Mississippi' and would look at it and shoot it for what it is. And also it was so behind the times. We could go down there in the 1970s and it was still like the 1930s; there was nothing we had to take down. I'd met Jean Boffety[13] in Paris, and to him Mississippi was beautiful! I liked the way he did the whole thing, just using the natural light outside and bare light bulbs inside. We didn't use a lot of lights.

The locations all look completely in period.

It was all filmed around Jackson, and we stayed for a while in a little town called Hermansville, about 70 or 80 miles away. Mostly we were in practical locations that we found, like the derelict church at the beginning. We just used what was there. I rarely storyboard. There's so much stuff that's just not in your mind; you have to *see* it. Every building down there had a Coca-Cola sign on it, because in the 1930s Coca-Cola would make and give everyone signs for free if they'd include the logo for Coca-Cola. Even the prison sign has 'Coca-Cola' on it. And there were Coca-Cola bottles everywhere; you couldn't move down there without kicking one. In the film you see a truck with a large bottle on it – we didn't make that up, we actually found that. They used to go around giving out bottles to kids. It was called 'dope', because in the early days it did have a little cocaine in it.

The pace of the film is very gentle.
I don't know if you can do this kind of stuff today, taking your time and being so leisurely about it. I don't know if you could really do it then. But *Thieves* had the pace that I think was exactly what it required. If I shot it today, I don't think I'd have the courage to do it.

Again, the film seemed to suffer from half-hearted distribution, even though it's much liked by those relative few who saw it.
I remember taking it to Phoenix, Arizona, for a sneak preview, which started at midnight, following *Last Tango in Paris*! There were only about thirty people there anyway, and eight of them stayed. United Artists knew the picture was a turkey – that was their attitude. But I felt if I could just show this to people, then I knew they would respond to it. People found the title odd: 'What do you mean, *Thieves Like Us*?' But it got some great reviews, and we went to Cannes with it, though we didn't win anything.

California Split

Although a film about gambling would seem perfect for you, I was surprised to discover that before it came to you the script of California Split *had been developed for Steven Spielberg.*
Yes, it was, though it doesn't seem likely to me either. The guy who wrote it, Joseph Walsh, was a gambler, and still is. And I was a bit of a gambler, my father was a gambler and I knew a lot of gamblers, and I kind of like that world. I thought those guys I have known were romantic. I've had a couple of good wins, but they don't compare to the losses. People only remember the wins.

Gambling is a way out of the security of life, bringing risk back into it. Luck is bad or good. You win a lottery, $26 million – 'Wow, my God, I've won!' But your brother walks down Madison Avenue and a brick falls off the top of a building, hits him on the head and kills him. Now the odds of that happening are the same as you winning the lottery. So you both won, only one of you is dead and the other is rich. It's Lady Luck – like any coin, it has two sides.

So you don't believe in the kind of lucky streak that Bill, the George Segal character, enjoys in the film?

It reflects a certain logic. But when people say, 'I've got to wear my lucky shirt, every time my team has won I've had this shirt on' . . . well, even to think that the shirt you're wearing has an outcome on that game simply isn't true.

The film's depiction of gambling situations certainly feels very authentic, but then you, Joe Walsh and Elliott Gould all gambled a lot, and many of the people we see in the games were actual players. I gather most of the extras in the casino were from an organization of ex-addicts.

Normally the audience sees gambling set up more dramatically, and what you have in *California Split* is the stuff you really see in those casinos. The poker club in the opening scene was a set built by Leon Ericksen in some dance hall, and we just set up these gambling situations and filmed them happening. None of the players' stuff was scripted. I think this film had the least amount of plot in it of any of my films, until more recent times. It's about character. And that was the fun of it, getting into these people. George brought a tension into it, because in a funny way he was in over his head . . .

34 Charlie Waters (Elliott Gould) and Bill Denny (George Segal) play blackjack in *California Split* (1974)

Given it seems to have informed your career, what is your attitude towards gambling today?

I think gambling is just action, and why not? What is there to hoard? I don't think I've ever jeopardized anybody's existence by my gambling. Actually, for the last fifteen years or so I've been kind of bored with it, because it doesn't mean anything – what's the most I could win? Buying lottery tickets, that isn't gambling. That's just throwing your hat in the ring. I don't think gamblers want to lose. But there are people who are addicted to it. At one time I could stand at a crap table for two days – the feeling is like sex. Compulsive gamblers lie to themselves, to everybody. I think I became embarrassed that maybe I was becoming a compulsive gambler. When I was making *Tanner '88*, I bet on every game on every day of the baseball season.

There's a moral blanket over gambling. It's considered immoral, it's not what you're supposed to do. I think the greatest theatrical opening scene ever was in *Rosencrantz and Guildenstern Are Dead*,[14] when the guys are tossing coins, and one of them wins every time. The odds are against that, yet they're not. Every time you throw a coin, the odds are fifty–fifty. When you say I've thrown heads six hundred times in a row, what are the odds of that happening? Well, mathematically they're tremendous, but to say that now you're going to bet on tails because the odds are way in your favour – the odds are *not* in your favour. So you try this guessing game, 'I've got a hunch, I feel it . . .' That was the whole point of *California Split*, when at the end George Segal turned to Elliott Gould and said, 'There was no special feeling.' He never felt it, because he has nothing to feel!

The reason I was so keen to do *California Split* was that for years I wanted to do a gambling film that had nothing but the ambience of gambling, and then point out it had nothing to do with money.

Nashville

If your previous films had broken away from their genres – a war movie, a Western, a thriller, and so on – Nashville really was a film like no other. What was its genesis?

First off I wanted to do *Thieves Like Us*, but United Artists weren't interested. They'd just bought a company who published country-and-western songs, and instead they gave me a script that was a vehicle for Tom Jones.[15] I read it and said, 'I won't do this, but I'll do my own country-and-western story if you let me do *Thieves* next.' Now I had never been to Nashville in my life, and country music to me was what we call 'hillbilly' music.

I was down in Mississippi with Joan Tewkesbury, who had written *Thieves*, and I said to her, 'OK, Joan, get on a plane and go to Nashville, and just keep a diary of what happens to you. And from that we'll write some Nashville movie . . .' She arrived at the airport, got in a hired car, and there was a traffic jam caused by a boat falling off a pick-up truck, so she was stuck on the freeway for three hours. That made a great scene to introduce many of the characters. And everything that was in the eventual script was like that, something that had occurred to her. That's pretty much the same way Barbara Turner put *The Company* together. So we wrote that script and gave it to David Picker at UA, who hated it.

Then Jerry Weintraub,[16] who was in the music business and was managing singers at the time, came to see me at my office and said he wanted to get into the movie business, how could he do it? I said, 'Well, here's a script about Nashville and country-and-western music. Get me the money to make that and you can produce it and you're in the business.' He came back in a day or two and he said, 'I got Marty Starger at ABC interested.' They came over to

35 Haven Hamilton (Henry Gibson) sings at the Grand Ole Opry in *Nashville*
(1975)

my house and I played him two of the songs that Keith Carradine had done, 'I'm Easy' and 'It Don't Worry Me'.[17] And they said, 'OK.'

How would you describe the subject of the film?
It was about the incredible ambition of those guys getting off the bus with a guitar every day, and like in Hollywood, trying to make it. Nashville was where you went to make it in country-and-western music. I just wanted to take the literature of country music, which is very, very simple, basic stuff – 'For the sake of the children, we must say goodbye' – and put it into a panorama which reflected America and its politics.

Nashville *was not an expensive film – you're on record as saying all the actors were paid either $1,000 or $750 a week, and they all knew the deal before going in.*
Nashville was the first film I really had total control over. It cost, I believe, $1.9 million. But I didn't have anybody standing over me, I didn't have any studio. I went and did it the way I felt it should be done. We shot over seven weeks. I gathered a group of actors together, twenty-four of them, and I had them write their own material. Everything was done on the spot, changed on the spot; it was indigenous to what was going on. We'd create events and document them. And we weren't paying the extras – if anyone turned up in a red dress, I couldn't change that. So it was very like a documentary, with a small crew moving fast. Today it would be so complicated; you'd need all the permissions. The scenes with Geraldine Chaplin wandering in the junk yard and among the yellow buses – I'd driven past those places every day and thought, 'We've really got to shoot there.' So we just stopped on the highway, threw Geraldine into it, and she improvised her rap.

Chaplin's Opal is the one character who interacts with all the others. Her slip of the tongue that she's working for the 'British Broadcasting Company' is the clue that she's a complete fraud, though.
Opal was our tour guide, the connecting tissue. She was based on a lot of people I've met at the Cannes Film Festival, who you never know if they're really who they say they are. I had to have some connection in my head why I was doing all these disparate scenes, so as a reporter with this ruse she was working for the BBC, she was able to go through this world and became the voice who could ask the questions the audience wanted answering. She was wonderful at improvising her scenes. I'm crazy about Geraldine.

36 Tom Frank (Keith Carradine) is interviewed by 'BBC' correspondent Opal
(Geraldine Chaplin) in *Nashville* (1975)

*Lily Tomlin, in her first screen role, also does some brilliant improvisations
in the film, like her description of the exploding eyeball at the Hamilton
party.*
Originally the part was going to be played by Louise Fletcher,[18] whose parents were deaf, so she knew sign language and that was the reason it was in
the picture. Just as we were ready to go, she backed out, but the deaf kids
stayed in. I think Lily gave a spectacular performance.

The father in the family couldn't deal with that situation. Ned Beatty had
been in my mind for a while, as I'd thought about him for a part in *McCabe
& Mrs Miller*. I'd given Jeff Goldblum one short scene in *California Split*,
and his character came from a grip on *Thieves Like Us*, who was always
riding around on his bike. Henry Gibson had been in *The Long Goodbye*,
and he convinced me he could do Haven Hamilton, which I had originally
offered to Robert Duvall.[19] And Timothy Brown had been in *M*A*S*H*. He
was a great football player but not a great singer.

37 Linnea Reese (Lily Tomlin) uses sign language to communicate with her deaf son Jimmy (James Dan Calvert), while her husband Delbert (Ned Beatty) looks on in *Nashville* (1975)

Gwen Welles, whom you'd previously cast in California Split, *gave an unforgettable performance as the hopeless Sueleen Gay.*
As Ned Beatty says in the film, Gwen Welles 'couldn't sing a lick'. It's very hard to take someone who can sing and tell them to sing badly. But I had Gwen take singing lessons from Richard Baskin, saying, 'You've got to be the best you can.' And she really worked at it!

Karen Black was probably the best known of any of the actors in the movie, and she wrote the three songs she performed.

You got some criticism for letting your actors write and perform their songs.
Richard Baskin was the musical director, and he helped some of those people write their songs. He arranged all the music in the film, and it was all shot live. I thought, 'Why should I go out and buy a lot of songs that were tried and tested?' And also, this wasn't about hit songs; most of the songs were not *meant* to be hits. Actually, one of them was a hit, 'I'm Easy', though Keith wrote that five years before we did the picture. But I wanted a

cross-section of songs, good and bad. The country-and-western people in Nashville all said, 'Oh, the music's terrible, it's no good,' to which I would reply, 'Well, I don't think your music is that good either ...' They felt I should have used their stuff. But I was satirizing them. Their stuff would have been too on the nose.

All that said, Ronee Blakley's songs really do stand out.
Yes, they're excellent. How's it go? 'He's got a tape-deck in his tractor and he's ploughing up his daddy's land.' At first we had just bought some songs from Ronee, and then when we got to Nashville she was there singing back-up. Susan Anspach was going to play Barbara Jean, but as the picture developed we couldn't afford her. She wouldn't drop her price, so we lost her. Then I saw Ronee after her gig and asked if she could stay around for a few days. So she hung out with us, and I was wondering if she could do the role, as she'd never acted before. Finally we gave it to her, and she was as good as anyone in the film. I guess she got her inspiration from Loretta Lynn. I remember the scene where she has her breakdown, she came to me in the morning and said, 'I've got some ideas for the scene.' And I was really wound up then and said, 'Ronee, I can't talk about this, just go ahead and do it.' We were running two cameras, we shot it four times, and I saw it just as she did it, and it was just great.

Nashville *introduced your first foray into mixing reality and fiction, with some actors playing themselves.*
Elliott Gould, Julie Christie and George Segal all came through Nashville while we were shooting, so I decided to give them those cameos. George didn't make the final cut. Sue Barton, who accompanied Elliott and Julie, was our actual PR person. Julie was really valuable for the scene where Karen doesn't recognize her.

How did you devise your invented political candidate, Hal Philip Walker and the Replacement Party?
Thomas Hal Phillips was a Mississippi novelist and writer I'd become friends with when I was shooting *Thieves Like Us*.[20] His brothers are all politicians from Mississippi. They're an incredibly wealthy family that owns trucking businesses and stuff, and he was the odd one out. So I asked him to create a candidate for me whom he would like to see elected as President of the USA and write his inaugural speech. So he did, a thirty-minute piece, and that's his voice you hear in the film. Then I hired a guy from Denver called Ron Hecht, who worked in the media, and told them both to put together a

campaign, which they did with a truck which they painted up, using the name of the 'Replacement Party'. And this was all before Jimmy Carter, who then had the same grass-roots kind of basis to his campaign. This was the stuff politicians don't say, so we might be actually interested in it. Then Nixon's resignation happened when we were shooting in the Grand Ole Opry.

I used this candidate figure throughout the picture, though you never saw him. He said all these great things, like 'Get the lawyers out of Congress,' and it worked really well, quite independently of me. I said, 'You can find my shooting schedule every day. You'll know where we're going to be, and if we're somewhere, bring along the girls dressed in their short skirts carrying their posters and signs, stick them up and get in our frame.' So, for instance, we're in the hospital with Barbara Jean, and through the window you would see their truck going by. So they were invading our shots just as they would if they were doing it for real, to get people's attention. Of course, I had more control over this than I care to say, but the idea was that this was something going on while I was shooting in the streets.

The most controversial element in the film must still be the assassination.
Of course, everything was set up for a political assassination, only I didn't assassinate a politician, I assassinated an entertainer. I called Joan in one day and said, 'Listen, there's something missing in this script. I think there's got to be a political umbrella on this, otherwise it's just gossip.' I wanted an assassination and I said I thought Barbara Jean ought to be shot, and we'd build backwards from that.

Polly Platt, the art director, was so outraged she quit the film because of that. She thought it was dumb and silly and irresponsible. But I insisted this was the way I saw it. Then, when John Lennon got assassinated a few years later, the *Washington Post* called me up and said, 'Don't you feel responsible for creating that situation, since you predicted an entertainer would be assassinated rather than a politician?' I said, 'I think it applies to all celebrities. Don't you think that instead of taking me to task on this you should look at yourselves and ask, "How come we didn't pay any attention to his warning?" '

The assassination is prepared in the film in the scene in the Exit/In where Lady Pearl, played by Barbara Baxley, talks about the Kennedys to Opal.
That's an example of how improvisation can really work. Barbara Baxley was a stage-trained actress, and she never said a word in a film or play that she hadn't rehearsed, studied, practised, analysed. But I knew in advance

from talking with her about her sentimental fanaticism over the Kennedy assassinations. I told her that in this scene I wanted her to go into her whole sense of her feelings about them. At the same time, she's carrying a gun in her purse! So she went off and wrote this thing, and then said she'd like to read it out to me so we could make any changes if I didn't like it. I said, 'Well, why don't we just film it, and I'll hear it as we're shooting?' I put the camera on her in a two-shot and we ran for ten minutes, a whole reel of film. I asked her to stop a minute, and then we ran another reel. I said, 'Fine, we're through,' because I knew I had what I needed, and I could always cut to the other people in the club. She was very impassioned and gave a great performance in those twenty minutes.

Do you have any thoughts on why assassinations happen the way they do?
I think that in a political assassination you know that someone out there is going to support you. I don't believe an assassin kills someone unless he believes there are other people on his side. It's the difference between assassination and murder. People have told you, 'This guy ought to be shot, he's terrible, he's ruining our country.' So the assassin feels he has at least a minor mandate, that what he's really assassinating is an idea, a public figure, and saying, 'I did that. I'm as important as the person I erased.'

I don't feel responsible for anybody's assassination. It defies logic. We have four or five people who have committed political assassinations still incarcerated, like Sirhan Sirhan, who shot Robert Kennedy, Hinckley, who failed to kill Reagan, and James Earl Ray, who may or may not have killed Martin Luther King. And nobody can tell you why they did what they did. We just don't know, and we accept that – it's because they're crazy or they're looking for attention through that act. It's a symbol for them – 'I shot so-and-so.' In *Nashville* everyone assumed it would be the political candidate who is assassinated, because that's something we can accept, we buy that. But he shot the entertainer, and we don't know why.

At the end, everyone just joins in singing 'It Don't Worry Me!'
Shit happens, and life goes on . . . I think that's what happens. We don't take any kind of lessons from these events. We accept whatever has occurred because it has occurred.

The power of the film was that it was a political picture, and the fact it was country-and-western music didn't have a lot to do with anything other than as metaphor. Now, if this had been a film for Paramount – who eventually distributed it – they wouldn't have run for that in a second!

Notes

1 Pauline Kael (1919–2001) has long been regarded as one of the leading American film critics, highly influential for her charged, passionate writing and steadfast advocacy of certain maverick directors. In the 1950s, while running the Berkeley Cinema Guild and Studio, an adventurous repertory movie theatre, she became noted for her writing of programme notes and occasional reviews in print and on radio, famously panning *The Sound of Music*. In 1967 she was hired by editor William Shawn to write reviews for *New Yorker* magazine, where she championed Brian de Palma, described the US première of *Last Tango in Paris* as an occasion 'comparable to . . . the night *Le Sacre de printemps* was first performed' and cruelly undermined Orson Welles's achievement in *Citizen Kane*. In the early 1970s, from *M*A*S*H* on, and with the exception of *Images*, Kael was hugely supportive of Altman's films and reviewed *Nashville* ahead of other critics after the director screened her a rough cut, describing it as 'the funniest epic vision of America ever to reach the screen'. She was attacked by critics Vincent Canby and Andrew Sarris for stealing the march on her colleagues, and the controversy harmed her reputation. Her advocacy of Altman dipped dramatically following her disappointment with *Buffalo Bill and the Indians*.

2 Susannah York (b. 1941) first made an impact as a screen actress in John Huston's *Freud* (1962) and Tony Richardson's *Tom Jones* (1963). She played the title role in the third adaptation for the big screen of Charlotte Brontë's *Jane Eyre*, with George C. Scott as Mr Rochester. It was directed by Delbert Mann and featured a score by John Williams.

3 John Williams (b. 1932), formerly known as Johnny Williams, has become established as one of the cinema's most successful and prolific composers. Beginning in television in 1950s – where he worked with Altman – he demonstrated his ability to encompass a wide range of styles, but became most famous for his music for *Jaws* (1975) and *Star Wars* (1977). Since then he has largely specialized in grand symphonic scores for adventure and fantasy movies, including the *Harry Potter* series, and won an Academy Award for *Schindler's List* (1993).

4 Raymond Chandler (1888–1959) was born in Chicago, educated in England and began as a journalist before writing short stories. His celebrated mystery thrillers featuring the Los Angeles private detective Philip Marlowe proved rich material for the movies – *Farewell, My Lovely* was filmed with Dick Powell in 1945, *The Lady in the Lake* with Robert Montgomery in 1947, and most famously *The Big Sleep* with Humphrey Bogart in 1946. Robert Mitchum appeared as Marlowe in versions of *Farewell, My Lovely* (1975) and *The Big Sleep* (1978). Chandler also wrote screenplays for Hollywood, such as *Double*

Indemnity (1944), directed by Billy Wilder, and *Strangers on a Train* (1951), directed by Alfred Hitchcock.

5 Elliott Kastner and Jerry Bick would go on to produce two more adaptations of Chandler novels, *Farewell, My Lovely* (Dick Richards, 1975) and *The Big Sleep* (Michael Winner, 1978), both starring Robert Mitchum as Philip Marlowe.

6 Clifford Irving (b. 1930) was an aspiring novelist who became one of the expat community living in Ibiza in the 1960s and 1970s. There, while married, he became romantically involved with Baroness Nina Van Pallandt, famous as one half of the singing duo Nina and Frederik, whose greatest hit was 'Puff the Magic Dragon'. He wrote a biography of another Ibiza resident, art forger Elmyr de Hory, which earned him an appearance in Orson Welles's essay film *F for Fake* (1975). Welles's film also made reference to Irving's subsequent book, a fake 'authorized' biography of the reclusive billionaire Howard Hughes. For this effort Irving was eventually exposed and spent fourteen months in prison.

7 Sterling Hayden (1916–86) was a leading man in Hollywood in the 1940s and 1950s and proved himself in John Huston's *The Asphalt Jungle* (1950) before falling foul of the House Un-American Activities Committee and naming fellow communist sympathizers in Hollywood. In spite of some fine performances that followed, such as in Stanley Kubrick's *The Killing* (1956) and *Dr Strangelove* (1964), he was troubled by his past actions and devoted much of his subsequent life to sea voyages on his private schooner.

8 Dan Blocker (1928–72) was a popular character actor who worked in a large number of TV western series until joining *Bonanza* as Eric 'Hoss' Cartwright from 1959 until his death. *The Long Goodbye* carries the dedication 'In Memoriam for Dan Blocker'.

9 Mark Rydell (b. 1934), a New York actor and sometime jazz pianist in the 1950s, became a television director in Hollywood and graduated to features with *The Fox* (1968). He subsequently directed *The Cowboys* (1972), *Cinderella Liberty* (1973), *The Rose* (1978), *On Golden Pond* (1981) and *Intersection* (1994).

10 Joan Tewkesbury (b. 1936) trained as a dancer and appeared as a young ballerina in *The Unfinished Dance* (1947). After working in dance and theatre, she joined Altman as script supervisor on *McCabe & Mrs Miller*. She made her directorial début with *Old Boyfriends* (1979), from a screenplay by Paul and Leonard Schrader, and has subsequently worked mainly in television.

11 *They Live By Night* (1948), the first screen adaptation of Edward Anderson's novel, was scripted by Charles Schnee, produced by John Houseman and directed – his début – by Nicholas Ray, who would later make *Rebel Without a Cause* (1955). Ray's version stars Farley Granger and Cathy O'Donnell as the young lovers and is a more overtly romantic interpretation of the subject, for all

its classic tones of a *film noir*. Like Altman, Ray began his film with a challenging sequence, shot from a helicopter. A song performed in Ray's version, 'Your Red Wagon', was also the working title for the film, and still appears on some prints.

12 Keith Carradine (b. 1949) was the son of actor John Carradine, brother of John and half-brother of David. After landing a role in the stage musical *Hair* in Los Angeles in 1969, he was given his screen début by Altman in *McCabe & Mrs Miller* and subsequently also appeared in films by Alan Rudolph, notably *Welcome to L.A.* (1977), *Choose Me* (1984) and *The Moderns* (1988). In Ridley Scott's *The Duellists* (1977) he appeared with his then partner, Cristina Raines, who also acted in *Nashville*. Shelley Duvall (b. 1949) went on from appearing in Altman films most notably to playing the terrorized wife in Stanley Kubrick's *The Shining* (1980) and producing her own television series, *Faerie Tale Theatre*. She now appears to have returned to Houston and retired from cinema and television.

13 Born in France, Jean Boffety (1925–88) was the cinematographer on Claude Sautet's *Les Choses de la vie* (*The Things of Life*) (1969) and *César et Rosalie* (1972), as well as Alain Resnais' *Je t'aime, je t'aime* (1968) and Claude Goretta's *The Lacemaker* (1977).

14 Tom Stoppard's play *Rosencrantz and Guildenstern Are Dead*, first performed in 1967, takes two supporting characters from Shakespeare's *Hamlet* and examines their life in an ironic comedy whose action runs parallel to the well-known tragedy. In one classic scene, they bet on the toss of a coin, which has landed heads up eighty-five times in succession.

15 UA's script was called *The Great Southern Amusement Company*.

16 Jerry Weintraub (b. 1937) had been the tour producer for Elvis Presley and Frank Sinatra. After *Nashville*, he went on to produce such films as *Oh God!* (1977), *Diner* (1982) and the lucrative series of films beginning with *The Karate Kid* (1984).

17 Keith Carradine wrote 'It Don't Worry Me' for the film *Emperor of the North* (1973), but it wasn't used. 'I'm Easy' was written while he was appearing in the stage musical *Hair* and won the Academy Award for Best Song, the only winner among the five nominations the film received.

18 Louise Fletcher (b. 1934) was married to producer Jerry Bick at the time of making *Thieves Like Us*. The same year Lily Tomlin was nominated for *Nashville* Fletcher went on to win the Academy Award for her role as Nurse Ratchett in *One Flew Over the Cuckoo's Nest* (1975). Though her subsequent film career has been overshadowed by that role, she has remained active in the cause of civil rights for the deaf.

19 Robert Duvall (b. 1931) would later play a washed-up country-and-western singer in *Tender Mercies* (1983).

20 When Altman first met Thomas Hal Phillips in 1972, he was chairman of the Mississippi Film Commission and would be of great help on *Thieves Like Us*.

Phillips (b. 1922) wrote his first novel, *The Bitterweed Path* (1950), for his master's degree at the University of Alabama. He followed it with *The Golden Lie* (1951), *Search for a Hero* (1952), *Kangaroo Hollow* (1954) and *The Loved and the Unloved* (1955). He subsequently worked as a screenwriter and in local politics. Maintaining his friendship with Altman, Phillips also appeared as a poker player in *California Split* and in a small part in *O.C. and Stiggs*.

5

Buffalo Bill and the Indians – 3 Women – A Wedding – Quintet – A Perfect Couple – Health – Popeye

With the success of *M*A*S*H*, Altman was able to form his own company, which he called Lion's Gate after the bridge that leads into Vancouver, so named because the mountain peaks that dominate the city create the form of a lion. The key figures in the company were Altman's regular collaborators throughout the 1970s, Tommy Thompson, Bob Eggenweiler and Scott Bushnell. Not only did Altman's office and technical facilities in Los Angeles (at first on Westwood Boulevard, then on South Bundy Drive) become a base for the creation of his own films, but it also enabled him to produce for others.

DAVID THOMPSON: *How did you find the experience of acting as another director's producer?*

ROBERT ALTMAN: It gave me more volume of work – in other words, it allowed me to keep more people in the company, and it was fun for me to do. I like most of the films that I've produced. I know enough about short cuts we can make, and all the films I'm involved with are made for less than anyone else can do them for. But I didn't have any artistic input into them, other than discussions at the script stage. Basically, it was just to enable things to happen. I didn't have a good experience with Robert Benton on *The Late Show*,[1] which wasn't too great. Then there was Robert Young's *Rich Kids*,[2] which was a really bad experience – I thought the picture was sappy, nothing but close-ups. So since then I've mostly produced Alan Rudolph's films, beginning with *Welcome to L.A.*[3] And that's been a lot of fun, and I hope I haven't done him any harm, because I'll do it again. I'm very comfortable with Alan's stuff.

Why do you feel so close to his work?

I like the fact they have so many layers, I love to see the elements to all the chords. And I just like him a lot – I've known him most of my life. He was second assistant director on *The Long Goodbye*, and then worked his way up to be writer on *Buffalo Bill*.

Buffalo Bill and the Indians

Buffalo Bill and the Indians, *which according to the titles was 'suggested by'*
Arthur Kopit's play Indians, *was the most expensive film you had made up*
to that time, costing about $7 million. This was partly to pay for the two
famous stars: Paul Newman as Buffalo Bill Cody, now a showman playing
on his mythical status, and Burt Lancaster as the dime novelist Ned Bunt-
line, who blew up Cody's reputation. How did the famous, not to say
notorious, Italian producer Dino de Laurentiis[4] become involved?
Nashville had been quite a hit and everyone was all excited about it in New
York, and Dino approached me and asked what I was doing next. And
Buffalo Bill came up; the producer David Susskind had the rights to the play,
and Dino agreed to back it. He said, 'Be sure there's plenty of action. I don't
read any action in the script.' I said, 'Oh, they're going to go on a posse hunt,
they're going to do this and do that . . .' But Dino was really disappointed. It
was more what I call an essay film, and we weren't seeking to involve the
audience with the main character at all. And those kinds of pictures are hard
to sell.

Although the credits mention the play Indians *by Arthur Kopit, there's not*
much evidence of it in the film.
The Sitting Bull speeches were from the play, and Arthur Kopit was around
for the shooting – actually, he's the conductor of the band . . . But it wasn't
his play we put up there. Our version was really about the beginnings of
show business. Buffalo Bill was the first manufactured American hero. He
was a good shot and an Indian scout. In the Old West, that was about as
exciting and significant as being a New York taxi driver. So here's some poor
schmuck who thought he wanted to be a hero, and once he got there he just
didn't have any idea how to handle it all. Ralph Waldo Emerson said you
have to be careful about what it is you want because more than likely you're
going to get it . . .

The film's subtitle was Sitting Bull's History Lesson, *and you've said that*
your intention was to take a close look at an American myth, taking off from
historical fact about the way Cody really was. The screenplay certainly has
some choice lines, like 'Truth is whatever gets the loudest applause'.
Alan Rudolph wrote all that stuff, and he's very funny with words. At one
point, they're walking along and they look up at the hill, and in the distance

you hear this boom, boom, boom – and there's a whole bunch of Indians up there, and one guy says, 'That's Brown Horse's funeral.' Now, Brown Horse was injured in the first stunt with the burning cabin. And Newman as Bill says, 'Remember, son, the last thing a man wants to do is the last thing he does.' Alan is just great with those lines.

What was your attitude towards Buffalo Bill? There seems to be a sly political reference at work here.
I think Buffalo Bill is a victim, more so than Sitting Bull. Most of the bad guys are victims, and I think the real perpetrator of evil is society. The more an individual wants to please society, the more he becomes the heavy, and that makes him a victim. Nixon was a victim, but he was the right president for a total democracy, because the majority of the people in the US were like Nixon – they wanted him, and he represented their views. Then, when he got caught playing dirty, everyone was shocked because they had been betrayed.

Given that most of the film is set within the circus, it has a very stylized look, more so than the films that had preceded it.

38 The stagecoach under attack in the Wild West Show in *Buffalo Bill and the Indians* (1976)

Everything about the film was consciously controlled – the wardrobe and the sets. I didn't want any blue to appear in the film; it was red, yellow and black, the circus colours, with the reds really saturated. I don't know what exactly I was after, just an antique look that corresponded to those period signs, but I knew I didn't want it to look like any other film.[5] We used a lot of telephoto lenses, and many times we were almost a mile away from the action with our camera, shooting what would be the long shot. Sometimes we were so far away that we had to communicate by telephone. But with the compressed lens, it really flattened the image and gave the whole film a strange, bizarre look.

Sitting Bull's entrance began about five miles away from the camp – his party started out of sight and it took about twenty minutes for them to get to us. Dino arrived on location the day we ran the dailies of those, hours and hours of this caravan arriving, and that was a disaster. It wasn't the action film he was expecting . . .

With such a large budget, and an important central role, you were going to need a star. I understand you talked to Marlon Brando and Jack Nicholson, but Paul Newman was your first choice. Buffalo Bill is a vain, dissolute liar, trying to live up to the myth that's been created about him. Was Newman happy with a role in which his star persona was deliberately deflated?

Absolutely, that's why he wanted to do it. He even said he was playing himself – Paul Newman, movie star. He was great on the film, no problems at all. Except that I hate read-throughs; they don't serve a purpose for me, and I only do them if they serve a purpose for the artists. Paul Newman loves to read everything and would always ask me, 'When are we going to have the read-through?' I'd say, 'Paul, I can't get the actors together.' So we'd do it, and half the actors wouldn't be there, and the read-through would turn into a discussion about one beer being better than another.

There are other ways to go about this. I try to be with the actors when they're going through their wardrobe, because then you can talk obliquely about the character through the boots they're going to wear.

It was another big ensemble company, including opera singers. I told everybody they had to learn to ride, and that's when Geraldine Chaplin, who was playing Annie Oakley, had an accident – her saddle broke, she fell off the horse and broke her shoulder. Everybody was saying, 'Who are you going to recast?' I said I wouldn't do that – 'She'll have to shoot left-handed.' It may not be historically correct, but emotionally it fitted the film.

Given the budget and the big names involved, why do you think the film failed to reach a wider audience?
It was released on 4 July 1976, which was the USA's bicentenary. Nixon had just resigned, the whole country was polarized by him, and now you couldn't find anybody who had voted for him! So there were no national celebrations, and the only big one other than private picnics was the Russian tall ships which were in New York harbour. The whole country was licking its wounds, and then I came out and said, 'You want to see what ass-holes you are? You want to see what politics is really about?' And it didn't succeed. The timing couldn't have been worse.

You had a three-picture deal with Dino de Laurentiis, and after Buffalo Bill, *you were going to do a film of E. L. Doctorow's* Ragtime. *What happened?*
Dino took *Ragtime* away from me. I was set to do it, with Joan Tewkesbury as the first writer. Then I had Ed Doctorow[6] do his own script, and it was over three hundred pages long, but it was terrific.

With its mixing up of the fictional and real-life characters in 1906 America, Ragtime *would have seemed a natural for you. Is it one of the projects you most regret not doing?*
Yeah, I think so. You know, the Atlantic pier in Atlantic City was then still the way it was in the old days; the wooden pier and the rides and the diving horse and all those things were just as they were before gambling came in. It would have been great to shoot there, in those grand hotels. The biggest problem, which we discovered when we went down there, was that I couldn't figure out how to record sound, because you couldn't take a step in any of those old buildings without the floor creaking. It would really have been a problem, but we never got as far as trying to solve it.

Didn't Dino de Laurentiis call you about another project?
Edgar Doctorow, my agent Sam Cohn and I flew from New York to Beverly Hills to meet with him about some great idea he had about the End of the World. He said, 'Doctorow, you will be the writer. Altman, you will be the main director. The other directors will be Kurosawa, Bergman and Fellini. Fellini will do the European section, Kurosawa will do the Asian section and Bergman will do all those northern countries. Altman, you'll do America.' He was so excited about it, but then Edgar said, 'You know, there's one thing you haven't thought of, Dino. There couldn't be a sequel, could there?' We never heard another word about the project from that moment on.

Wasn't Breakfast of Champions *another project at that time?*
Yes. Alan wrote a script for me from Vonnegut's book,[7] but we never got
that made, and we lost the rights. But then twenty-five years down the line,
Alan got to make it with Bruce Willis. And I thought it was good, though it
was hated by everyone. But the things they criticized were because Alan
stayed a little too close to the book.

But at this moment you found an ally at 20th Century Fox.
Alan Ladd Jr[8] took over. I would go in with a pitch for a film, saying, 'This is
what I want to do, and it will cost a million and a half dollars.' And I would
do it for that. So the studio was never in a situation of things running over
budget – that was *my* problem. Laddie liked me and stuck his neck out for
me, and even lost his job because of me. Just after *Quintet*, there was a
stockholders' meeting in Monaco. Princess Grace was on the board of
directors, and she said to him, 'How could you let Altman make that awful,
awful film with my friend Paul Newman?' And Laddie got up and said, 'Oh,
fuck you,' and he quit. Maybe he knew he was going to lose his job anyway,
but that's the story.

3 Women

You've always said 3 Women *was a film you dreamed before you made it.*
It's true I dreamed it up, but it was not the content of the film or any emotion
in it, just that it was about personality theft. I had a film cancelled on me at
Warner Brothers.[9] I needed to make a film badly, and then my wife Kathryn
got very sick. We took her to the emergency hospital at four in the morning,
and it seemed very serious at the time, though it all turned out fine in the end.
But I returned to my house on the beach in Malibu and went to bed feeling
kind of desperate, and I dreamed I was making this film. I dreamed the title,
the location and that there were three women, and I knew two of the cast,
Shelley Duvall and Sissy Spacek. Part of the dream was that I kept waking up
and writing these things down on a notepad. And then I told two of my
production people, Tommy Thompson and Bob Eggenweiler, to check out
Palm Springs. When I really woke up, there was sand in the bed, because my
son Michael, who was eleven then, had joined me, and he was spending all
his time on the beach. So that's probably where the desert location came
from.
   I had done a painting in the late 1950s or early 1960s and it showed three
women, just their faces. Each one was skinny-necked and ethnically each

one was different. I lost that painting because I gave it to a friend, and when he died his estate said it was listed as being worth $600. They were willing to sell it to me for that, but I said, 'It isn't worth $600, I can tell you that!' But that painting was probably the genesis of *3 Women*.

The next morning I called my associate Scott Bushnell and said I had a terrific idea for a film: I'd read this short story – which was a lie – and briefly outlined what it was. She thought it would be great for Fox. So I went out to Fox, told Alan Ladd Jr about it and walked out with the deal. I had no story at that point, just an ambience and an atmosphere. I knew it would be about identity theft, or personality theft, so I just sat down and wrote it. Patricia Resnick[10] did a treatment, but I was essentially the author. I started with a thirty-page outline. I knew every scene that was going to take place, but those scenes weren't written until the day we shot them.

How significant was the location you found for the film?
When we found that spa where the old people were looked after by young women, I knew that would be where they worked. The spa and the other locations, the bar and the ranch, expanded the story. So it was an organic process. Even the heat down there contributed to the film. I can safely say

39 Two out of *3 Women* (1977) – Millie (Shelley Duvall) contemplates the pregnant Willie (Janice Rule) in the empty swimming pool

that in any film I've ever done, if you take the six high points of that film, those things were never in the script; they were accidents that happened during the shooting or some deviation or suggestion that came from a grip. Mostly they come from the actors themselves.

Isn't a famous example in this film the way Shelley Duvall constantly traps her dress in the door of her car?
That happened the first time we shot her getting in the car. Tommy Thompson called 'Cut' as soon as she drove off, but I said, 'No, that's good, let's use that.'

The cast clearly played a large part in the creation of the film. Shelley Duvall – who went on to win Best Actress at the 1977 Cannes Film Festival – was extraordinary.
Shelley wrote all of her letters, all of those recipes, all of her diary stuff. I don't know any writer who could have done it better. She was wonderful in it. She allowed the fool in her to show itself, what I call the 'pink stuff', what you normally don't show people. Real actors show the 'pink stuff'. Millie's a victim of women's magazines and movies and everyone around her. She just repeats things that she thinks will make people like her, but she's totally alone. Both Pinky and Millie were lost souls trying to find an acceptable way to live. Pinky was like an alien who had arrived on the planet and said, 'How do I hide myself in this world? I'll become *that* person.'

Alan Rudolph had used Sissy Spacek in *Welcome to L.A.*, and I just thought she was irresistible. I'd been watching her in his dailies and I had her in my mind. The two girls were just remarkable. They worked very well together.

Janice Rule was an experienced New York actress, so she invested quite a bit in her character, Willie. I had written several monologues for her, but I cut them before shooting because I wanted her to be an enigma, telling her that she was probably impregnated when she got into that pool with all those creatures in it. And she got that, playing it with a sadness, as if she knew her pregnancy would end in a stillbirth.

Bob Fortier was the key male presence. What made you think of him?
I think his character was named Edgar after Edgar Doctorow, whom I was working with at the time. Bob was an actor, dancer and one of the funniest people I've known, yet when he was on camera that didn't happen. I originally suggested that he came down to help build the set, but then I asked him to learn all the gun stuff. And I think he really knew that I had him in mind for this part. There was a kind of macho sadness about him, and that was the

40 Two women – Alma (Bibi Andersson) and Elisabeth (Liv Ullmann) – in
Ingmar Bergman's *Persona* (1966), a great influence on Altman

41 Sissy Spacek as Pinky and Shelley Duvall as Millie in *3 Women* (1977)

character – as much a fake as Millie was to become. He played that ineptness really well. Most actors try to give their characters some dignity, they really want to be loved, and Bob had that vulnerability.

The textures and colours of the desert are beautifully caught in the film.
Chuck Rosher, the cameraman, was very good at capturing the consistent light that exists in the desert. We overexposed the film, up to three stops, and then printed it in the lab to give it a desaturated look. We were very aware of the colours in the desert, especially the yellow and the purple sage. The designer was Scott Bushnell, who made the costumes and picked those colours too, the yellows, pinks and purples. The art director was James Vance, who was recommended to me by Burt Lancaster. He's a great water-colourist, and he made Willie's sand paintings. I'd met an artist called Bohdi Wind and saw some of his drawings, and when we found the swimming pools were empty, I got him down to paint those sexual monsters. But it was so hot the paint would boil, so they had to be done at night under lights. Those images really reinforced the dream idea. A few years later he stepped off the kerb in London, looking the wrong way, and was killed.

The music by Gerald Busby was the most unusual score you'd had since Images.
I don't know much about atonal music; I'm more a Gershwin man! But I wanted something I was unfamiliar with, and I thought Gerald's score was really compelling. It was exactly the mood I wanted to set in the audience's mind. His score was mostly heard when we deal with the dream element.

The dream sequence is a decisive moment for many people, and the point where some critics felt the film went astray.
Most of the dream sequence was shot through one of those kitsch water machines that actually contain coloured oil, which tip back and forth making waves. It tied into the way a foetus would be, immersed in liquid. Other shots were taken from elsewhere in the film and re-imaged in various ways. The dream is certainly the weakest thing in the film for me – it's a little pretentious and contrived. But the dream came back to the idea of a dominant male figure, with the females as victims. All the characters are like a rare species, lonesome, looking for a place in the world. The image I have in my head is of three female seals who have just kicked the last male seal off a rock. What the film's really about is what happens when the last male dies, with the three women becoming the family in three generations. But I

look at it more like a painting. You're not saying here's a beginning, a middle or an end. It's an impression. And trying to make films like this is very difficult. I wanted it to be cyclic, and that's hard to sell to a mass audience!

A Wedding

On the face of it, few films could be further removed from 3 Women *than your next,* A Wedding.

To me, *3 Women* and *A Wedding* are very closely related. We did them one directly after the other, and you'll often see how I've transferred the casts from one to the next, because you work with somebody and you get to like working with them. Or you think, 'Oh, they'll be good, let's do a film with so-and-so.' In *A Wedding*, instead of Mia Farrow I originally had Sissy Spacek, and instead of Pam Dawber I had Shelley Duvall. Then neither of them would do it. Shelley wouldn't do *A Wedding* because she was living with Paul Simon, who had rented a house in the Hamptons, and she said, 'No, he won't let me come and work because we've already paid for this house for the summer.' The reason that the Vittorio Gassman character was Italian was because Ben Gazzara had originally been cast – he was married to Janice Rule, and had been on location with us when we did *3 Women*. John Cromwell and Ruth Nelson were both in *3 Women*, and I put them right into *A Wedding*. So it's all very incestuous! It's not just casting those actors to fit the part; I actually wrote the part to fit the actors in all of those cases. I even cast the composer Gerald Busby.

When we were shooting in Chicago, all anyone cared about was Carol Burnett, because she was the big TV star of the time.[11]

Like 3 Women, *didn't* A Wedding *also have an unlikely genesis?*

A journalist from *Mother Jones*, a Texas magazine, came up to me when I was shooting *3 Women*. She was dressed very like Opal, covered in black shawls with beads flying everywhere – in fact, she looked like Omar Sharif riding across the desert! She said, 'What's your next film going to be?' I had an awful hangover, it was a really hot day, I didn't know at the time if I could complete *3 Women* and I was so exasperated that I just said, 'Oh, I'm going to do a wedding next.' And she said, 'What do you mean?' I said, 'Well, I'm going to take my crew and when somebody gets married they hire me and I shoot their wedding.' And she didn't take it very nicely, and I was very rude about it, but when we broke for lunch I went back into my motel room with

42 Altman directs the opening ceremony of *A Wedding* (1978), with John Cromwell as Monsignor Martin behind him, Mia Farrow as Buffy Brenner on the left and Vittorio Gassman as Luigi Corelli on the right

a group of people and said, 'That's a great idea, let's do it, let's do a wedding.' I called Laddie about it, and he said, 'Great, go ahead.'

So what appealed about a wedding as a subject?
It's hard to disguise yourself when you don't know what's expected of you. It's a unique situation, it's not something you do every Friday night. Everyone wants to be on their best behaviour; they're wearing tight shoes and wondering what people will think of them. They're over-hyped by the importance of the event and by the fact that they want to look at their best. Then they have a few drinks, time wears on and they get bored. The hilarity and joy break down, and things come out.

Who worked on the screenplay?
John Considine, who played the role of a security man, wrote the original script with me. Then Allan Nicholls, who played Lauren Hutton's cameraman, and Pat Resnick, the security woman in the shades, came in too. Each of us took care of a different set of characters. I knew the story outline, who each individual character was, what their secrets were and their inner rela-

tionships, but their scenes evolved as we were shooting. I told everyone to fight for their space, and there was a lot of improvisation going on. The scene with Pat McCormick and Carol Burnett dancing, I didn't really know what exactly they were going to say and do until I photographed it. It was as fresh to me as the audience who sees the film. I thought of *A Wedding* as having a very geometrical structure, beginning with the symmetry of the wedding ceremony, followed by a disintegration of this sense of order, and then bringing the pieces back together again.

What was the idea behind doubling the number of characters who had appeared in Nashville?
It was a caprice, a conceit. We had forty-eight characters, two families: one nouveau riche and the other old money. Americans don't believe there are differences between the classes! I couldn't have made *A Wedding* without the experience of having done *Nashville*. Like in *Nashville*, I put together a group of people who normally wouldn't meet each other and united them at a wedding. This time Geraldine Chaplin as the wedding co-ordinator played a kind of director, because a wedding is like a theatrical spectacle.

Where did you film?
We filmed at Lake Bluff on Lake Michigan, in a real 1930s mansion that we didn't need to dress. The only invention was Vittorio Gassman's underground taverna, which we built there ourselves. Nothing was specially created; all the clothes and gifts came from stores specializing in wedding fare.

The tensions in the families are not just financial – there's also racism.
Regina, the Nina Van Pallandt character, became pregnant one romantic night in Rome, and since Gassman passed his blood test, he was allowed to join the American family but not allowed to see his own family.[12] Twenty years on, he's tired and bored, and she has become a morphine junkie after the birth of twins. When Gassman, now a very rich man, meets his brother again, he realizes that America doesn't really have anything more to offer him. But then it's always a case of 'the grass is greener'.

I didn't kill off the newlyweds in the car, but I made the event both a shock for the audience and the families. When the couple come down the staircase, safe and sound, everyone's overjoyed. Only Vittorio asks, 'Who was in the car, then?' Because they're outsiders, no one gives a damn. Nina Van Pallandt says that they had no right to take Dino's car, and everyone leaves to celebrate with champagne. Only Vittorio stays behind. So I'm pointing a finger at the audience, saying, 'You're as racist as these people!'

43 Altman as a child at his Aunt Pauline's wedding in 1928. His father B. C. is third from the left, his mother Helen second from the right

44 The line-up for *A Wedding* (1978)

Some critics felt you were very hard on, if not contemptuous of, these characters.

I really don't hate these characters. I know them all; I've seen people like this all my life. When I was three years old I was the ring-bearer at the wedding of one of my aunts. I can't remember anything about it, except there is a photograph of the wedding with me in a little satin suit. But my father's family is similar to the Sloans, and my grandmother on my father's side was also called Nettie like Lillian Gish[13] in the film, and she was a kind of matriarch. My aunts were all sent to Europe for their 'education', but they were really only dilettantes. My mother's family was originally Irish, Welsh, French; they were among the first to colonize America. So they resembled the Brenners more.

I wanted to show the old money that can be found in Michigan and Illinois, which came from the men who felled trees along the Mississippi. They are very conservative and are against the nouveau riche as well as the grand international families like the Rockefellers and Fords who became wealthy in industry. However, my family were never as rich as the Sloans. By the time I was born they weren't rich at all, though that way of life persisted.

I showed *A Wedding* to those of my aunts who were still alive, and they didn't recognize anybody in it! So the connections I make are both true and false.

Quintet

In your original statements about Quintet, *you described it as a dark spy thriller set in an underground Chicago, like 'Graham Greene with a little Kafka and Camus'. The actual film seems a long way from that, especially in its bleak, snowbound setting.*

We were in Montreal, thinking we could find stranger exteriors than in Chicago. Then we looked at what remained of Expo '67, and I called Leon Ericksen to join me there. Most of the décor of the film was already there, including the sculptures and the photographs tracing the history of mankind. The ice had preserved everything for twelve years. And I forgot one thing: that when we would be filming in the winter, everything would be frozen! But that seemed perfect for the film. It was awful cold, and we even ended up inside the Arctic Circle above the tree line for those last scenes.

In some ways the film feels like a Western, with snow and ice replacing the sand dunes.

Yes, it's a Western or a samurai adventure. But I really see it as fairy tale. The hero, Essex, comes from outside and discovers a world falling apart that he doesn't understand.

You've commented that you may have been affected at this time by the death of your parents.
My father died from cancer just before we left for Montreal. My mother had died two years before. I'm sure that influenced the tone of *Quintet*.

That tone is very bleak. We seem to be looking at the last gasp of humanity on earth.
We asked ourselves, what would people live on in these conditions? The only food would come from the sea; anything that gave warmth would be extremely precious. Then, as in any community surviving under extreme conditions, there would be a game they would play, taking the place of religion.

Where did the game of Quintet come from?
It was a pretty good game that I invented myself. There is a pentagon pattern; you shook the dice and you could move either way. There were certain places you were safe and others you'd get killed. The unique thing was that one person becomes the 'Sixth Man', who advises the players, but his strategy would probably be to advise the strongest player wrongly, because whoever was left would play the 'Sixth Man'.

After the film's release I gather that you heard people were actually playing the game.
There was for a long time, especially up in Minnesota, a group of people who formed clubs to play the game. The attraction was you made your own markers. They designed their own boards, and they were quite detailed with the inlays. Actually, a game was manufactured by Parker Brothers, but when they saw the picture they realized it wasn't going to go anywhere, so they stopped it being sold widely.

Do the names you give the characters have a deeper significance?
The characters were identified by the pieces they carried around to play the game. Francha came from 'French A'. Deuca from 'Deus K'. 'SX' was Essex, a heroic name for Anglo-Saxons. Grigor brought connotations of the Orthodox Church, St Christopher the papacy or the leader of a sect. Vivia was life and hope, as she was the only one carrying a child. This is a society

45 The deadly game in *Quintet* (1979). Paul Newman as Essex plays with
Nina Van Pallandt as Deuca, while Bibi Andersson as Ambrosia looks on

without procreation, so that's why they make such a fuss about finding a girl
being pregnant. I got that whole idea by reading about elks in Lapland:
suddenly these herds would stop reproducing, and no one could figure out
why.

*Your casting of distinguished European actors – Fernando Rey, Vittorio
Gassman, Nina Van Pallandt, Bibi Andersson, Brigitte Fossey – was that
another game?*

Yes, that was a game. I decided that English would be the language of the future, but each character would speak with a different accent. And not just accents but also different colours, so that St Christopher and Grigor speak a more archaic form of English.

It seems the response to the film was in the main negative.
It's a difficult film. It has a game at its centre, and it is a game. But the thing about *Quintet* that most people don't get, or didn't at the time, though it had a cult following in Europe, is that in my mind it takes place on a different planet from the one we're on. I totally understand why people hate it, although I don't.

I've read an interpretation of the film that suggests the Newman character is you as an independent versus the studio, trying to survive the game, even when the odds are against you?
Maybe. At the end of the film, as he follows the goose, he's told, 'You will die out there.' And he replies, 'Well, you know that, but I don't.' That was pretty much my philosophy at the time.

A Perfect Couple

Again, there's a huge contrast between the style and tone of Quintet *and* A Perfect Couple.
Instead of taking a break after *Quintet* and sitting by a pool in Palm Springs, I decided yet again to make a film completely different to the previous one, something light and frivolous and musical. I wanted to show the cultural and musical clash between my two heroes. Paul Dooley's background is in the classical world – his sister is a cellist who plays in the Hollywood Bowl – and Marta Heflin, who's the niece of Van Heflin, is a back-up singer in a rock band. And they meet through a video-dating service. It was the opposite of *A Wedding* – two unlikely people who come together for good reasons. I wrote it with Allan Nicholls, and it was shot very quickly, in about seven weeks.

It was during *A Wedding* that the idea came about, as Dooley and Heflin and Nicholls were in it. Dennis Franz, too, was in *A Wedding*. He was a Chicago actor I found, and he went from a tiny part in that to a pretty good career.

A Perfect Couple *is certainly a romantic film, but not in any conventional way.*

46 *A Perfect Couple* (1979) – Alex (Paul Dooley) and Sheila (Marta Heflin)

The whole conceit of the film was that it starts out at this concert. You see
this very attractive couple sitting there in the Hollywood Bowl, drinking
their wine, and the camera comes in as if towards them. She drops something, and he bends over, and then the camera goes over to this improbable
'romantic' couple. And that's who we follow, rather than the attractive pair.
Why do we always end up having to follow the attractive couple? The reason you have to is because that's what the public want to see. They didn't
want to see the other couple, and the results of the movie were such! And we
had issues like the gay couple having a baby, which at that time were normally dealt with as a joke.

The band in The Perfect Couple *seem very much of their time.*
It's soft, middle-of-the-road rock music, but I like it. It's indigenous to
what the picture was. Ted Neeley had been the lead singer in *Jesus Christ
Superstar*, and the band, Keepin' 'Em Off the Streets, was put together for
the film by Allan Nicholls, who wrote the songs with them. I think it's a
terrific musical – it's what *I* call a musical.

Health

*Your last film to be bankrolled by Fox was filmed at the Don Cesar Hotel in
St Petersburg in Florida, where you created a bizarre convention of health
fanatics. The name of the nutrition nuts' national organization was an acro-
nym for 'Happiness, Energy And Longevity Through Health'. But all is not
that simple, as weren't the two rival candidates for presidency of the organization, played by Lauren Bacall and Glenda Jackson, based on historical
figures who once faced each other off in the US presidential elections?*
Yes, Dwight Eisenhower and Adlai Stevenson.[14] I was very involved in the
campaign for Stevenson, and it was a great shame we lost him as president
and got Eisenhower. Betty Bacall, who knew Stevenson and was also a big
supporter of his, played Eisenhower, however, who did fall asleep giving a
speech. Glenda was Stevenson, and many of those speeches of hers were
right from his words. It was a thinly disguised satire of political conventions
in the US, and the film should have been released in 1980 when they were
being held.

So where did the idea of health food come in?
The health-food craze was very prominent at the time, and Frank Barhydt,[15]
who wrote it with me, was the editor of a health magazine and was trying to
get out of it. I suggested doing a health convention and bringing in the
political parallels. So many of my films have been done this way. It wasn't
honing a screenplay and bringing someone in to do a rewrite to sharpen it
up; it was anti the professionalism when everyone was getting too serious
about movies. What I'm often doing in films is making them like documentaries, going into a situation and saying, 'OK, let's take what's there;
how do we make a movie out of it?' rather than trying to adapt a great idea
and attempt to make everything fit the movie.

In Health, *you had the once popular chat-show host Dick Cavett playing
himself as our tour guide. Why him?*

47 Dick Cavett hosts his show in *Health* (1980) with, from left to right, Lauren Bacall as Esther Brill, Carol Burnett as Gloria Burbank and Glenda Jackson as Isabella Garnell

He was a cultural icon whom we were talking about at the time, and he seemed to fit the health world. He was pretty much doing what he does. For me, the character who really understands what's going on is the public-relations girl, played by Alfre Woodard.

The film featured a song, 'Exercise the Right to Vote', which you used again in Tanner *'88.*
That's because I owned those songs and didn't have to pay for them! But it worked well in *Tanner*. The songs were specially written by Allan Nicholls and me for the Steinettes, who were a group I found busking on the streets of New York and decided to put into *Health*. Most of this stuff you end up putting in pictures is expedient, because you can't afford to use anything else.

Health *must have had the worst release of any of your films.*
It basically never got released. There was a whole change of management at Fox. Sherry Lansing came in, and they felt there was nothing in the picture

that was going to attract an audience. Mike Kaplan[16] and I eventually did a small release ourselves.

Popeye

Popeye was originally introduced into a comic strip called 'Thimble Theatre' in January 1929 by Elzie Crisler Segar, and he became the chief character until his creator's death in 1938. The first movie cartoon featuring Popeye appeared in 1931, again first as a guest character. But he soon became popular enough in his own right, with Paramount insisting he down a can of spinach in every one. Robert Evans had been developing the film for three years at Paramount, with cartoonist and playwright Jules Feiffer writing the script and Dustin Hoffman and Lily Tomlin originally cast as Popeye and Olive Oyl. Both Mike Nichols and Arthur Penn passed on it before Altman showed interest.

The promotion for Popeye *suggested that in the first attempt to recreate the cartoon character in a live-action film, to be true to Segar's style you and Jules Feiffer had made 'a musical without professional singers and dancers, a comedy without jokes, and a fantasy with a minimum of special effects'.*
I was familiar with the comic strip and then the cartoons. Jules and I definitely wanted to do more of the early Segar things than the cartoons through which most of the public knew Popeye. We kind of started with a level of reality, and then the longer he stayed in Sweethaven, the more it turned into a cartoon land in which he was trapped. It was an oppressed community, with a tax collector, a sheriff – Bluto – who terrorizes everyone, and everything run by a dictator they never saw. To me, if Segar had seen this community, he would have drawn his strip from it. The storyline was that Popeye blew in to shore in a storm, looking for his pappy, and eventually found out in Sweethaven that his pappy is the dictator. But his motto remains 'I Yam What I Yam.'

The actors often seem to be performing as if in a cartoon strip.
I brought in a trainer as you would for a dance troupe. We set up about four Quonset huts. One was a rehearsal hall – all the costumes were manufactured there – one was a special-effects building, one was for wardrobe and one was where we ate. Everyone I hired and brought to Malta, thirty or so of them, were all clowns or physical entertainers. About five of them came from the Big Apple circus, clowns and jugglers, people who did weird things. Then, with everyone in the rehearsal hall, we would have sessions that I called 'pick a tic'. So I would say to someone, 'You can only show two

dimensions. You cannot show any depth of character whatsoever – so how do you want to walk?' And we would work it out so that each person had their own way to walk or would look or sing a certain way. I figured that if you were to stand everyone up on the hill, then from miles away you could tell who each character was by their silhouette. We had the mayor who made a lot of noise but had no authority, the photographer in his raincoat whose flash never worked, and so on. And the costumes were very faithful to the way the characters looked in the cartoon strip.

What I didn't want was for *Popeye* to look like a Broadway musical. I wanted a simplicity to it; it wasn't about good dancers and great voices. I wanted the sense that, in this community, no one could rise to the level they aspired to. It didn't matter if they sang badly. Shelley couldn't sing, but when she did 'He Needs Me', she was wonderful.

Who was responsible for the casting of the two lead roles? Up to that point, Robin Williams was famous chiefly for the TV comedy series, Mork and Mindy.

Robin Williams was Bob Evans's idea, and he was the perfect choice at the

48 Robin Williams as Popeye and Wesley Ivan Hurt, Altman's
grandson, as Swee'pea, in *Popeye* (1980)

time. Robin is a master of improvisation, but he was trying hard to hold back, and I had to tell him he was playing it all too tight and that he should improvise more. Then he loosened up, and I let him talk to himself a lot, and I meant for it not always to be understandable. He wasn't thirty yet then and had to look much older. It took a long time to get his arms right, so I had to begin shooting all the scenes where he had his coat on again and again. That led the American crew to quit, but eventually the problem was solved and we carried on with the Italians.

For Olive Oyl, the studio wanted Gilda Radner, but I felt Shelley Duvall *was* Olive Oyl. I rang her in London when she was making *The Shining* and

49 Shelley Duvall in the role she was 'born to play', Olive Oyl, in *Popeye* (1980)

said, 'Shelley, I want to give you the role you were born to play!' As a child she'd been called 'Olive', like a lot of very thin girls. Jenny Beavan, who did the costumes on *Gosford Park*, created her shoes with the big toes.

And Swee'pea was your grandson, Wesley Ivan Hurt.
My daughter showed up with her baby, who at the time had Bell's palsy. So when he laughed he had this unusual expression. I thought I would have more control over a kid if he belonged to my own daughter, because Swee'pea had to be woken up at three in the morning, he was left floating in a rowing boat, and many things happened to him that another mother wouldn't like her child to go through. Actually, the things that might have scared him, like the octopus, he loved. He cried when he was around Robin and just loved being with Bluto, who was this guy Paul Smith. He was less than a year old when we started, but during the shoot he learned to walk, so we had to tie his feet under his dress.

The music for the film was composed by Harry Nilsson, who described what he did as 'Walking Music – not rock and roll, not old American musical, but music that walks along with Popeye throughout the film'.
Popeye was a true musical, though it's not thought of that way. I brought in Harry Nilsson[17] because I loved his work, the simplicity of his songs. He had done a little animation film with Fred Wolf called *The Point*, which was about a kid with a round head who lived in a land populated by people with pointed heads. There were a lot of double entendres about the point . . . Van Dyke Parks was the musical director.[18] We had a Quonset hut where we set up our own recording studio for the cast, and we would watch dailies there, too.

What drew you to shooting in Anchor Bay, Malta?
We had to do it some place and build everything. They had a huge water tank there. We talked about Florida and other places, but Malta was best, and as we were there almost a year, it was fairly safe politically, as the basic religion was Christian. Remember, this was Gaddafi time, and he made a visit while we were there, with thousands of ships.[19]

It was a long shoot, six months in all, and the press gleefully reported a lot of excessive behaviour and heady consumption of drugs.
Well, there was an awful lot of that going on. It was in the middle of the cocaine thing, and all of those guys, especially the musicians, were indulging. Harry, in particular, was incorrigible.

The production designer was Wolf Kroeger, who'd begun working with you on Quintet. *The construction of Sweethaven is strongly reminiscent of the town in* McCabe & Mrs Miller.

It was similar in that we built a town from scratch. I had the same character of the town drunk – Robert Fortier – who danced on the ice, wearing the same clothes. And I took a lot of the look of Sweethaven from *McCabe*, especially the Presbyterian church that no one attends. Also, when Popeye went into the brothel, there was a woman smoking an opium pipe like Mrs Miller and looking at a vase just as Julie did at the end of that film.

Giuseppe Rotunno,[20] the cinematographer, was famous for his work with Fellini. What did he bring to the film?

He shot in a rounded way, and the colours were saturated. We knew there would be problems with the weather, and I wanted a lot of lamps so that we could achieve that bright light you see in puppet films. The town was monochrome so that the costumes in primary colours, like Olive Oyl's red dress, really stood out, putting these two-dimensional characters into relief.

The bad weather you encountered caused many delays during the shooting in the first half of 1980, pushing the final cost to something between $20 and $25 million.

I've always been under or on budget. Rarely have I gone over, unless it was intentional, like on *Popeye*. We began with $13 million, but with that I said, 'I can't do this.' Bob Evans said, 'Just lie to them, because they're not going to stop the picture.' So I said, 'OK,' and that's what we did. The set alone, which took months to build, cost $2 million.

What did you make of the film's reception? It was released in December 1980 in the US by Paramount, and in the rest of the world by Disney, in a version in which you removed three songs. It's often referred to as a flop, and yet it actually made money worldwide – according to Variety, *it brought in $50 million in the US alone.*

It came out with the second *Superman*, and that was a cartoon film, and nobody had seen what we were trying to do before, really making the actors into those Segar characters. It was probably a dumb idea, but the studio didn't lose any money over it. It just didn't meet their expectations. It's a terrific babysitter now. When kids reach two years old their parents throw them into the Popeye room, put the tape on and know that it will keep them quiet for two hours. Through the years I've met children who can recite every line of the movie.

Notes

1 Robert Benton (b. 1932) began his film career as an established screenwriter with his writing partner David Newman, most notably on *Bonnie and Clyde* (1967) and *What's Up, Doc?* (1972). As a director he made his début with *Bad Company* (1972), and followed this with the Oscar-winning drama *Kramer vs Kramer* (1979) and *Places in the Heart* (1984). More recently he directed *Nobody's Fool* (1994) and *Twilight* (1998).

2 Robert M. Young (b. 1924) began his film career making documentaries for television before forming a partnership with director Michael Roemer in the 1960s. Young's début film as a director was *Short Eyes* (1977), and he followed this with a number of films generally on the theme of social injustice, including *Alambrista!* (1977), *The Ballad of Gregorio Cortez* (1982), *Triumph of the Spirit* (1989) and *Caught* (1996).

3 Alan Rudolph (b. 1943) officially made his directorial début with *Welcome to L.A.*, which featured many key Altman actors, though in fact he has two earlier films to his name, both low-budget exploitation exercises: *Premonition* (1972) and *Barn of the Naked Dead* (1973). To date, Altman has produced four more of his films: *Remember My Name* (1979), *Mrs Parker and the Vicious Circle* (1994), *Afterglow* (1997) and *Trixie* (2000).

4 Dino de Laurentiis (b. 1919) began his career in the Italian film industry at the age of seventeen, and by the 1950s had become an established producer following the success of *Bitter Rice* (1948), which starred his first wife, Silvana Mangano. With Carlo Ponti he produced Fellini's *La Strada* (1954) and *The Nights of Cabiria* (1957), and then moved into making expensive spectacles, building his own studio, Dinocitta. In the 1970s he moved operations to Hollywood and was responsible for *Three Days of the Condor* (1975), the remake of *King Kong* (1976), *Flash Gordon* (1980), *The Bounty* (1984), *Dune* (1984), *Manhunter* (1986), *Hannibal* (2001) and *Red Dragon* (2002).

5 In the DVD of *Buffalo Bill and the Indians*, the transfer fails to represent the original colour scheme, instead seeking a more general balance of the spectrum.

6 Edgar Lawrence Doctorow (b. 1931) has had a number of his novels adapted for the big screen: *Welcome to Hard Times*, *The Book of Daniel* and *Billy Bathgate*. *Ragtime* was eventually made by Milos Forman in 1981, with a screenplay by Michael Weller, and was notable for the return to the screen of James Cagney after a long retirement.

7 Kurt Vonnegut's hallucinatory novel *Breakfast of Champions* (1973) is set in a fictional Midwest town and deals with the converging lives of suicidal Pontiac dealer Dwayne Hoover and pulp science-fiction writer Kilgore Trout. Released in 1999, Alan Rudolph's film adaptation, from his own screenplay, cast Bruce

Willis as Hoover and Albert Finney as Trout. It failed to win either critical approval or commercial success.

8 Alan Ladd Jr (b. 1937), the son of actor Alan Ladd, began as an agent and then an independent producer, operating from England in the late 1960s until he was put in charge of production at 20th Century Fox in 1974. In 1979 he formed The Ladd Company, and then went on to high positions at MGM, Pathe and Paramount.

9 The cancelled film was *The Yig Epoxy*, based on Robert Grossbach's novel *Easy and Hard Ways Out*, with a screenplay by Alan Rudolph. It was a black comedy about military-industrial complex red tape. Warner Bros constantly questioned the script and Altman's choice of cast: Peter Falk and Sterling Hayden.

10 Patricia Resnick went on to write the screenplays of *Nine to Five* (1980) and *Maxie* (1985), and wrote and directed the TV movie *Grandpa's Funeral* (1994).

11 Carol Burnett (b. 1933) became a success in Broadway shows in the 1960s and then had her own television series, *The Carol Burnett Show*, winning five Emmy Awards. Her film appearances have been sporadic, including *Pete'n' Tillie* (1972), *The Front Page* (1974), *The Four Seasons* (1981) and *Annie* (1982).

12 Vittorio Gassman (1922–2000) was a stage actor before the cinema, and then made a great impact in *Bitter Rice* (1948) and *Anna* (1951). His marriage to Shelley Winters in 1952 led to a brief spell in Hollywood, where he projected a very macho image, and back in Italy he formed his own company and directed himself in *Kean* (1957). In more recent times he became celebrated for his comic roles.

13 Lillian Gish (1896–1993) has become legendary as 'The First Lady of the Silent Screen', and along with her sister Dorothy, she became famous in the films of D. W. Griffith, notably *The Birth of a Nation* (1915), *Broken Blossoms* (1919), *Way Down East* (1920) and *Orphans of the Storm* (1921). She also appeared in Victor Sjöström's *The Scarlet Letter* (1926) and *The Wind* (1928), but with the advent of sound she became more of a stage actress, with only the occasional film, most memorably Charles Laughton's *The Night of the Hunter* (1955). Her last film was *The Whales of August* (1987), directed by Lindsay Anderson and produced by Mike Kaplan.

14 Dwight D. Eisenhower (1890–1969) was born in Texas and had a glittering army career, culminating as Supreme Commander of the US troops invading France on D-Day, 1944. As a Republican presidential candidate, he achieved a sweeping victory in 1952. After steering the US through the most intense period of the Cold War, he was re-elected in 1956, but he suffered a heart attack and left office in 1961. Adlai Stevenson (1900–65) was brought up in the north and educated in law at Harvard, after which he became counsel to the Agricultural Adjustment Administration of Roosevelt's 'New Deal'. Following his involvement in the creation of the United Nations, he ran as presidential candidate for the Democratic Party in 1952 and again in 1956, when he won the largest

popular vote of any losing candidate in US history. He was always noted for his fine oratory and strongly held liberal views.

15 Frank Barhydt Jr, the son of Frank Barhydt, former production head of the Calvin Company, joined Altman as a writer on *Quintet* and *Health*. He subsequently worked on the screenplays for *Short Cuts* and *Kansas City*.

16 As publicity director for MGM, Mike Kaplan first worked with Altman on *Brewster McCloud*. He was then invited to act in *Buffalo Bill and the Indians* (he also appears in *The Player*), and joined Lion's Gate and worked in distribution and the marketing of all the films made with Fox. He was an assistant producer on *Short Cuts* and made a feature-length documentary with John Dorr on the shooting of the film, *Luck, Trust and Ketchup* (1994).

17 Harry Nilsson (1941–94) began writing songs for others before producing his own albums, much admired by the Beatles, including *Pandemonium Shadow Show* and *Aerial Ballet*. His fame grew with his cover of the song 'Everybody's Talkin'', which was used in the film *Midnight Cowboy* (1969), as well as his album-length children's fable that became the soundtrack for the animated film *The Point* (1970), directed by Fred Wolf, in which a boy is born with a round head in a village populated by people with pointed heads – a parable about prejudice and conformism. After a hit single 'Without You' and two more successful albums, *Nilsson Schmilsson* and *Son of Schmilsson*, his career suffered from his growing intake of drugs and alcohol, and he died from a heart attack.

18 Van Dyke Parks (b. 1941) was born in Mississippi, but his family moved to Hollywood when he was thirteen, where he worked as a child actor (he appeared in *The Swan* in 1956), and then moved into music, producing singles for West Coast bands in the mid-1960s. In 1966 he began a collaboration with Brian Wilson of the Beach Boys and provided lyrics for the uncompleted album *Smile*, which was finally remade in 2004 and performed live to great acclaim. Parks also worked with Arlo Guthrie, Ry Cooder and Randy Newman, developing his musical styles. For Altman, he worked with Nilsson on the songs and music for *Popeye*, returning in 2002 to provide music for *The Company*.

19 Colonel Mu'ammar Gaddafi seized power in Libya in a bloodless coup in 1969 and has remained the Arab world's longest serving leader. A fervent Arab nationalist, his first dream was to unite Libya with Egypt, Tunisia and Malta, and he offered economic support to Malta throughout the 1970s and 1980s, although the island remained an independent republic. His relationship with the US has been consistently fractious, and in the 1980s there were several incidents involving military aircraft over the Mediterranean.

20 Giuseppe Rotunno (b. 1923) worked as a camera operator on several highly prestigious films, including Visconti's *Senso* (1954), before becoming one of Italy's leading cinematographers. His credits include *Rocco and His Brothers* (1960), *The Leopard* (1963), *Fellini's Roma* (1972), *Fellini's Casanova* (1976), *And the Ship Sails On* (1983), and outside of Italy, *Carnal Knowledge* (1971), *All That Jazz* (1979), *Regarding Henry* (1991) and *Sabrina* (1995).

6

Come Back to the Five and Dime, Jimmy Dean, Jimmy Dean – Streamers – O.C. and Stiggs – Secret Honor – Fool for Love – The Dumb Waiter/The Room – Beyond Therapy – The Caine Mutiny Court-Martial – Tanner '88 – Vincent & Theo – The Player

In 1981 Altman closed down Lions Gate, selling the facility to producer Jonathan Taplin for $2.5 million, and moved his operations to New York City, where he opened an office on 59th Street. At the time he said, 'I left the major studios, I didn't leave movies.' Among his projects at that time, one, *Lone Star*, based on an off-Broadway comedy by James McClure, was cancelled by MGM. The money fell through for another, *The Easter Egg Hunt*, which was a story set in a girls' finishing school in Britain in 1915, written by Gillian Freeman, who later published it as a novel. For some years Altman hoped to make films from two scripts by Jim Leonard, one based on his play *The Diviners*, about the relationship between a brain-damaged boy and a former preacher set in the Midwest in 1931, the other an adaptation of Thomas Berger's novel *The Feud*, a comedy set in 1940.

In the meantime, Altman had accepted an invitation to direct a double bill of one-act plays by Frank South – *Rattlesnake in a Cooler*, a monologue, and *Precious Blood*, a two-hander in which the characters never speak to each other – at the Los Angeles Actors' Theatre.

DAVID THOMPSON: *You did these plays in June 1981 in Los Angeles, and then again in New York, at the St Clement's Church off-Broadway, after which you taped them for ABC's Cable Arts Network under the title* Two by South. *Already then you were using simple filmic techniques that marked them apart from the usual stage to tape transpositions.*

ROBERT ALTMAN: That was the first time I shot on video. When I did the *Two by South* plays, I actually rehearsed and performed them in an office space. We'd literally pull the furniture back and put about twelve chairs out.

But this wasn't your first time directing in theatre, was it?
No. Back in the 1950s, when I was in Kansas City, I worked in the Resident Theatre, which was the only theatre in the city, located in the Jewish Com-

munity Centre. They'd do three or four plays a year, and I got myself integrated into that group. There was a summer programme in which I directed three one-act plays: two by Tennessee Williams, *Hope is a Thing with Feathers* and *Portrait of a Madonna*, and the third was by me. And in the process I tried to learn a little more about actors.

Come Back to the Five and Dime, Jimmy Dean, Jimmy Dean

After Precious Blood, *in 1982 you went one further and directed Ed Graczyk's play* Come Back to the Five and Dime, Jimmy Dean, Jimmy Dean *at the Martin Beck Theatre on Broadway with an exceptional cast, including Cher in her stage début. The play chronicled a reunion of a Texan James Dean fan club, in which one of the members, played by Karen Black, has since undergone a sex change. Although you received some negative reviews, I believe it was a success with audiences.*
It ran about sixty-five performances, and we did OK. Frank Rich, the critic of the *New York Times*, never let up on us and we never got good reviews, but we had full houses all the time.[1] It was mainly the actors that came into it who convinced me to do it. However, Sandy Dennis was certainly not a star, Kathy Bates hadn't done much at that time, and Sudie Bond was known around the theatre world but not Broadway. And Cher was a pop star. But then Cher was kind of the public draw.

When did you decide to make a movie of it?
I hadn't envisaged that at first, but after I saw it running I said, 'I want to film this.' So literally a week after we closed the play we were shooting the film. We only had to reblock a little, as everything was basically set. We shot it in about seventeen days with two cameras in a Manhattan studio. Pierre Mignot[2] shot it in Super 16, which we then blew up to 35mm, and I think it cost about $800,000.

One of the exceptional devices in the film is the use of the mirror image we see of the dime store in the past.
When I did readings of the play there were mirrors all round my office, and I kept watching the actresses through these mirrors. That's how that idea of crossing time through the mirror came about. And it was much easier to do that when I made the film.
In the play there were people who played the 'mirror' side, while in the film I was able to use the actual reflection. It's a Mylar mirror that reflects

50 The hardy Juanita (Sudie Bond), the ever-pregnant Edna Louise (Marta Heflin) and the mysterious Joanne (Karen Black) in *Come Back to the Five and Dime, Jimmy Dean, Jimmy Dean* (1982)

until you put light behind it, and then you see through. I don't think I could have used Mylar in the theatre – I believe it was just gauze there – but in the studio all those effects were done live.

The cast arguably make up for the deficiencies in the play, in which perhaps there are too many awful revelations.
Well, I didn't think it was a great play. I didn't like the writer very much. It had a Tennesse Williams/William Inge aspect to it, with each character having their say, and I thought that would be interesting for the actresses. It's pretty simplistic. The James Dean thing was very strange as, of course, I did *The James Dean Story* and then I subsequently worked with James Franco, who played James Dean. And there sure are similarities.

Streamers

From an all-female cast, you went to an all-male cast in the next play you filmed, David Rabe's Streamers,[3] *which dealt with the tensions between young air-force recruits in a barracks. Was that contrast part of your interest in the piece?*
I don't know. It was always a matter of whether the play would work with a fourth wall. For me, many plays don't. And the success of the film of *Jimmy Dean* encouraged me to do *Streamers*. It had already been a success on stage with Mike Nichols directing, but I never saw it; I just read it. It had been brought to me some years before, and I just kept putting it off. We cast it in New York and shot it in Dallas in twenty-one days, on a set built in a new studio there, Las Colinas. It was brought to me by Geisler and Robadeau, and these guys proved to be dreadful.[4] I'd been shooting for two days and I found out they didn't have any money. They came in and wanted to take everything away from me. We spent a whole day in a lawyer's office, and finally I had to pay them half a million dollars to get the rights from them. My agent at the time brought in this rich guy, Nick Mileti, who owned basketball teams in Cleveland. He came and put up the money for it, saved my bananas.

You were reported as saying at the Venice Film Festival, 'I did M*A*S*H *in 1969. Basically, I'm telling the same story, but it just isn't funny any more.'*
I don't like the idea of these young men being sent off in political armies around the world. And I don't think I could have made the film had the African and Central American situation not been what it was at the time.
    When I was in US Air Force as a pilot during World War II, I was eighteen years old. There was always the threat of being attacked by the Japanese, though I was never in that kind of situation. But I remember being in a barrack room and sleeping next to somebody I didn't know, and that can be frightening because you're not sure of yourself and you try to act the way a bunch of rough fellas do. Being an individual can lead to a lot of problems. The boys in *Streamers* are in a real pressure cooker. Everything is based on fear. It was more about that than Vietnam.

The whole cast won the Best Actor award at the Venice Film Festival in 1982.
That was good, because I took the point of view that there was no leading character; each of the boys was as important as the other. I must have inter-

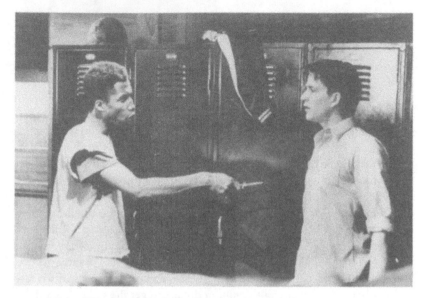

51 Michael Wright as Carlyle threatens Matthew Modine as Billy in *Streamers* (1983)

viewed about a hundred actors for the lead roles. I had two casts lined up, and I said to my wife, 'I'm going to sleep on it.' The next morning, I'd completely changed my mind. Now I can't see the film being done by anyone else.

I don't think that I *direct* anything, because by the time the film is cast, about 85 per cent of my creative work is finished. I remember Mitchell Lichtenstein, who played Richie, came up to me and asked, 'How shall I play this scene?' I wouldn't give him a direct answer. I said something like, 'Are you going to wear those boots? Let's see if we can't get *brown* boots.' Anything to divert him, because the minute I say something specific, I've taken 360 degrees of possibilities and narrowed it down to six. And afterwards, if someone says the film's no good, the actor would say, 'Oh, I just did what he told me to do.' What I want to see is something I've never seen before, so how can I tell someone what that is? I'm really looking for something from these actors that can excite me. I think that's valid and truthful. If I see what is at the height of my imagination, and the whole film is done that way, it's not going to be a great film. The real communication in this quasi-artistic medium comes from the performers, the actors. They're the ones that can say something or walk a certain way, and if you in the audience are hooked you'll react with, 'I don't know what this is, but it's *right*.' And that's the kind of emotion that we're trying to give to the audience. I have to encourage the actors, make them trust me, so they know they can go further and step over the edge. And I have a safety net – I won't let them crash or make fools of themselves.

Do you see your stage adaptations as more than a visual record of theatre pieces?
You can't just film the stage, and theatre is totally different. You're playing for an audience, and it's live and three-dimensional. I made *Streamers* in the same way as I did *Jimmy Dean*; that is, not trying to open it up but simply making it a film. The subject matter demanded they remain claustrophobic. What I attempted to do was to put the audience among the characters. In a close-up, you can tell so much about a person.

It's a different medium. I wouldn't let television make a visual record of any of the theatre pieces I've done. I didn't allow it on the operas I did, neither *McTeague*,[5] which I staged for the Chicago Lyric Opera, nor *The Rake's Progress*,[6] which I did at the University of Michigan in Ann Arbor. You can't just film the stage. And the experience of theatre is totally different. You're playing for an audience, which is live and three-dimensional.

How did you get involved in directing operas?
Unbeknownst to me, the composer Bill Bolcom,[7] who lives in Ann Arbor, had suggested to the Michigan people that they get me to direct *The Rake's Progress*. He kept saying, 'This guy should do opera.' They called me, and I said, 'No, I don't know how to do this.' It was a Saturday, so I hung up, tried to get back to sleep, and then I thought, 'No, I *could* do this.' So I called him back and said I could do it if they let me have eighty to a hundred people on stage! So that's how it happened. I can't read music, so I had to approach it as theatre.

How was that first experience of directing opera?
Oh, I found it terrible! Those people are tough, and everyone's concerned about the music and the singing. That said, I had a good time, but the stagehands, the unions would fuck us up all the time – 'Oh, we can't work on Saturday, we want double time,' and so on. After doing *The Rake's Progress*, I got a call from La Scala to direct *La Traviata* with Placido Domingo. I said, 'Why? Musically I can't help them. These performers come in knowing the part, and I can't turn around and restage it, because they know where they're going to stand to sing this and this, and I don't know

how to direct that. If it's an original piece that hasn't been done before, and I can develop the whole thing with them, *then* it makes sense.'

That production in Ann Arbor of Stravinsky's The Rake's Progress *came out of a period in the early 1980s when you were a visiting lecturer at the University of Michigan. You then took that production to Lille in 1986, and I believe it was the source of your contribution to the portmanteau film* Aria, *in which you observe a badly behaved eighteenth-century audience at a performance of Rameau's* Les Boréades *at the Renelagh Theatre.*
That's true. I took all those rags I had from those costumes – prosthetic tits and so on.

O.C. and Stiggs

In 1983 you made a film for MGM, O.C. and Stiggs, *based on a* National Lampoon *article called 'The Ugly, Monstrous, Mind-Roasting Summer of O.C. and Stiggs'. It wasn't released until 1987, and it remains one of the least seen of your movies – why?*
It was about how two teenage boys spend their summer, and it was also about cultural anarchy. Teenage exploitation films were all the rage at the time. It was offered to me by MGM, and I agreed to do it because I hated teenage movies so much. I thought I could do it as a *satire* of a teenage movie. But of course it was *sold* as a teenage movie. It was a suspect project from the beginning.

Secret Honor

In 1983 you saw Philip Baker Hall playing Richard Nixon in a one-man play called Secret Honor *written by Donald Freed (a political activist who had extensively researched the Kennedy assassination and the CIA) and Arnold M. Stone (an ex-government attorney) and directed by Robert Harders. The play followed Nixon through a post-Watergate drunken night examining his past and his conscience.*
I saw the play in Los Angeles at the LATC theatre run by Bill Bushnell, at a preview with about twenty-five of us in the audience. It ran about two and a half hours, and when you walked in you had to cross the set to get to your seat, so there was no way out! Generally one-man performances about famous presidents are tiresome to me, but I thought it was terrific, so I brought it to

New York. I put it on off-Broadway, in the Provincetown Theatre in the Village, where I ran it for about a month in October/November.

Everything in the play was truthful, if not factual. For the hard content, there was strong evidence that he said or thought these things. No one sued for libel. There was nothing really sympathetic to Nixon in *Secret Honor*, yet a lot of little old ladies used to come to the theatre in New York and one of them even knitted a sweater for Philip, because it was the middle of winter. And they were all fans of Nixon: they thought it was terrific, even though he was up there saying, 'Fuck it! Fuck it! Fuck it!' But Philip was just brilliant.

I then took it to the University in Michigan, where it played for five performances, and immediately afterwards we moved it right into an old women's residential hall, which my son Stephen re-dressed to serve as a set, and I shot it in seven days with Pierre Mignot. We made a course out of the production, and students had the opportunity to see what was happening on TV monitors in an adjacent hall linked to a camera in the ceiling of the room. Most of the crew were graduate students, and the dailies were open to everyone. The music was composed by one of the professors and played by the student orchestra. The success of the piece exceeded all my hopes, but even if it hadn't, I believe it was a worthwhile project.

A fascinating aspect of the film version was the use of all the TV screens. Was that your major addition to the stage production?
Yes, the screens came in when we did the film. That idea came up about two days before shooting began, and I think they saved the film. The big problem was that a one-man play gave me no cutaways, so what was I going to cut to if I wanted to truncate it, eliminate pieces of dialogue or just not be bored? The students at Michigan set up these monitors for me, and that proved a real good solution. I liked the bad quality of the image; it almost gave the impression we were watching old films of Nixon's television appearances.

They were like security cameras, and it also allowed me to show his paranoia. And Nixon was a president who governed with the aid of television. They're like a character in themselves – as are the drink and the microphone.

For all that it's one man in a room, it's certainly a very filmic piece right from the beginning, with the camera prowling around the set like a private investigator.
To keep the visual interest and prevent it seeming slow and static, we worked out as much movement as seemed logical, but never for its own sake. We shot with a zoom lens and a jib arm in 16mm.

The slow opening was to give time for the audience to think about Nixon. There was nothing historical about his keeping a loaded gun; it was just a dramatic device that would serve its purpose at the end and would keep the audience in their seats through the not so interesting parts. Everything was very arch until he takes out the tape recorder – and, of course, everybody associates taping with Nixon.

Before making *Secret Honor*, and before the tapes were released to the public, a friend of mine, Dick Tuck, got hold of some pirated copies and we listened to lots of them. Nixon would stay on the phone so long, you could hear him getting progressively drunker. He was talking late one night to Haldeman, who clearly didn't want to talk to him, and Nixon said, 'Supposing John Dean comes in and he's wearing a tape recorder? I'd better be careful what I say!' So the paranoia broke through; the person who was doing the taping suspected everyone else of taping, just as the thief worries about everyone else stealing, because he knows about the possibility.

Though no fan of Nixon should approve of the film, you present him as a complex, tortured individual.
Most villains never think of themselves as bad guys, and I'm sure Nixon didn't, and we establish early on that his attitude was as if he was a benevolent person. He was ashamed of his family. He had a great connection with his mother, though I don't think he liked her very much, he was jealous of his brother, and his father was a failure. He thought you couldn't become a president with his background, and yet he did. Then as he gets drunker, he becomes proud of himself and more caught up in his fantasy and further away from reality. He believes he was doing what he was told to do, that he was a hired gun. But then he didn't trust the people around him – he felt out of the loop, it seems to me. It was always how 'they did this to me', and what he did for them, and how he won in spite of everything being against him. His credo was that he could be a winner because he was a loser, like the people who voted him in. And the American system is to win regardless – it's all to do with greed; personal ethics have to be buried.

Did you do any research into Nixon's account of himself?
I've never read any of Nixon's books nor thought of reading them. Maybe we could learn a lot about him from them – I'm sure there's a lot of material between the lines! In the play, he's always excusing himself and he's very sentimental. I don't think he was smart or intelligent. I think a great deal of the fiction in the play is his awareness of himself. I don't think most of us can

52 Philip Baker Hall as President Nixon, overshadowed by Henry Kissinger, in
Secret Honor (1984)

analyse ourselves that well, but Donald Freed was able to step back and
approach Nixon in that manner.

Nixon was a man duped by his own plan, and it is the Willy Loman
tragedy.[8] Arthur Miller's play nailed it; it could have been about Richard
Nixon. I view him as a tragic character, and I'm personally more

sympathetic to Nixon than I am to Ronald Reagan. Although Reagan came closer to saying, 'I'm just hired to act this part', he thought he knew *how* to act, though he was a bad actor. Nixon was taught how to act; it was the same thing – you posture and make people think you do it well so that the content is lost to the delivery. The important thing is the presentation, and that will always be true when millions of people look to one person to lead them.

Originally the play was called The Last Tape (and Testament) of Richard M. Nixon. *Where did the title* Secret Honor *come from?*
That was my idea, because Nixon's defence was that he had to become unelectable, to a point where he was almost impeached, to keep himself from being re-elected. The people who controlled him, the Bohemian Grove people,[9] when they saw the power he had achieved, they were going to make him President again. He saw what was happening and felt that was basically wrong, so the only way to stop it and the only 'honourable' thing to do was to get himself caught. I was shooting at the Grand Ole Opry in Nashville when the news of his resignation came through, and one of the musicians went inside his room and locked the door – he sat and cried and played his violin, he was so upset, and we couldn't shoot for about an hour. Most people kept quiet about it because they had been disgraced, and the vast majority of people had voted for him. This was democracy at its height.

Philip Baker Hall[10] gives a tremendous performance.
Philip's a terrific guy, and he was born with the gift of a golden voice. He developed his performance with Bob Harders. They worked on it together for a long time, and it really had nothing to do with me. I never looked at a script; I only ever heard it as it was performed, and I made cuts as we did it. Of course, Philip doesn't look anything like Nixon, but after five minutes you forget it's him or any actor. And I agree with people who say his performance is on a Shakespearean level.

His screen career has now been boosted by his roles in the films of Paul Thomas Anderson,[11] who was a big fan of Secret Honor *and whose work clearly owes a debt to you in their multi-character, multi-plot complexity.*
Philip knew Paul Thomas Anderson's father well. And when he made *Hard Eight*, Paul insisted on using Philip, though he was asked not to. Paul has become a friend, and he says I've influenced him, that he's ripping me off. And that's very flattering. He used the song 'He Needs Me' from *Popeye* in his film *Punch Drunk Love*.

Fool for Love

After *Secret Honor*, two projects fell through for Altman: *Biarritz*, about an American who has married into high society and begins an affair with a French opera singer in the French resort; and *Heat*, a thriller scripted by William Goldman and starring Burt Reynolds (it was finally made in 1987, directed by R. M. Richards). But funding for his next film came from Cannon, the overambitious company run by Menahem Golan and Yoram Globus, who briefly dominated cinema exhibition in Britain and financed films by such maverick talents as Andrei Konchalovsky, Norman Mailer, Jean-Luc Godard and John Cassavetes.

Sam Shepard's play Fool for Love, *about a washed-up rodeo star in an incestuous relationship with his step-sister, was originally produced in New York by Shepard himself and the Magic Theatre of San Francisco in May 1983, with Ed Harris and Kathy Baker in the central roles. I believe it was Shepard[12] who contacted you about directing a film version because he admired what you achieved with* Jimmy Dean.
Yes, I saw the play in New York, when Shepard directed it. But it was a year later after two projects had fallen through that I called him to see what we could do with it. I never talked to him about his own ideas about the play, as he wouldn't tell me, and I had my own. What I found irresistible was having Sam playing the main part, because he's a terrific actor. When I suggested he play the lead role, he refused at first, but two days later he said yes.

Kim Basinger really wanted the part of the sister, and I remember she came to see me in my hotel room in California and campaigned hard for it. She was terrific, I think. She reminded me of Marilyn Monroe, very sexy and uninhibited. Harry Dean Stanton was great too, but we didn't get along – we had some conflict over his conception of the character. As I see it, his character had two wives and two children, and they become incestuous lovers, and he thinks he's responsible for this. In a way, it's close to *3 Women*. Everything about the play was incestuous, and I was making the film spiral into itself and out.

The film, not least because there's a lot of exterior filming, has more of a 'movie' look to it than your other stage adaptations.
It had the most film-like set of all my theatre adaptations, because we had all that space to play with. We shot it in Santa Fe, where Sam was living, and since we couldn't find anything we liked, my son Stephen built a motel with all these cottages by this road where you couldn't see anything around. We

53 Sam Shepard as Eddie confronts Kim Basinger as May in *Fool for Love* (1985)

made a junk yard of old cars and trailers, which also served as dressing rooms. At first Robby Muller[13] was the cinematographer, and he's great, but he was making a different film to the one I wanted. He was more interested in the composition of the frame. I had to replace him with Pierre Mignot, who understood better the fluid camera movements I like.

The screenplay for the most part keeps to Sam Shepard's original dialogue, but you depart from the single set a great deal.
There was a screenplay, but really it was just his play. The only real difference from the play was my decision to illustrate the monologues. What people say is Sam's text, but what I showed in the flashback often contradicted that. It was my idea to bring the family from twenty years ago into the motel and mix up the time periods. Sam's reality is an imaginary one, and when you hear what people say and then see it for yourself, you realize that it's not always the truth. I think most people lie when they tell stories of their past, even if it's not malicious.

Did you find yourself being typecast as a film director specializing in putting plays on to the screen at this time?

I did keep searching those things out. And certain ones you find you can do . . .

The Dumb Waiter/The Room

You and Harold Pinter[14] might seem an unlikely combination – deliberate pauses rather than overlapping dialogue, for one thing – so how did you come to direct two of his early short plays on film?
I was a big fan. This guy from ABC called me and said, 'We want you to do an hour-long play for the ABC theatre slot, anything you like.' And I said I didn't think I wanted to do something for the network. But he insisted, anything I want, so I said, 'OK, I want to do Harold Pinter.' And I said that as a kind of smart-ass response. They said, 'OK, which play?' I said I wanted to do *The Room* and *The Dumb Waiter*. So it was a deal. I started casting and figuring out the shooting and the budget, and then they came back and said, 'We've read them. Are you *sure* you want to do these plays? Because we don't understand them.' And I said, 'Don't worry, you will when you see them.' They ran one on Christmas Eve and the other on New Year's Eve, I believe. And then I put them together and released them myself as a kind of feature called *Basements*.

What was Pinter's reaction to them?
He was fine, except he hated my casting of Tom Conti, because he said they were supposed to be two Cockney guys. And I said I felt that Tom had this Scottish accent and that we should just let him use it. So that pissed Harold off.

What about John Travolta as a Cockney, then?
He was great, John was really good. And I had Linda Hunt, Donald Pleasence and Annie Lennox in her first dramatic role. All these choices were mine, over a lot of people's heavy objections. I said, 'What difference does it make? We're making little frothy things. I don't think the search for perfection or making something bigger or better is important; it's just something that occurs to us and we do it.' And I say *we* advisedly, whoever *we* are – 'Let's get together and put on a show, and that's the fun of it. And if in our secret hearts we know this isn't going to change everybody or make a lot of money . . .' Really, it's doing it for me. If that's arrogant, I can only apply the arrogance because I want to do it that way. And why should I do it any way other than the way it occurs to me? I know what

they mean, and I understand it, and I'm always trying to overcome those odds, but . . .

In 1985 you moved office to Paris, hardly a predictable decision.
Well, I wanted to do a movie on the fashion world for ten years, which became *Prêt-à-Porter*, so I was over there a lot seeing shows. I had different people writing scripts, including Susannah York. I didn't have any place else to live, and I liked it then, but I don't care if I ever go to Paris again. I was always an American in Paris. I never could come close to mastering the language, and that made me feel dumb.

Beyond Therapy

With Carol Burnett and Amy Madigan, you filmed the play Laundromat *by Marsha Norman, who had won the Pulitzer Prize for her previous play* 'Night, Mother *in 1984. Since it was an interior piece, staying mainly within the confines of a laundromat where two women meet one night, it was no problem to film it in Paris. Yet you also made a film adaptation there of a very New York-centred play, Christopher Durang's* Beyond Therapy.
Beyond Therapy was shot in Paris, though Paris was standing in for New York. Then at the end I gave away the conceit – or else they moved the Eiffel Tower! I was offered the financing, and I said I'd rather do it there rather than New York. We had an office in Paris with editing facilities, and that's where a lot of it was shot. I felt they'd shot pictures in New York about London, Paris or Rome, so I thought, 'Why not do it the other way round?'

It's generally regarded as one of your weaker films, mainly because of the source material. Were you a fan of the play?
Not particularly. I screened the film to an audience of four hundred psychoanalysts, and they all laughed during the picture, but afterwards, when they analysed it, they didn't like it so much.

The unfortunate part about *Beyond Therapy* was that when I came to release the film in America, the day it opened *Time* and *Newsweek* magazines came out with AIDS as their cover story. So AIDS opened too, and that finished the film because of the bisexual attitude in the play. It was about a bisexual guy in love with the guy he lives with and a girl who comes into his life. The first person I knew to die from AIDS was my costume man on the stage production of *Jimmy Dean*.

The Caine Mutiny Court-Martial

I think one of your strongest films of this period, but one not so widely seen, was your version of the Herman Wouk novel and drama, The Caine Mutiny Court-Martial, *famously filmed in 1954 as* The Caine Mutiny *with Humphrey Bogart. Was that famous precedent a problem for you?*
I took the play; I didn't think about the movie. Many of the actors said to me, 'Listen, I don't like these lines. They're awkward, I want to change them,' and I'd say, 'No, say exactly what's written.' They said, 'Why? We've worked with you before. This isn't what you usually do!' And I said, 'The reason is that when you're on the witness stand, you're not talking like your usual self, you're using words that are beyond your vocabulary, words you have read or heard but you don't use in your everyday speech. So if you're uncomfortable, that's great.' The only scene that was difficult was the last scene, where the guy gets drunk and makes a long speech. Both the play and the movie were done that way. So I just had him come through drunk, using all of the dialogue, but no one was listening to him.

We were shooting up outside Seattle in Washington state, and Herman Wouk even came up to visit. And he just loved the way we were doing it.

You had a very strong cast, and Brad Davis[15] in particular was very moving.
Brad Davis was excellent. He had AIDS then. He was in a scene in *The Player*, in the background, but he looked bad. He weighed about four pounds, and he was dead six months later. So I took him out.

Tanner '88

Although you had relocated to Paris, you were back in the US in 1988, following the presidential campaign trail with a fictional candidate, Jack Tanner, for a series for the burgeoning cable channel Home Box Office (HBO). On this you worked in collaboration with Garry Trudeau, famous for his satirical cartoon series Doonesbury. *This was the first time you had gone into making something entirely for television for some time, and it contained quite a few surprises.*
I think it broke the existing parameters because we took a fictional group of people and put them into a real situation. We took Jack Tanner and his campaign, all his staff and crew, and we went to New Hampshire and Detroit and Atlanta, following the real campaigns. If we heard Gary Hart or

Bob Dole were going to be talking in a factory, we'd go over there, and Tanner and his daughter would shake hands with them. We dealt with real people and mixed reality with this *faux* reality. It was structured by Garry Trudeau, who wrote the episodes as we went along. I would take that script and go to Detroit, and if I could do something real I would replace what he had written with reality. If I ran out of reality I always had his fiction to fall back on. But we were always looking to find a reality to push into it, and that was really exciting, for while it was scripted, we were making it up as it went along and bringing our fictional people into real situations and constantly blurring the lines.

We edited as we were shooting, and the shows were on the air within days of being shot. There's a lot of danger in that, and being new and naïve at it, we just did it. We didn't have to think too deeply about it. I think its descendants are many, television shows such as *The Larry Sanders Show*,[16] which have successfully crossed over between reality and fiction. I certainly think they owe us a nod, even if they didn't copy us. But we did set up that convention.

Did you know Garry Trudeau before Tanner '88?
I didn't know him personally, but while in Paris I needed my daily fix of *Doonesbury* in the *Herald Tribune*. When Trudeau was approached by HBO to write a comedy about a presidential candidate, he proposed that I collaborate with him. So we got together and came up with this notion of mixing up the fictional and the real, and very soon after we were shooting.

I remember going through the telephone directory searching for a name for the candidate, and that was how we found Tanner.

Trudeau has said that Doctorow's Ragtime *was an influence in that it had real and fictional people rubbing up against one another. Was that true for you too?*
Yes, but that approach can be dangerous. It's fraught with traps. The non-fictional people in *Ragtime* were actually fictional people by the time we got to them. For example, J. P. Morgan would appear to be a fictional character, whereas today it would have to be Donald Trump.

Was Michael Murphy always in your mind for Jack Tanner?
When we first came up with Tanner, Garry Trudeau said to me, 'What about your friend Michael Murphy?' And he was the kind of guy I had in mind, but I was a little reluctant to bring him up at first. He had been in a number of my movies, and in *Nashville* he had played the dark side of Tanner in John

54 Michael Murphy as Congressman Jack Tanner on the road in *Tanner '88*
(1988)

Triplette. When Garry suggested him, I thought that was perfect, and we never thought of anyone else. Michael had that Kennedyesque quality. And he really caught the fever – he was running for president! He took it very seriously and worried about not being as well informed as he should be. We simply hoped that if he made mistakes, then it made him look just like the real guys.

Most of the cast had worked for me before. Daniel Jenkins and Cynthia Nixon had been in *O.C. and Stiggs*; Matt Malloy had been in *The Caine Mutiny Court-Martial*. I met Pamela Reed at a party, and she turned out to be as tough and hard-talking as anybody, so she was perfect for T. J. Cavanaugh.

And how well did the real politicians play along? The sequence with Bruce Babbitt, for example, is extraordinarily convincing.
Cynthia Nixon was great, because she would walk up to anyone and say, 'Hi, I'm Alex Tanner, you must know my dad,' and everyone would follow on. Then Kevin O'Connor, playing the reporter, approached Pat Robertson and said, 'What's this about "playing Christian hardball"?' And Robertson snapped. He said, 'I used to be a boxer, blah blah blah.' And that was the first rush I got that we were getting something real on camera.

There was a small team of three who went ahead to prepare the ground, and mostly people trusted us. The mandate was always not to tell people what to say. Bruce Babbitt's people wanted to know what the script was, but we explained there was no script, he could say what he liked. And the sequence was entirely improvised. But everyone in that world is so inured to television cameras. If you'd taken our crew into the men's room at the convention and gone down the line of men at the urinals, they'd all have turned round to say 'Hi!'

I think the most important thing we ran into was in Detroit, where there was this show of robots, and as we were always looking for material for the title sequence, we shot that. Then we got into the 'So Sad' event, with mothers who had lost children to gunfights. The police escort would not go with us to that neighbourhood. A woman at the head of 'So Sad' put together the rally, and this was the first time I heard rap music. We found these kids, brought them to New York, and they wrote that rap for us.

The series felt very fresh, very innovative.
I think it was probably the most creative work I've ever done, and of all my work, this took the biggest leap.

Vincent & Theo

After Tanner '88 you took on another television project: a mini-series about the relationship between the artist Vincent Van Gogh and his art-dealer brother, Theo. Did you feel you were now going to be completely immersed in television again?
No, I was just riding the wave. There was a script by Julian Mitchell[17] and a French producer named Ludi Boeken, who had a deal with European television companies, including Central Television in Britain, to make a four-hour television film. I said, 'I'll do this, but I want to cut a theatrical film out of it.' The long version of the film takes in more of the early years in Holland and his beginnings. In the theatrical version we cut more to the later life.

Vincent & Theo I felt was quite an accomplishment, made for no money.

One of the film's strengths was your casting, using British actors who were not big names at the time.
I went to London and I sat in the Athenaeum Hotel and started interviewing people. I didn't want American actors for the main parts. British actors have the right training for this kind of film. Tim Roth and Paul Rhys were among the first I saw. I didn't think anyone could be better than them. At first I was worried about Tim's strong accent, but he was so powerful I was convinced.

Were you inevitably drawn towards using the letters for the screenplay?
We have all these letters that the brother saved, and you can read them all on the internet. There wasn't one letter in which Vincent wasn't asking for something, whether by inference or directly – 'You've got to send me some money.' Yet he didn't keep one of Theo's letters. So we don't really know what Theo's attitude was, except that he felt he had this burden to carry. And I think he did come to believe in Vincent's work, but not as a critic but because he was his brother.

Actually, the only time the letters are mentioned in the film is when Theo refuses to read one to his wife on the grounds that they're only meant to be read by the person they're written to. She gets angry, so he picks up a whole sheaf of them and throws them at her. I didn't really want to use the letters as a source, one reason being that people don't write the truth in them.

What, then, was your overall view of Van Gogh?
My view was the film was more about a desperate person who felt they had failed than a great artist. Van Gogh never sold a painting in his life, except to

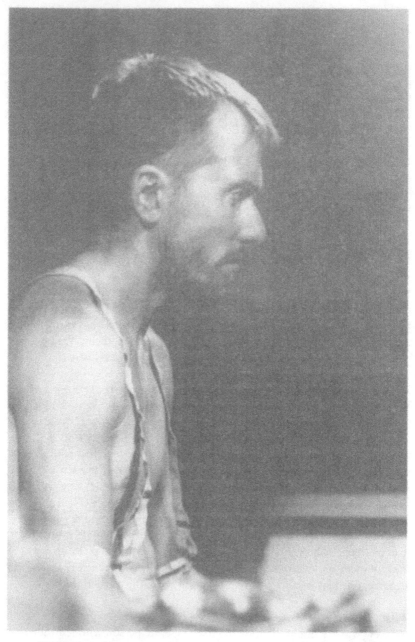

55 Tim Roth as the 'unsuccessful' artist Vincent Van Gogh in *Vincent & Theo*
(1990)

his brother, which was not a sale. I felt you had to take the position that these paintings aren't valuable. At first I wasn't going to show any paintings, but then I thought it was obligatory that we had evidence of his work, so that was the level on which we dealt with it. We became a little sacrilegious about it and decided to treat the paintings just as he would have treated them himself. Now, of course, if you say a painting is a Van Gogh, everyone gasps. So I had my son Steve, who lives in Paris, and a bunch of students produce fifty Van Gogh paintings, and I said they didn't have to be traced or photographically exact because you were never going to see them flat on, only obliquely. And then I said I wanted them thrown on the floor and stacked in the corner and left out in the rain and stepped on to get away from that thing of how today, if you were to pick up a Van Gogh, oh my God, you'd need three people . . . You know, when Van Gogh left Holland, he left behind a trunk with his mother, full of finished canvases. And she had the whole trunk burned, and some forty-odd paintings were destroyed. That was my main take on the situation, not to revere his work.

Isn't it tempting for you to identify to some degree with Van Gogh, in the sense that you've often wondered if your films will last?
I do think *Vincent & Theo* has something to say about the relationship between art and life. It's relevant to anyone like me who either likes or makes art. When you make art, you're perceived as different. And the moment you go off the usual path, of course, you're seen as *crazy*. I didn't deal with Vincent as if he was mad. He certainly had fits and some problems, but a lot of that came from his family. Theo probably had more mental problems, because he was trying to conform to society and keep everything under control.

In editing the film, was there a special challenge in making two versions?
Not really. There's always a certain chronological line that you have to follow, but that can be violated with time warps and flashbacks. Editing is just taking the raw material and putting it together, and it always seems to work. There are four stages to film-making. One is getting the idea, which is the ugliest and the toughest. Second is the shooting, which is fun and enlightening, during which the picture is changing and you begin to see the three dimensions to it. But by the time I get to the end of that, I couldn't go another day, no matter what – I've used all of my energy up. Then I start on the editing process, which is a whole new adventure, so a whole new energy and sense of excitement begins. And then the last is the forty-five seconds of

enjoyment that you get when you can smile and say, 'Look, I did this, isn't it good?' But that doesn't last for long . . .

This was your first collaboration with Geri Peroni, who became your most regular editor up to The Company.
I was editing with French film-makers, and the language was just defeating me. I said I had to have someone with whom I could communicate, so I called an editor who had worked with me on *O.C. and Stiggs* and asked her over, but she had just got married. So she suggested Geri, who had been an apprentice at that time. I liked her and I knew I could talk with her, so I brought her over to work with the French editor. Marcello Mastroianni once turned me down on a film I didn't make, but when he did *Prêt-à-Porter* he said, 'I've got to have my hairdresser.' I said, 'Shit, I can't do that.' We solved it through his lawyer. I said I'd hire his hair person if she would be the head hair person. Not that she had to do anyone else, but that way if any other actor made the request, I could say it wasn't possible, or otherwise thirty of the crew would be hairdressers! Then Marcello and I became friends, and he confessed he didn't mind about his hair, but in the morning when he was having his coffee, for the first hour of the day, he needed someone to speak Italian with him. I said, 'I know exactly what you mean.'

The Player

Until *Vincent & Theo* brought Altman fully back into the game, projects in America had continued to prove elusive. In 1987 Jerry Weintraub suggested Altman make a sequel to *Nashville* provisionally called *Nashville 12*, taking some of the characters on twelve years later. But it never happened for the lack of a script everyone could agree upon. Then a screenplay by Michael Tolkin[18] based on his novel *The Player*, about a studio executive who murders a writer, became a possible return to home territory.

How did The Player *come into your hands?*
I'd come back to the US from France and had an office in Los Angeles. I'd written *Short Cuts* – it was then called *L.A. Short Cuts* – and cast most of the parts, but I just couldn't get the film financed. Then I was offered *The Player*, which was really a dreadful script. I didn't want to do it particularly, but I said, 'OK.' I put *Short Cuts* aside and took many of the people I had cast in it, like Tim Robbins,[19] and put them in *The Player*. I hired a couple of writers to do dialogue for some scenes, whom nobody knew about, and I worked

with Michael Tolkin on the structure. We were rewriting it constantly as we shot it, because we never had a script that made any sense to me. It was about halfway through that we came up with the ending, which to me was a cyclic wrap-around that made the film valid. There was no ending in Michael Tolkin's book nor in the screenplay. It became a movie about movies, and the structure was like a snail that turns in on itself. At the end, Griffin Mill in the car is giving the pitch for the film you just saw. The idea came out of a conversation with Tim about how I ended *M*A*S*H*, making the audience aware that they have been watching a movie. And since it was a satire on movies, inside the film I was able to use movie-plot elements and movie behaviour and movie styles and movie music to reflect upon the attitudes of people who work in the movies. You see posters and titles everywhere. So it's all mirrors.

Were you aiming to paint an accurate picture of Hollywood?
What we show in *The Player* is a very, very soft indictment of Hollywood, an unrealistic look at that arena. It's really more of a farce, because although we did lift up a few rocks, Hollywood is much crueller and uglier and more calculating than you see in the film. It's all about greed, really, the biggest malady of our civilization, and it was Hollywood as a metaphor for society. What's the accomplishment in making $200 million, as top executives do? But my tongue was firmly in my cheek when we were making *The Player*, and frankly I'm still very surprised when people say, 'Oh my God, you really got Hollywood' – because it's just a funny conceit, that film, and the truth is much, *much* worse. People said, 'Oh, I'll bet you're going to be tough on agents.' Well, I was – by not including them in the film at all! That's another story, because they really run the business. I cast Brion James as the studio head as he was always appearing in B-movies as a villain, and he, of course, played a replicant in *Blade Runner*,[20] so that helped the satire.

As for Hollywood, they sell shoes and I make gloves. So we really aren't in the same business, and we're not dealing with the same audience. I can't tell you who runs the studios today. What they would want me to do, I'd fail at, I'm afraid I'd be late for work. When Griffin Mill delivers his speech about the art of motion pictures, it's the same hypocritical speech they all make, what every studio says every year about how they're going to be provocative and socially responsible . . . They're shameless about it, and they believe it. I asked my son Steve to come up with something really dumb for a motto, and he devised 'Movies – now more than ever'. Two years later ABC were using it as their theme. They probably didn't even know we did it.

56 Tim Robbins as studio executive Griffin Mill under threat from an aggrieved writer in *The Player* (1992)

You've certainly established a reputation for yourself as the outsider, or at least someone who only does his own thing.
Well, you do develop a reputation. And I am a liar. When they say, 'Are you

going to do this picture the way the script is?' then I say, 'You're goddamn right I am. I love this, it's going to be terrific.' And I mean that, sort of ... but I know it's going to get better – because if it doesn't, it's not going to be any good in most cases. Also, I feel I'm trying to do what they want, because they don't really *know* what they want, except a result of some kind. And I feel if I do what they want it's going to fail, and that's no help to them. So I've become sort of a double-crosser.

Do you ever feel you've been wrong in your judgement of what you did?
No. Every film I've ever done I really like. That's not very modest and not the way you're supposed to be, but you invest so much in them. I liken them to your children. You might say, 'Well, don't you wish he was taller?' 'He isn't.' 'Don't you wish she had blonde hair and blue eyes?' 'But she doesn't.' And you do tend to love your least successful children the most. So I love all my films.

But you do recognize why your films can prove unpopular?
That people got bored with them or didn't get them. In most cases I think they don't really get attended – in every sense. Many of my films, I feel you're not going to get them unless you see them twice. And that's almost an impossible thing to ask. The worst statement to my ears is when somebody asks, 'Do you want to see this movie?' And someone else says, 'Oh, I've seen it.' If you've seen a film once, and it has any quality whatsoever, you haven't really seen it. Because the first time you watch a film, no matter how savvy you are to movies and techniques, you're playing 'Whodunnit?' You're playing a guessing game: 'Oh, she's going to leave him. No, she didn't. Well, she's probably a lesbian. Oh no she's not.' And you're going through the film and finding out how all these suppositions are wrong. Well, now you know and you go and see it a second time: you're not faked out by the plot, you're able to deal with corners of the frame, with the nuances – which is what I feel the film is really about.

We don't have this attitude to music. You don't remember a piece of music from hearing it once. Every piece you can think of you've heard more than once. Paintings you see more than once. It brings something to you, and you bring something to it. It bounces something to you every time you look at it. But you can't ask this vast paying public to see a film twice. If they don't, however, then they're missing out on something. So it's a dilemma: do I worry that people are only going to see it once? Or do I go my way and think about the twenty-five people who might see it again and say, 'Hey, that was really good'?

But Hollywood remains obsessed by the quick fix, the movie that has to be an instant hit, and everyone's looking for the golden formula.

This system of trying to make films in Hollywood, in the context of studios and agents and those people who really control all of that – other than a few exceptions in terms of independent productions, or the case where the studios might have a property with which they feel they might attract a big star – they don't much care what you make or what they make. It's who you put in it and what the ad's going to be. You can come in with the one-sheet and say, 'This is the way we're going to advertise this picture.' They're not going to read the script. They're not capable of it. But they have these edicts that say that on page 32 there has to be a high point, and somehow all of this work has been formulated. By whom, we don't know. But somebody says, 'Well, such-and-such a picture made a lot of money, and twenty-two minutes into that there was a car chase.' And that suddenly becomes a statement. I know a lot of people who go to film schools are actually taught that, and I don't think it's true.

A script to me is a tool, just a reminder as to what kind of picture you've decided with your collaborators to make. So you kind of pay attention to it, but I'm desperately trying not to shoot the script, whether it's by me or someone else. If I come to work in the morning and I'm foggy and in a terrible mood, and I can't get my act together, then I'll follow what the script gives us. If I wake up with a little bit of a hangover, if I didn't get much sleep and I don't feel so good, then I come in and I say, 'What scene are we doing today?' Then we do it, but if it had been scheduled for the day before or the week before, I dare say it would have been a different scene. But generally I feel it's my obligation to try to take the elements that have been gathered together – actors, the props and the weather – and do something like the scene in the script. But I don't try to make the script; I try to make the film knowing that I have the script as a platform, something to fall back on. It's like an architect's rendering or a blueprint. You might say, 'This is the building,' but no building has ever gone up exactly to the plan. Somebody will say, 'Well, we've got this beam here, why can't we do this with it?' So there's a little addition put on.

It's like plays in the theatre: you go buy a copy of the play, and what that is is a transcript of the play as it appeared on its opening night. But during the weeks of rehearsals before – which consisted of blocking and learning lines and seeing what works and casting and firing people, and so on – there was this process to make these words work as a three-dimensional living presentation. And the number of theatre pieces that have been changed by the actors and the directors and the circumstances of the sets or costumes, and then presented . . . It's a working process, not a fixed text, and if you pick up the play and say, 'Boy, whatever's here is what you do', that isn't true. I guess some people work that way, but I don't – I'm really making it up as I go along.

I don't think that's bad, because over the time you work, there'll be balance. With a script as your sketch, it's like a painter attacking a canvas, with flowers over here and in the corner a dead monk. Well, say you have trouble painting the dead monk, so you let him live. Then you add a horse, then another, and then, in order not to have them running off the edge of the canvas, you paint a fence. And it might seem that that is far away from your sketch, but when you look at it, it is surprisingly similar to what you started with.

You introduced a lot of real-life movie people into The Player – *about sixty-five of them! Was that inspired by what you had achieved in mixing fiction and reality in* Tanner '88?

Yes, and I'd done that in *Nashville*, with Julie Christie and Elliott Gould passing through. In *The Player*, I thought if they were going to be naming movie stars that didn't actually exist, that wasn't very realistic, and it would heighten the reality of the film to have famous actors playing themselves. I began calling up a lot of people I knew and told them, 'I'm making a film about a studio executive who murders a writer and gets away with it, and it has a happy ending. Come to a party, and I'll pay you scale.' All the money was donated to the Motion Picture Home. Taking care of all these people took up a lot of our time. I just asked them to be themselves, and they all improvised their own scenes. Some I had to cut out, like Jeff Daniels and Patrick Swayze. But what developed was they weren't just playing cameos, smiling and passing through; they played themselves – and people like Burt Reynolds and Malcolm McDowell brought a really acid attitude towards the fictional characters. In the scene with Malcolm meeting Griffin Mill, originally he was just going to be walking by, but I said, 'Why don't you have a go at this guy?' And Malcolm said, 'I know exactly what to do. I'll just tell him to stop lying to me. That's what they all do.' And he just did it. When it came to actors like Dean Stockwell and Richard E. Grant playing parts, we had to introduce them as a little over-the-top, as caricatures, so that the audience would buy them. And I think it works.

For the big benefit party, we told everyone to wear black and white, just because I thought visually it would be interesting. But then when I invited Cher, I was trying to think of something that would make her think she was a little more special than everyone else. So I asked her, 'Please wear red, but I don't want anyone else to know about it, so that it's as if you did it on purpose to stand out from that crowd.' What I didn't realize at the time was that actually she never wears red!

The opening scene of the film – one very long take using a camera on a crane which introduces the characters and sets up the plot – drew immediate comparisons with the opening of Orson Welles's Touch of Evil, *which is even referred to in the scene.*

I was never really a great fan of Orson Welles. In fact, the opening shot of *Touch of Evil* isn't even that long – only about four minutes. When it comes to long tracking shots, I prefer to think of Max Ophüls.²¹ Really I was making fun of myself and all those pretentious people who think these things are important. The shot itself was a conceit; it becomes story-telling in itself rather than an element within it.

I did that shot right at the beginning of the shoot. I had a little model made of the lot area, and then we had a crane in scale, so I could figure out where I could have the camera for each of these moments. The whole sequence was a complete reel of film, about eight minutes long, and it involved about eleven miked-up actors. We rehearsed it for a day, lit it and shot it the next morning. We did about fifteen takes, ten of which were completed. Of those ten, I think five were good. They were all different because of the improvisations going on. Annie Ross was just visiting for the day, so I asked her to be a studio executive walking along with Frank Barhydt and Mike Kaplan. You saw Joan Tewkesbury and Pat Resnick pitching script ideas, and those were their own stories. Alan Rudolph and Buck Henry did the same thing. It was all a matter of timing. The best take, I felt, was the last one, but I used the next to last because the last was too contrasty; we were losing the light by then. You see on the clapperboard that it was Take Ten. It was a great way of getting the audience's attention, and I knew it would also create comment on the movie.

I believe you were in conflict with Michael Tolkin over Greta Scacchi's character?

I don't remember Tolkin's idea, but I was not very fond of him. I found him a humourless guy. To me, she was an ice queen, so she did ice paintings. We made her come from Iceland and named her Gudmundsdottir, which is the most common name there, like Smith. Griffin Mill's attraction to her was the classical idea of taking over the girl of the guy he defeated. It's like something in classic drama. And we wanted her to be a little strange and alien, a perfect woman who makes no demands and who has no interest in movies, because it's as if Griffin invented her. That was difficult for Greta, because she wanted to play her as real person.

For the obligatory sex scene, I shot it all in close-ups on their faces and said, 'Let's make it as erotic and as real as we can.' I didn't want to see those scenes you always get in movies of simulated intercourse. She was actually wearing a track suit. We did two takes and everyone went home.

It's notable that although Greta Scacchi is an actress famous for doing nude scenes, she wasn't the actress who appeared naked in the film.
The reason for nudity in the scene between Bonnie Sherow and Griffin Mill was both a comment on their relationship and a comment on nudity in the movies, in that she's not the kind of girl Hollywood usually asks to take her shirt off. I'd cast Cynthia Stevenson because she didn't look like a Hollywood glamour actress, and she was great about it. She said, 'Why me? Nobody's ever asked me to be nude before.' I said, 'That's the reason.' That's why you didn't see Greta Scacchi naked. Paul Newman's comment was, 'You don't get to see the tits you want to see, and you get to see the ones you don't want to see.' And that was it, it was all about movies and people's expectations of movies. Putting them together in the jacuzzi was a Hollywood thing in itself.

Whoopi Goldberg as the investigating cop was interesting casting.
I always wanted a woman to play the detective, who I don't think was written as strongly in the original script. I think I approached Joan Cusack first, but she wasn't available. Whoopi came to me and asked to be in the movie, and it was the only part left. The scene when Griffin Mill is taken to the Pasadena police station, that wasn't really written at all; I didn't know what we were going to do. Whoopi came up with the thing about playing with the tampons right there on the set, and she was the star of the scene. It was like reverse sexual harassment! I had cast Lyle Lovett in *Short Cuts*, and he hadn't acted before, so I made him the other detective in *The Player* to help him prepare for that.

Is the Richard E. Grant character, the writer Tom Oakley, in a way representing your opinions, at least before he sells out? 'No stars, no pat Hollywood ending'?
Yeah, that's what all directors say! 'I want this to be new', 'Everything for art', and then in the end we sell out. I would hope we wouldn't have an ending like the one in the movie-within-a-movie, *Habeas Corpus*. But we're all guilty. And if this is a happy ending with Griffin Mill and June married

and she's pregnant, then I think the baby is Damien [from *The Omen*]! And he'll become the head of a studio . . .

Personally, I don't know any happy endings. The only ending I know for sure is death, and that usually isn't associated with happiness. There are ambivalent endings, but to me it's just a stopping place, not a real ending. People's lives go on. If wedding bells are ringing, and they run down the aisle and they're happy, well, four weeks later they find out they're sexually incompatible or they have a terrible fight or they're divorced or she murders him. To me, it's just a stop on the curve. The river keeps going.

The final scene of Habeas Corpus *always draws a huge laugh, as you had a cast every producer in search of a hit would die for!*
That was shot on the one set we used, which was built in a warehouse in Santa Monica. After the title 'One Year Later', you see Susan Sarandon and Peter Falk, and everyone wonders, 'What are they doing in this movie?' Then we dolly back, and you see we're on Death Row. Bert Remsen as the old retainer goes in to check the chamber, and we pan over to a cell and see Rene Auberjonois and Louise Fletcher, and Ray Walston as a priest, and there's Julia Roberts! So now we know for sure we're in a movie. Then

57 *Habeas Corpus*, the film within a film – starring Julia Roberts as the heroine facing the gas chamber – in *The Player* (1992)

it's Bruce Willis! They were both my first choices and were very generous doing it.

Did The Player *really function as a kind of comeback for you? It certainly won awards and had a lot of press attention.*
I think it could have made a lot of money if they'd spent more on marketing, but sure, it got *Short Cuts* made. And then *Short Cuts* led to *Prêt-à-Porter*, and so on. After *M*A*S*H*, I remember there was an article in which the writer referred to flash-in-the-pans and promised that Altman wasn't going to come up with anything afterwards of any value. *McCabe* was not a successful film, but it survived because of the critics, so it saved my reputation. Similarly with *Nashville*, I guess that kept me up there for a bit. The highest-grossing film I did was *M*A*S*H*, the second being *Popeye*. *Gosford Park* may have supplanted it now. For myself, I've had five Academy Award nominations, and though people won't believe me, I'm thrilled I haven't won. I wasn't at the time, but I'm much better off for it, as it seems to put an end to everything. This way, if you don't win, you've got your friends who say, 'Ah, you got screwed, you should have won, you were the best!' I didn't even go for *Short Cuts*, as the picture wasn't nominated and nobody else was, so I had no reason to go. How can you be nominated for best director and the picture not be nominated? I don't get it. There's no truth and justice in it. There's no difference between the Academy and the *National Review*, and nobody knows who those people are. They're just a bunch of head waiters. When you put up what are supposed to be the top five films of the year, then that means four of them are losers.
We make too much of it. There should at least be categories for the films.

But your films are hard to categorize.
They *should* be hard to categorize. It's like comparing tangerines and apples.

Notes

1 Frank Rich, then the all-powerful theatre critic of the *New York Times*, described the stage production of *Come Back to the Five and Dime, Jimmy Dean, Jimmy Dean* as a 'dreary amateur night'.
2 Canadian-born Pierre Mignot (b. 1944) began his career as a cinematographer in the 1970s, mainly shooting French-language films. His credits include *Anne Trister* (1986), *À corps perdu* (1988), *Nô* (1998) and *The Blue Butterfly* (2004).
3 *Streamers* won the New York Drama Critics Award as Best American Play in

1976. The title refers to the song parachutists are supposed to sing when their 'chute doesn't open – "Beautiful streamer, open for me". David Rabe served in Vietnam in 1966 before embarking on a career as a journalist and then a playwright, beginning with *The Basic Training of Pavlo Hummel* (1971). His other plays include *Sticks and Bones* (1972) and *Hurly Burly* (1977). He wrote the screenplays for *I'm Dancing as Fast as I Can* (1982), *Casualties of War* (1989) and *The Firm* (1993).

4 Robert M. Geisler and John Robadeau (who died in 2002) were involved in the New York theatre and occasionally branched into producing feature-film projects. Their most successful venture was Terrence Malick's long-awaited third feature, *The Thin Red Line* (1998).

5 *McTeague* was based on the 1899 novel by Frank Norris, which was famously made as *Greed* by Erich Von Stroheim in 1925. The libretto was by Altman and Arnold Weinstein, and the music composed by William Bolcom. An abridged version of the opera, using extracts from the stage production and clips from *Greed*, was produced by Frank Barhydt for PBS Television.

6 *The Rake's Progress*, Igor Stravinsky's only full-length opera, was given its première in Venice in 1951. Composed in his neo-classical style, with allusions to Mozart and Donizetti, the opera had a libretto by W. H. Auden and Chester Kallman after the engravings by Hogarth, and has remained firmly in the repertory of major opera houses.

7 William Bolcom (b. 1938) is an established American composer specializing in chamber music, vocal works and opera. His most famous opera to date is *A View from the Bridge* (1999), based on the Arthur Miller play. His most performed concert piece has been a setting of William Blake's *Songs of Innocence and Experience*, and with his wife, mezzo-soprano Joan Morris, he has recorded many songs from cabaret and stage musicals.

8 Arthur Miller's classic play *Death of a Salesman* premièred on Broadway in 1949. Its story of Willy Loman, an ageing salesman who is downtrodden and heavily in debt but refuses to give up hope in his belief that 'personality wins the day', has become the tragic flip side to the American Dream.

9 The Bohemian Grove is a retreat in Monte Rio, California, where the power players of America – largely Republican, extremely wealthy and exclusively male – meet for discussion, high jinks and cultish rituals. The subject of much speculation by conspiracy theorists, this group has acquired the reputation of being in control of the country and deciding on the appointment of future presidents. Nixon was a member from 1953 but on the tapes was later heard famously to describe the gathering as 'the most faggy goddamned thing you could ever imagine'.

10 Philip Baker Hall (b. 1931) built up a solid reputation as a theatre actor but only became really noticed with *Secret Honor* and subsequently through his appearances in the films of Paul Thomas Anderson, who cast him in the principal role in his feature début, *Hard Eight* (a.k.a. *Sydney*). Baker Hall's other

credits, as a very distinctive supporting actor, have included *Midnight Run* (1988), *Air Force One* (1997), *The Truman Show* (1998), *The Insider* (1999), *The Talented Mr Ripley* (1999) and *Dogville* (2003).

11 Paul Thomas Anderson (b. 1970) has proved to be one of the best of the new generation of independent American film-makers, making his début with a film starring Philip Baker Hall, *Hard Eight* (1996). In his subsequent films, *Boogie Nights* (1997) and *Magnolia* (1999), the use of multiple plot strands and a large canvas of characters clearly owes a debt to Altman. His next film, *Punch Drunk Love* (2002), made extensive use of the song 'He Needs Me', sung by Shelley Duvall, from the soundtrack of *Popeye*.

12 Sam Shepard (b. 1943) developed his craft as a playwright in the underground, pop-influenced world of New York in the late 1960s and early 1970s, and was first noticed for *The Tooth of Crime* (1972). *Buried Child* won the Pulitzer Prize in 1979 and was followed by *True West* (1985), *A Lie of the Mind* (1985) and *Simpatico* (1999). He wrote the screenplay for, among others, *Paris, Texas* (1984) and became established as a film actor with *Days of Heaven* (1978) and *The Right Stuff* (1983).

13 Dutch-born Robby Muller (b. 1940) was noticed as a cinematographer thanks to his work for Wim Wenders in Germany, notably *Kings of the Road* (1976), *The American Friend* (1977) and *Paris, Texas* (1984). His painterly, textured style was also evident in Jim Jarmusch's black-and-white films *Down By Law* (1986) and *Dead Man* (1995).

14 Leading British playwright Harold Pinter (b. 1930) first came to prominence with *The Caretaker* (1960), which was adapted for the screen three years later. Films were also made of his plays *The Birthday Party* (1968) and *The Home-coming* (1973), and he also wrote the screenplays for three Joseph Losey films, *The Servant* (1963), *Accident* (1967) and *The Go-Between* (1970). Prior to agreeing to let Altman film his two short plays, he told the director that *Secret Honor* was one of the best films he'd ever seen, and he subsequently directed plays by Donald Freed on stage.

15 Brad Davis (1949–92) began his acting career on stage and then made a dramatic film début in *Midnight Express* (1978). He subsequently appeared in *Chariots of Fire* (1981) and *Querelle* (1982).

16 *The Larry Sanders Show* was created by Dennis Klein and Garry Shandling, with the latter playing the eponymous talk-show host whose vanity has no equal. Shown on HBO (and consequently very strong in its language and subject matter) from 1992–8, the show's highly successful ploy was to have real guests playing themselves mixed with the show's regular personnel played by actors.

17 Julian Mitchell (b. 1935) is a novelist, playwright and screenwriter. His most successful play has been *Another Country* (1981), later filmed, and he was a key writer on the *Inspector Morse* television series. His screenplays have included *Arabesque* (1965), *August* (1995) and *Wilde* (1997).

18 Michael Tolkin's novels include *Among the Dead* and *Under Radar*. He wrote and directed two films, *The Rapture* (1991) and *The New Age* (1994), and has written several screenplays, including *Deep Cover* (1992), *Deep Impact* (1998), *Changing Lanes* (2002) and *The Punisher* (2004).

19 Tim Robbins (b. 1958) has established himself as a leading American actor and also, with his wife Susan Sarandon, as an outspoken activist. His film credits include *Top Gun* (1986), *Bull Durham* (1988), *Jacob's Ladder* (1990), *The Hudsucker Proxy* (1994), *The Shawshank Redemption* (1994) and *Mystic River* (2003). He has also directed *Bob Roberts* (1992), *Dead Man Walking* (1995) and *Cradle Will Rock* (1999).

20 *Blade Runner* (1982), directed by Ridley Scott, has become a benchmark in the design of science-fiction films, depicting a futuristic Los Angeles dominated by immensely tall buildings and constantly under rainfall. The story was drawn from the Philip K. Dick novella *Do Androids Dream of Electric Sheep?* and dealt with a world in which replicants prove very hard to distinguish from humans, among them one played by Brion James.

21 Max Ophüls (1902–57) was a German-born director from a Jewish family who, mainly because of historical events, made films in Germany, Hollywood and finally in France. His rich, elegant style, famous for its long, flowing tracking shots that would encompass an entire scene, was particularly evident in such films as *Letter from an Unknown Woman* (1948), *La Ronde* (1950), *Madame de . . .* (1953) and *Lola Montes* (1955).

7

Short Cuts – Prêt-à-Porter – Kansas City – The Gingerbread Man – Cookie's Fortune – Dr T and the Women

Short Cuts

DAVID THOMPSON: *How did you come to think of Raymond Carver's short stories as material for a film?*

ROBERT ALTMAN: I was on an airplane, flying back from Europe in 1990 after a project in Italy had collapsed,[1] and I said, 'Give me something to read, give me some short stories or something.' So I had a pile of books, and one of them was a collection of Raymond Carver stories,[2] and I read them on the way to New York. And I said, 'Oh Christ, this is what I want to do!' They were terrific because he made stories out of small incidents. None of these people were extraordinary, but mundane events could have an important emotional significance. And these stories were so unstructured that no one would automatically say, 'Oh, let's make a film out of this.' But I saw them as a movie right away, using them as a basis, shuffling images and lines, with a piece of one story and a paragraph from another, and I started writing it with Frank Barhydt. We colour-coded each story and placed cards on a board, so we could see if there was too much of the same colour! I felt by cutting back and forth the audience would always carry the story they've just left in their minds, so there's a continuous sense of lives going on.

I pitched the film and got a certain amount of interest. But there wasn't any obvious pattern to it; there weren't a lot of other films you could say, 'This is like that.' Having all these different characters touch but not really be part of the same story ... Even in *Nashville* the arena was tighter, as they're all getting off the bus with the guitar. And this was Los Angeles, which is spread everywhere, and we were dealing with the suburbs – Downey, Compton, Watts, Pomona, Glendale. Carver's stories were all about Seattle or less populated northern towns, and I felt I had to put them into one venue and then to fracture them, mixing up the nine stories and the poem 'Lemonade' we used. But the life we show applies equally to people in non-poor countries like England or France. They were mostly characters who hadn't made it, losers – in fact, a lot of Carver's stories are about alcoholics. Carver didn't make any moral judgements on these people, and neither do I. The Tim Robbins character is an awful misogynist, but he takes responsibility for his family, and his wife stays with him. Audiences can't make easy decisions about such characters.

In your opinion how faithful did you remain to Carver?
Everything that was in there was his stories or pieces or lines from the stories, which is why it says in the credits 'Based on the writings of Raymond Carver', not on any particular story. I called it a 'Carver soup'. We invented at least two characters Carver never dreamed of, Tess and Zoe, so that the music could come from within the film. We scrambled all the stories, and there was only one complete story in there that was kind of the main clothes line of the film, which was the one about the Finnigans, whose boy gets hit by a car and later dies. It's the most intact of all the Carver stories in the film. But everything was inspired by Carver's work, and there's even a scene that's still in the film when across the street you see a guy walking along with two kids pushing a bicycle – that's another Carver story. So you always know you're in Carver territory.

Some people asked, 'How can you add your input to a great author?' That's fair enough, but his widow Tess Gallagher, who edited and also wrote many of these stories with him, was with us all the time, and she felt what we were doing was very close to Ray's stuff. I never got to know him personally, as he was dead before I began on the film. But you can't make a pure film of someone's writing. You can be true to it technically, in a way, but that doesn't mean you're being true to it emotionally.

I think that *Short Cuts* was very well realized, in that we achieved exactly what we set out to do. It was like *La Ronde*[3] or *Tales of Manhattan*.[4] I was never very interested in bringing a novel into a film, except *Thieves Like Us*, and that I wanted to do just the way it was. With *The Long Goodbye*, I used pretty much the same kind of style that Chandler used, which was stringing a lot of little thumbnail essays along a line. These multi-character films have always been the most interesting to me – *Nashville, Short Cuts, Prêt-à-Porter*.

You had twenty-two actors in Short Cuts. *What constantly attracts you to working with these large casts?*
My smart-ass, cynical view of it is that in a multi-story, multi-cast film, if a scene didn't work, I could always cut away to something else. If two actors are really happy with a scene and say they really want to do it, and we shoot a six-minute scene, and they're happy they have put a continuity into that, as long as I have something to cut away to, an escape hatch, I can get out of it

and come back where I want to. And you don't need as much information as you're given in most films. If you're given all the information, you don't have anything to do yourself. I think it's far better when you have just a hint of something.

We have this thing about movies having to be two hours or an hour and fifty minutes long, and everything has to be fitted into that, and I don't believe you can do that with most novels. It's hard to condense and do a good adaptation; there's usually so much information there. I think short stories fit themselves to film very well. It's like paintings: 'What kind of painting are you going to do? Are you going to do something very realistic?' I look on all this as mural work – you just put all the stuff in, and I don't much care what the subject is. I found the same interest in digging into the world of ballet, and I knew nothing about it, though I have an emotion for it now.

Do you prefer not to know too much about the arena you're going into?
Yes, because then I'm discovering something that I can enthusiastically recommend and pass on to the audience.

Short Cuts *was a relatively low-budget film – $12 million, raised independently – yet you assembled an amazing cast for the film, some of the busiest actors around.*
That was actually kind of easy to do, because nobody worked more than eight days, and they all worked for the same fee. I could say to you, 'Come and work six days,' and you'd say, 'OK, that'll be fun, I can do that.' I used recognizable artists for all the characters so that the audience would remember who they were. And I had a good reputation with actors, so I was able to attract them. After I had all those cameos in *The Player*, people would say, 'I'd love to be in one of your films, because I don't have to go to the North Pole and live in an igloo for eighteen weeks.'

But it also meant I couldn't shoot in sequence. I would work with Lily Tomlin and Tom Waits and do their stuff, and they're gone. Then we'd start overlapping with Tim Robbins and Madeleine Stowe, and then they're gone. If there were seven earthquake sequences, we did the earthquake seven times.

Where did the idea of the earthquake come from?
I don't think that was in any of Carver's stories. I did it to tie all the stories together. It was just another earthquake; no one got hurt. But it got your attention, and it was the glue for all those stories, giving all the characters a

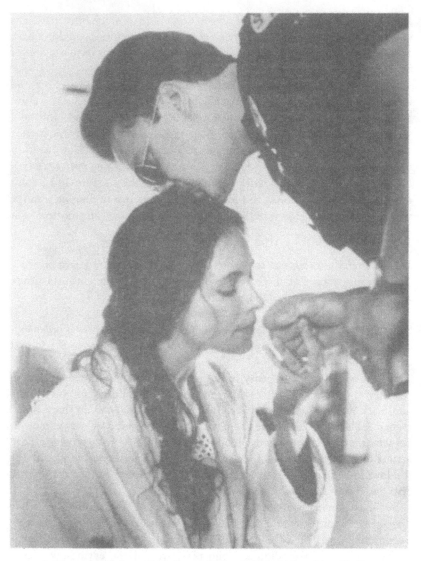

58 The unfaithful cop Gene Shepard (Tim Robbins) kisses his wife Sherri (Madeleine Stowe) as she sniffs his hand in *Short Cuts* (1993)

common experience and wrapping it all up. I'm sure that for every earth-quake that happens there's a dramatic event in somebody's life.

Did you have other characters in mind for the film whom you had to drop?
Originally I had maybe five characters in two other stories that were threaded through the film, one of them based on a Carver story, one based on a story of my own. Before we shot, I felt the script was too long, so I put it up on a board and I eliminated both of those. One was about someone selling cosmetics door to door, and the other was about an alcoholic judge. That's how the chauffeur played by Tom Waits got in, as he was the driver for the judge. I knew a guy like this. He was a periodic drunk who would tear whisky ads out of magazines and put them in his desk. Then he'd show them to his secretary, saying, 'This stuff looks really good, this Three Crown Bourbon. Go out and get me two bottles of that.' So he'd amass this whisky, then he'd say he was going home to do some briefs, and he'd lock himself in and drink for eight or ten days. Then as he was sobering up, he'd fill his refrigerator with beer, and his secretary would come by in the morning to make sure he was detoxing himself . . . The Ann Archer character was to be his secretary, so I took that out and made her the clown. That was prompted by Tim Robbins, who suggested having a clown arriving at the Finnigans' house after the child had died, and though I didn't think that would play, the clown idea stayed with me. It helped me bring her character into the hospital.

I still often read about the offence that Julianne Moore's nude scene caused. It clearly got to a lot of people.
Well, that's their problem, isn't it? That was not from a Carver story, except those characters *were*, but I think it really is the best thing in the movie. This couple are waiting to see this other couple. She spills a drink on her dress and takes her skirt off to iron it, and he keeps on to her about this affair she'd had. The idea of her standing there in front of him, naked from the waist down, talking about and admitting to this indiscretion, was just irresistible. I wouldn't have done it any other way.

I first offered that part to Madeleine Stowe, and she called me to say, 'I can't do this, Bob.' I said, 'I understand that.' But she wanted to be in the movie, and I said, 'That's OK, you'll be in the movie.' Then I called Julianne Moore in New York. I said, 'I've got this script, and I've got a part for you, but before I even talk about it, there's a scene in it that's mandatory in which for about five minutes you have to stand naked from the waist down.' There was this pause on the phone, then she came back and said, 'I can do that.' So

I said, 'Great, let me send you the script and see what you think of it.' Then she said, 'Oh, Bob, one more thing – I've got a bonus for you.' I said, 'What's that?' She said, 'I really am a redhead!' And then Madeleine Stowe said, 'I don't mind being naked, I want to be in the picture.' So she played Julianne's sister, married to Tim Robbins the cop, and in one scene she's posing naked while Julianne is drawing her. And she insisted that she be naked. It wasn't the nudity that had bothered her. She said she didn't feel able to keep her concentration to play that other scene if she was standing there in front of the crew.

That scene when Matthew Modine bursts in on the sisters, and they respond with a conspiratorial laugh, had a real sense of the women's power over the men.

All those things added to what the film is about. That scene was never in Carver, it was never in my stories, but in the way we made the picture we arrived at moments like that, and they made for a terrific scene. I don't think it would even have occurred to me to have her posing naked for her sister if we hadn't had that conversation. And if she hadn't insisted. I mean, we had one kind of sex scene with Tim when they're interrupted by the kids, and she showed a little breast then, but this was something else.

Sex is dealt with in the film in a very open, honest way, which is not always comfortable to witness.

Most of it is not overt, but there's always an undercurrent of it. In Jennifer Jason Leigh's character's case, she's just a woman picking up $15,000 a year doing sex calls at home, apparently with the approval of her husband. It seems to be without meaning to her, but underneath I believe it has. Even from watching those scenes in the film, I feel that there's a lot below the surface. I asked Jennifer to write all that stuff herself, because she was the one who had to say it. And she went down to one of these jerk-off call centres. I don't know whether she took calls herself, but she came on the set and said, 'Well, shall I tell you what I have?' The whole crew were standing around, and she started talking, and then suddenly she stopped and said, 'That's all.' Everyone was stunned. I would never have been able to write something like that. I said, 'That's great. Now change the baby's diaper when you do this!' It was a great comment on pornography.

Did you ever consider making two films out of Short Cuts?

I thought about it, just as I did with *Nashville* and a lot of other times.

59 Lois Kaiser (Jennifer Jason Leigh) performs phone sex in her home in
Short Cuts (1993)

During the editing, I thought, 'I've got a lot of stuff . . .' And with *Nashville*
it was going to be *Nashville Red* and *Nashville Blue*, but it wasn't sequel-
ized. You could see them in any order, although the climax was basically the
same in both films, shown from different points of view. When *Nashville*
was sold to network television, they couldn't do it in one screening, and I
said, 'I can make two parts and I can add stuff.' That's when the rumour
came out that there was a four-hour version, which wasn't true, because if it
was shown one week, then the following week a certain amount of it had to
be repeated to allow you to catch up. We did a script and an edit that way,
but then the network decided against it.

*Wasn't the problem of length what caused problems in adapting Tony
Kushner's hugely acclaimed play* Angels in America[5] *to the screen?*
I was working on that when I went to Paris. My position was I would only
do it if it was going to be two pictures. I wouldn't truncate the whole thing.
And that's what Mike Nichols did at HBO, and I think that's the right thing.
It would be like cutting Tennessee Williams – if you were to pare it down to
the story, it would disappear.

Personally, I felt that in adapting Angels in America *for the screen, scenes that may well have played effectively at length on the stage were just a little too stretched.*

Well, you may be right, but it can be a question of comparing it with what you're used to. It's like going into a restaurant, and you see a new thing on the menu, and it turns out to be something that's inedible, but then you find that's what they enjoy eating in Somalia!

It was around this time you made Black and Blue, *which was a record of the Broadway musical revue featuring an all-black cast of singers, dancers and musicians at New York's Minskoff Theatre.*

That was done for David Horn for PBS, and to shoot it we really put it back together on the stage, brought the people back with their costumes and filmed over three days. The way we shot it was not a lot different from what I later did on *The Company*. I would shoot the end of a number, so people would be coming off stage, then the new number, and then at the end of that number those people coming off. So we'd have all the entrances and exits, but stop in-between those. They got rehearsals in the meantime while we were setting our cameras for the performances. But for the backstage stuff, which to me is what validates it, I just had Pierre Mignot by himself with a camera, shooting whatever, and I didn't even have access to that footage till later.

Prêt-à-Porter

Prêt-à-Porter – *or* Ready to Wear *as it was eventually titled in the US – a comedic look at the Paris fashion scene, had been on the back burner for a while.*

I'd worked on the idea for years, ever since my wife took me to a show in Paris in 1984 when I was in Europe promoting *Streamers*. I really had no interest in going at all, but then the lights went out, the music began, and I thought, 'So that's it, it's a circus. I've got to make a film about this!' I went backstage and met Sonya Rykiel, the designer, and just couldn't get the idea out of my head. Eventually I hired Barbara Shulgasser, a critic on the *San Francisco Examiner*, to write a screenplay, and it wasn't good enough. When Harvey Weinstein[6] bought the project, I sent him the script thinking, 'If they read this, they'll cancel it.' But they read it and said, 'We love this!' So I thought, 'OK, I've got the money, let's make it.' And we reinvented it as we were making it.

You famously ended the film with a fashion show featuring entirely naked models, which suggests you do not have a high opinion of the business.
The film was all about why we wear clothes, that it's just covering our nakedness, and what we wear is all a kind of disguise. So for me the final scene with the nude models was the most important scene in the film. It was a very loose essay film, a farce merged with reality. But it wasn't so much about the designers and models as the people who surround them, the press and media who have the power to make them. Not the artists, but the pure hype artists. People who go into that world fall back on acts and clichés, so you can't go very deep with it. You could even call *Prêt-à-Porter* a mockumentary, because I was using real names and mixing them in with the fiction. All the fashion people are very used to cameras being around their own shows, so they know how to do their thing. It was more a case of getting our actors not to act than getting the non-actors to act. And then there was the murder-mystery spoof element too.

That strand of the film enabled you to cast Marcello Mastroianni, as an Italian tailor from Moscow upon whom suspicion falls of murdering the president of the French Fashion Council, and Sophia Loren, as the president's widowed wife, and put them together as lovers.
I particularly liked the Marcello/Sophia scenes, in which she did a striptease and he sat on the bed and howled. That scene, the wardrobe and everything, was a direct lift from De Sica's *Yesterday, Today and Tomorrow*.[7] I needed a cast with famous faces the audience would recognize, as there were so many characters and no plot to speak of. If I'd had brilliant actors no one was familiar with, then the audience wouldn't have known who was who.

You told Lauren Bacall you wanted her to 'play' Diana Vreeland, and there was an obvious film-a-clef aspect to Prêt-à-Porter: *Anouk Aimée's character seemed based on designer Sonia Rykiel, the trio of Tracey Ullman, Linda Hunt and Sally Kellerman could be loosely linked to Alexandra Schulman, the editor of British* Vogue, *Suzy Menkes, of the* International Herald Tribune, *and Liz Tilberis, the editor of* Harper's Bazaar; *Stephen Rea parodied photographer Steven Meisel; and your 'tour guide' was Kim Basinger playing a ditzy, incompetent version of Elsa Klensch, CNN's fashion reporter.*
We shot five shows in fashion week in Paris. In the first cut I didn't use any of them, and then I realized I had to, because they were the reality that made the farce valid. Kim Basinger had no time to prepare for her first scenes, and everyone was appalled at how messy it all was, but then I realized her

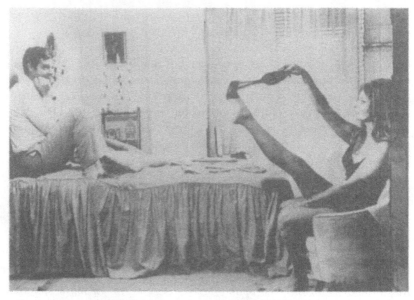

60 Sophia Loren stripping for husband Marcello Mastroianni in an effort to keep herself pregnant in Vittorio de Sica's *Yesterday, Today and Tomorrow* (1964)

61 Altman brings Marcello Mastroianni (in bed) and Sophia Loren together again as former spouses Sergei and Isabella in *Prêt-à-Porter* (1994)

mistakes and ignorance were very honest and made her very believable. And when she ends her final soundbite at Simone Lo's show, saying 'What the hell am I talking about? What's going on here? This is fucking fruitcake time, is that fashion? I have had it' – that, to me, vindicates the whole film.

You had the fashion world very heated up about the film and the image it gave them. Karl Lagerfeld banned you from his shows, as did Valentino and Yves St Laurent, and leading fashion-magazine editors asked to be seated out of the range of your cameras.
The fashion world has to reinvent itself twice a year, so it's very tough for them. I didn't go courting people like Karl Lagerfeld. And, of course, taking on that world opened me to critical attacks, as it was the easiest thing for female journalists to take me to task on, as they did later on *Dr T and the Women*.

The critical reception for the film was one of harshest in your career, with the usual line being that the film was too loose and chaotic. Certainly Richard E. Grant's diary suggested that, even by your standards, the larger part of the film was improvised.

62 Kim Basinger as Kitty Potter demonstrating her lack of skills as an interviewer with real-life designer Jean-Paul Gaultier in *Prêt-à-Porter* (1994)

Almost every scene in the film was improvised. We had no control over what the real people would say, but even with the actors, there was so much going on there was never any rehearsal. We'd just turn two or three cameras on and pretty much deal with what they did as if it were a documentary. But I like to go into everything that way; it's more fun for me, and the only interest for me in commercial success is to give me the wherewithal to continue making films. It's the doing of it that is the real joy, not the results or the prizes – that's a little pain-or-pleasure or sado-masochistic area that's about 2 per cent of the film. If I have a film out and the reviews start coming in and they're great, after about five of them I don't read them any more. I'll say, 'Is this a good one or a bad one?' If the reviews are bad, I'll read the first few, and then it's over. I get tired of that.

You've said that, for you, the real movie is when you're watching dailies or rushes.
Oh, it is, yes. Seeing everything, that's what's great. Because it's like that's what is in your mind, and then you encapsulate it to pass it on. It's like, 'Tell me what it was like to be on that ship when the storm came up?' Then I tell you, but I'm not telling you everything, because you can't. The story is the details you select, and no single one is more important than the other, although some are more tell-able than others. There does have to be a certain amount of selection. Fellini once said to me that a film is in its best state when you just put all the dailies together, and after that it diminishes as you edit them. I could watch hours and hours of what I shoot for my films, but a lot of people would like them to last as long as a trailer!

You're famous for inviting everyone involved in the film into watching rushes.
I've always done that. Not in television, because you didn't have any rushes. But on every film, I'm screening the stuff and pulling together a sympathetic audience, people I think will like it or want to like it.

Quite a few directors would prefer the actors not to look at rushes, as they feel all they will do is look at their performances and become excessively self-critical.
I've heard that, but I think quite the opposite. The reason I do it is that you find people start rooting for each other, and they realize they're part of a bigger thing instead of competing. There are some actors who won't look at rushes. They don't want to – Tim Roth wouldn't, Julie Christie, Richard Gere. Mostly – I hate to use the word 'bond' – but if suddenly they're seeing

this stuff, they're there in the soup together. And it discourages paranoia. It's very important to me because I can see what I'm doing, and I have an audience that is *simpático*. I remember there was a scene in *The Player*, and when we shot it we all thought it was great, but then when everybody saw it in the dailies, it was just dreadful. But instead of being embarrassed by the situation, it became a joke – it just showed us how fallible we could be.

There have been a couple of times when I've said, 'I'm not showing this scene' – for instance, in *A Wedding*. John Cromwell, who was about ninety, had a scene with Lillian Gish. He had a page of stuff to do, and he couldn't get through it. Lillian Gish was in bed, his wife was lying on the floor, and you'd see him look down, and she'd say, 'Say the line,' and he'd say, 'OK, old girl.' And I didn't show those dailies. I had the scene edited first, because I felt it would just be an embarrassment.

And there have been a couple of times, when I've filmed nudity or something like that, when I haven't shown the dailies. But in most cases I do. And that's why I like going out on location. You've got a captive audience, because these people don't have anything else to do. When I went to England to do *Gosford Park* I was very upset because my dailies almost became a legend, that I built elaborate projection rooms and provided lots of booze and food.

Didn't that reputation begin with a location report on McCabe & Mrs Miller, *which described you all as having a great party with booze and pot?*
Yes, we did on that. But I think it helps teach the actors what kind of picture it is, the level we're working on. Mainly it takes away the paranoia, the guessing. It's not that there's a right way or a wrong way. There were no dailies on *The Company*, though once a week I'd show them the dance sequences.

How do you feel about using the video assist when you're directing?
I love it. Alan Rudolph and I talked about it for years. I don't think I've looked through a camera in ten pictures, now. I don't record it, and for years I had a black-and-white monitor. But I can at least see what is in the frame and what's not, so I'm not surprised afterwards. Alan felt he should be always right behind the camera, but he's changing a little bit. It's a conceit – he says he wants to see it live because he believes he can see more, and there's probably truth in that.

Some actors feel they then perform to the director.
Yes, but they shouldn't be performing to anybody. Just think about the

theatre: no two people in the audience are seeing the same thing. In film, everybody sees exactly the same thing: what the camera sees.

How long have you been shooting with two cameras?
I used two cameras on *McCabe & Mrs Miller* and on almost everything since. It saves on how many times you have to do a scene, and if it doesn't inhibit your lighting, what difference does it make? The type of the film you're going for dictates those things. On *Gosford Park* I used two cameras constantly, and on some of the dailies you'd see the other camera coming into frame.

Was your technique of constantly moving the camera and using the zoom so freely a reaction against what you had been told to do when you began as a director?
For years on television, as we were taught, I would have to shoot a master shot, then over-the-shoulder shots and close-ups, and someone else would decide how they should be edited. But I didn't like that. We were using way too many close-ups, because with close-ups you can get away with almost anything. The same scene close-up might be intense in a way it could never be from further away. For example, the film with Al Pacino and Robin Williams, *Insomnia*[8] – I could have shot that in Topeka, Kansas. They didn't have to go to Alaska to shoot it. Everything was close-ups.

But in your case it's not just a matter of a shifting image that may stay wide; it's also cutting from moving shots to static shots, which I don't believe is in the rule book.
Well, the rule book is wrong. Nobody told me not to do things like that, but in the early 1970s I got a lot of heat about zoom lenses. I said, 'They show what I want to see.' There are all these different kinds of films. And it's like painting: there are rules, but most painters don't obey the same rules. All the rules have been broken, successfully and unsuccessfully.

Kansas City

Kansas City, which was originally titled Blondie, *was co-written by you and Frank Barhydt, who also grew up in Kansas City. In it you recreated the world of jazz and crime in Kansas City in 1934. You would have been nine years old then. How far was the film autobiographical?*
It represents an exaggerated kind of memory of the time. It has a lot to do

with my father – the character of Stilton is partly based on him – and stories he told me. I would go duck hunting with him, and he'd be with these notorious people like Frank Costello.[9] I heard these people talk for the first time and it was all to do with gambling and prostitution, illegal activities. The city was run by Boss Prendergast,[10] and everything was corrupt. During Prohibition, they didn't take the signs down or close the doors. The Mafia had their territory, and the blacks their neighbourhood too. So I have a glamorized, teenaged view of that world. I fantasized about it, and of course the music has always stayed with me.

In Kansas City in the 1930s they had the largest amount of whorehouses and prostitution anywhere. This was during the Depression, and they paid for the bands when no one else would, so jazz musicians went to Kansas City because they could get jobs there. For jazzmen it was like a crossroads where they could get twice the money they were offered elsewhere. Count Basie was a piano player who performed with different bands, and many of these bands were abandoned or broke up – in other words, it was all one-night stands. They would start in Kansas City and go south into Oklahoma and Arizona, then over to Los Angeles, then come across Colorado and back into Kansas City. I don't know how many high-school proms I went to that had really famous musicians playing, like Lester Young, because they weren't famous then. Many times they'd start out and go broke, or the manager would run away with the money and leave them stuck in a city. So Basie, when he started the Count Basie Band, was just stuck in Kansas City, play-ing piano gigs around town. I think it was when Benny Moten died that he took over that great band called The Blue Devils. Moten died 'prematurely', whatever that means, in 1935, when he had his tonsils taken out by a doctor friend of his, and the guy clipped an artery and Moten bled to death. The story was they were both drunk at the time. And people drove the doctor out of town.

Did you have any direct contact with this society of jazz performers?
When I was fourteen, fifteen years old, I used to go to those jazz places. They'd allow us in the balcony, though they wouldn't serve us drinks. Though we were white kids in a black venue, we were treated well. I felt very accepted by the black community. Some great music came out of that period, though I couldn't remember the names of anybody. Later, there was Julia Lee, Baby Lovett, Jay McShann – people like that who'd stayed in Kansas City through the war period. In fact, in the first film I made, *The Delinquents*, I had Julia Lee and a three-piece band, the Bill Nolan Quintet Minus Two, in the opening scene.

Has jazz always been your favourite music?
Oh yes. I mean, I have no education in any of this, but I've always liked jazz. The three Bs bored me![11] We had a black maid whose name was Glendora Majors, and she was very important to me, maybe more so than my mother. I remember there was a footstool in the house, and when I was eleven she sat me down when Duke Ellington was on the radio doing 'Solitude' and said, 'Now, Bobby, sit down and listen to this, because this is the best music there is.' And I sat there and listened and I got it, I guess. I put her into the film – Charlie Parker greets her at the back door of the club.

Music really informs the structure of this film.
I look at *Kansas City* like a musical piece, a fugue, with each character represented by an instrument. Harry Belafonte[12] was the trumpet, Dermot Mulroney the trombone, Jennifer Jason Leigh and Miranda Richardson were tenor saxophones doing a duet, and in a way their dialogue was like variations on a theme that didn't have too much to do with advancing the plot. And I put in this six-minute duel between Lester Young and Coleman Hawkins that served as an act break in the film and as a musical counter-point to the murder. But I think there was a dichotomy in the film: there was too much music for the people who wanted action-melodrama, and too much melodrama for the music fans.

The story itself was a fiction, though kidnapping was a common practice then, at least until the Lindbergh case, which brought in the death penalty. The Jennifer Jason Leigh character, Blondie, models herself on Jean Harlow. All her life is based on the movies, including handling a gun. And Carolyn, who's based on the mother of a kid I grew up with, takes laudanum as a form of escape, and so she's in a kind of haze about what's happening to her.

Why did you cast Harry Belafonte as Seldom Seen, the major gangster in your story?
I'd been working with him for some time on a project called *Cork* about the popular radio show *Amos'n'Andy*,[13] and he was cast from the beginning in *Kansas City*, writing a lot of his own lines. All the business about making fun of Marcus Garvey, the black politician who wanted everyone to return to Africa, came from Harry. Seldom Seen was a real character. He was always surrounded by his men, carried his money around in a cigar box and died at the age of ninety-eight. Harry's uncle Lenny was a gangster who ran numbers in Harlem, and he used him as a model as well.

63 Harry Belafonte as the menacing Seldom Seen at the Hey Hey Club in
Kansas City (1996)

The muted reception of the film suggested, as you say, that people had trouble with the mix of music and crime.
I shot the picture that way and probably overdid it, but I think that film is as good a film in all its elements as I've ever made. I think there will be a day when someone will discover it for what it really is. The musicians who saw it didn't care to think about the plot. It was just the music they were listening to, and they don't combine the two. And the jazz world has a little trouble taking it because all those great players were performing the kind of music from that period of the early 1930s, before bebop, yet they were playing their own music, not an imitation of it. I think that made sense, for the reason that the music was correct and everything else was like the memory of a fourteen-year-old kid. Being in Kansas City to shoot the film and living there for the first time since I was a kid, all of that fed into it.

You also made a music-performance film out of what you shot.
Hal Wilmer, who did the music for *Short Cuts*, brought together these jazz players, like David Murray, James and Ron Carter, Victor Lewis, and most of them had never performed together before. All the music was recorded live in the club, and there wasn't much time for rehearsal. The arrangements

were only fixed just before filming began. I put all the performance into a documentary, *Jazz '34*, and had Harry Belafonte do a narration.

How closely do your performers recreate the style of the 1930s musicians?
I think it was pretty accurate. Some of those events, like the 'cutting contest' between Josh Redman, who was playing Lester Young, and Craig Handy, playing Coleman Hawkins – that story was famous. Coleman Hawkins came through Kansas City in a new Buick convertible on his way to a gig in St Louis, which is probably a four- or maybe six-hour drive. He got into one of those jam sessions, and that very famous cutting contest between him and Lester Young was legendary. And he was late when he finally got going, so to get to his job in St Louis he ran that Buick on the floor and burned the engine out. Actually, Charlie Parker was there that night and played badly, provoking the drummer Jo Jones into throwing a cymbal at him. They showed that in Clint Eastwood's picture, *Bird*.[14]

It's always tempting to see a parallel between the freedom of jazz and your approach to film-making – taking a well-known theme, and through elaboration and improvisation, spinning off in different directions to make something completely fresh from the source material.

64 Altman and his jazzmen in the Hey Hey Club in *Kansas City* (1996)

That's probably true, but in jazz there is a breaking away from the conventional or the standard. And from where I come, there's no standard, is there?

Around the time of Prêt-à-Porter, *it was noticeable that you had lost weight, and it was reported you had cut out alcohol. But then the heart condition that had plagued you for a long time became worse on* Kansas City, *after which you underwent a full transplant, which clearly was a great success, though few people knew about it then or later.*

I was pretty sick when I was making the film; I was on a respirator at night. It was terrible. I shot the picture and rested. I finished all the work on the film on a Friday, and I was sitting around the house in Malibu wondering what the hell I was going to do next. I couldn't start another project. At midnight on Saturday I was bored to sobs, and then I got the call that they had a heart for me. I remember I got in the car and drove to the hospital, and the next morning they wheeled me in and gave me the new part. I'd gone in on 4 December and I was home by the sixteenth. On Christmas Eve I drove into Malibu village and walked around and did my Christmas shopping!

The Gingerbread Man

On the surface, a John Grisham[15] story about a lawyer being embroiled in an inheritance fraud might not seem the kind of material you would normally take on.

When I look for something that will interest me to make a film, I try to find some genre that I have never done before. I'd never done a thriller before. When The Gingerbread Man came along, it was a dreadful script, a screenplay that I believe John Grisham had done before he'd ever written a book. But he was hot then because of *The Firm*. He didn't want anything to do with what we made.

Kenneth Branagh[16] had been paid a lot of money to do it by Polygram. He had control of it and choice of director. He had turned down almost all of the directors they could get, but when my name came up, he'd said, 'Sure, Altman would be great.' When they offered it to me, I said, 'I can't do this.' And I called Ken up – I didn't know him then – and said, 'Do you really want to do this?' He said, 'Well, frankly, I could use the money. I'm building a house.' I said, 'I'll do it if I can rewrite it, but you have to be willing to become a flawed character in this, and then I'll do it with you.' And he said,

'Love it.' And that's how we got into it. He played a Clinton-like figure who couldn't keep his dick out of trouble.

I went to Cannes for the fiftieth anniversary, and Venice and Deauville, made several stops around Europe doing promotion for *Kansas City*. I found this writer Clive Hayes, and he went around with me working on the script. Then he used his brother's name as a credit for some reason. It's been suggested Al Hayes was a pseudonym for me, but that's not true, except that I did have an input on the script. In the Grisham script, it had the classic beginning with the girl coming into the lawyer's office and saying she's in trouble. We wanted to do something different and show him being sucked into the plot. The seduction scene, which I shot in one take, was one in which the lawyer didn't realize what he was getting into, involving himself with people from another milieu entirely. The Embeth Davidtz character never smiles, and we're never trying to ingratiate the audience in the usual thriller way.

I like the picture and had a lot of fun making it. There was nothing about Hurricane Geraldo in the original script. We had this idea of emphasizing the impending storm, with television sets everywhere that were only ever reporting the weather. It was actually plotted for us by a hurricane group in Savannah, so it was absolutely authentic.

65 Encountering Mallory Doss (Embeth Davidtz) in the rain, lawyer Rick Magruder (Kenneth Branagh) is lured into her trap in *The Gingerbread Man* (1998)

Why did you choose Changwei Gu[17] as your cinematographer?
Some agent called and said he was available, and I'd liked what he did on *Farewell My Concubine*. He was terrific, and working with him wasn't difficult, as we had a really good translator, whose mother had been born and raised in China because his grandparents were American communists who'd left the country. My son Bobby worked as the operator, as he has on several of my films. Changwei brought his own eye to what is not his normal territory, and I was anxious to get a look that was different, very dark, with little accents of red here and there – his car, his umbrella, his bathrobe.

The opening shots are wonderfully mysterious.
My son Stephen, who was the production designer, found this area and showed us it on video. I wanted to disorient the audience, and the music contributed to that. You could be orbiting the planet or looking in close-up at gingerbread cooking in an oven, but that might be my fancy because of the title. When the river appears, you recognize you're looking at the Earth.

Did you know Savannah?
I'd never been there. What I liked about it was the trees that would come up over, creating tunnels, and this moss hanging down everywhere. The book *Midnight in the Garden of Good and Evil* had been a big bestseller, though I didn't like it very much, and it was set in Savannah. I said I'd do the film as long as I could shoot there before Clint Eastwood made his film of that book. So we were ready and got in there before him. The original script wasn't set there, and we made Savannah another character in the picture. And every lawyer and judge in the film was played by a real judge and lawyer, including Vernon Jordan and Sonny Seiler, who was portrayed by Jack Thompson in *Midnight in the Garden of Good and Evil*.[18]

Mark Isham's music really adds to the atmosphere of the film.
I originally shot the film so that I thought I wouldn't have to use music, and I put in as much of the rain and wind sounds as possible, all the elements. Then I brought in Andrew Allen King to work on the film in the initial editing, and he put in synthesized musical sounds that mixed with the sound effects. But we felt even that result would have been a little tough on the audience, so Mark came in and we discussed where he could bring in his music to complement these sounds, folding the music into the effects. I think it was a whole new way of working for him, and he did a great job. He also did *Short Cuts* for me and most of Alan Rudolph's films.

Wasn't this a rare instance of your editing of the film being challenged?
The film didn't test well. Most of the comments were about the central character's morality. They kept saying to me, 'Make it shorter.' Then the film company took the picture away from me and had it re-edited, taking ten minutes out of it. They hired a guy who was the head of the Editors Guild, and I spoke to him, saying, 'I don't want you to do this, and I think you're making a big error in taking it on. Because if this starts, when a company can take a picture away and give it to someone like yourself and you can come in and cut it without my approval, then that's a mistake.' He never answered me. Geri was the editor, but her assistants stayed on. They made the cuts and mainly filled the picture up with close-ups. When that version was screened, they got worse scores than they did for my version. Then they cut it again, and the scores were even worse.

So I met with the head of the company and said, 'You're making a big mistake with this.' And because they figured Grisham wasn't supporting the picture, it hadn't tested well and it was going to go down the tubes anyway, they gave it back to me. They said, 'Do what you want, but we want this, this and this.' I'd already filed with the Directors' Guild to take my name off the picture, so I said, 'No, no, no, I'll finish the picture. I'll take into consideration what you've asked, but what I give you back is the film.' They had to agree to that, so I put it back to the way it was. The film opened to great reviews and good business in New York and Los Angeles, but there was no advertising to follow through. I heard Polygram wanted it buried, because they were embarrassed by all the stories going around about how they had to give it back to me.

Has this really been such an unusual occurrence in your career?
That's the only time it went that far. I've never had any of my films cut or edited by anybody. When *Popeye* went to Europe with Disney, some musical sequences were taken out because of the language, but in America with Paramount I had approval. And Dino had the rights to cut *Buffalo Bill and the Indians* in Europe but not in America, and that pissed him off – he felt the picture was too long. Then it won first prize, the Golden Bear, in my version at the Berlin Film Festival and was going to open in the truncated version in Germany, but Michel Ciment, who was on the jury, made sure that the award was only to 'Robert Altman's version', so it couldn't be used in advertising on a cut version.

You have to give up something in order to keep control, but I prefer to give whatever it is up first, because my main motivation in making the film is that I want to do it my way.

Cookie's Fortune

How did your association with the writer Anne Rapp begin?
I knew her and her husband Ned Dowd for about seven years, around the
racetrack, really, as he was kind of a junkie gambler. On *Fool for Love*, he
worked for me as an assistant director, and I remember she was around the
swimming pool . . . She had been a script supervisor, had worked for Sydney
Pollack on a lot of pictures. When she and Ned separated, she quit the
business and went to the University of Mississippi and took a course in
short-story writing with Barry Hannah, who was a writer I had worked with
years before. When I heard that, I called her and said, 'Listen, I've heard
you've written some short stories, so let me look at them.' 'Oh, Bob, they're
not ready. My God, they were just written for the class.' So eventually she
sent me three or four of her short stories – one of them was just one page
long – and I thought they were terrific. So I put her under contract just to
write for me, and we took the one short story called *All the President's
Women* – this was in the Clinton days – and I directed it for a television
series on which I was executive producer called *Gun*, in which there were six
films.

*Created by James Sadwith, Gun boasted some impressive names in the casts,
with James Foley and Ted Demme joining you as directors. How did you
become involved?*
That was when I was staying out in California for a while, recuperating from
the heart operation, and every three months I had to go in for check-ups. I
was approached about being executive producer on *Gun*, and I did it
because it gave me an office right there, as I still had Sandcastle running in
New York. I think they wanted me in because I would attract talent and it
was an anthology series.

Before that ended, we did a pilot for Fox TV called *Killer App* with Garry
Trudeau, which didn't sell, though it was good. It was about a space-age
computer company in Silicon Valley, a group of nerds, and the 'Killer
Application' was a big event. The things we talked about in that pilot have
happened – how you can stream directly, storing information on telephones.
The research on it was very good and accurate.

Did you find a great change in television after leaving it thirty years before?
Well, it was basically the same thing – when you talk to people there, they
are so fucking rude, so arrogant. But in terms of the form, I've always liked

the way you can carry things through, so situations and people become familiar to you. I've always fallen for it, but I've never had a success with it. I always get intrigued with shows in which there is not a single story, in that the story is not the important thing. If you had two stories taking place in the same arena, then each of them strengthens the other one, and if you have three it can get stronger, and so on. One evening Pat Birch, who is a choreographer, said to me she wanted to do a thing called *Saturday Night*, and it would be just the different things people do on a Saturday night. I said, 'Well, that's like *Short Cuts*. That's the tie: these people don't have any tie together yet they can cross.' And I woke up the next morning and thought, 'That's not a bad idea . . .'

So how did Cookie's Fortune *grow out of this diversion into television?*
Anne had had another idea for *Gun*, but when the whole series fell apart, I said, 'Let's just take that and make it into a feature.' So she wrote the script. We'd talk it over for a few hours, then she'd set to writing. There was some criticism that the film began very leisurely, so you didn't quite know where it was all heading, but that was deliberate. I didn't want it to be a suspense film. We took a long time to set up the characters and give the audience a feeling for them before Cookie kills herself. We played against the melodrama of the situation, using bright Easter colours throughout, to emphasize it was more of a character piece than anything else, just ordinary people living their lives.

The Easter production by the amateur theatrical company makes more explicit the darker side of this essentially good-natured community.
That was Anne's idea. The play being performed, Oscar Wilde's version of *Salome*, with changes made by Camille, was chosen to reflect aspects of the main story, with prejudice and intolerance always just beneath the surface. I found an acting group in a neighbouring town and asked them to put the play on, so what you see was actually directed by a local guy.

How did you assemble the cast for Cookie's Fortune?
The first people I sent it to were Anjelica Huston and Frances McDormand, but when it came time to do it, they both wimped out, in a funny way. Then I approached Glenn Close and Julianne Moore. But Charles Dutton and Patricia Neal were cast first. And once we knew the three-dimensional characters that were in the film, we did quite a bit of rewriting, with Anne on the set all the time, and used them to follow the story. Chris O'Donnell had great comic timing, like the young Jack Lemmon. I loved Liv Tyler for her

innocence and honesty, and she agreed to cut her hair for me! I saw Charles Dutton in the role of Willis from the beginning. He was always the guy. He's our tour guide, and he's what the story is all about really. The townspeople make it look like a murder because suicide was unheard of; it would ruin everybody's reputation. I think they would have let him be tried for it, even though nobody believes he could have been responsible. There's the line, 'How do you know? Because I fish with him.' And that was all Anne's stuff. Although Anne's from Texas, she has a real feel for this part of the South, with all its rituals and attitudes and that way of behaving as if you don't know what is going on but you really do. Her script reminds me of Flannery O'Connor and Eudora Welty,[19] those southern writers where the melodrama is less important than the behaviour of the people.

The location of Holly Springs, Mississippi, is like a major character in the film.
We shot the whole film there, and it was as if we were living on the set. Everyone there helped out on the film. The locale was a large part of the story. Cookie's antebellum house was pretty much as we found it. It had been empty for two years after being left to an eleven-year-old girl by her

66 Emma (Liv Tyler) comforts a wrongfully jailed Willis (Charles S. Dutton) in *Cookie's Fortune* (1999)

grandmother. I was fascinated by the exterior of a cotton warehouse. The red colour astonished me, so that became a major location. Changwei Gu wasn't available, but I brought in Toyomichi Kurita, who'd shot films for Alan Rudolph, and his work was great.

The whole film feels very relaxed, as if you made it with no sense of strain.
You never know . . . if I show up on a Wednesday to shoot a certain scene, and then we don't do it, and I return on Thursday, the scene will be entirely different. It's all about the moment. But I remember on this film we shot a scene and I staged it in a certain way, and it was OK, I liked it. We went on, and then we went back to that same location to do another scene, with almost the same cast, and the light was a certain way, and we shot that. But when I looked at the dailies of those scenes, I thought, 'My God, I must be losing it,' because these scenes, I did them both alike, they were staged in almost the same way. So I was not only copying from myself, I was copying three days later from myself! Now that scared me a little bit. When the film was finished, people said, 'That was just great, those scenes were so similar that we all got what you were trying to do!' I thought, 'Hmm, yeah . . .'

Cookie's Fortune *was premièred at the Sundance Film Festival and was the opening-night film. Was that like a vindication that you were a truly independent film-maker?*
Yes, I've always been independent – even those films I did for Laddie at Fox, I had closed-in deals, so I had control of the film. Really the only film I made where I was on the lot hired by the studio was *M*A*S*H*. I think the rise of independent cinema has helped everybody. I was reading today how the majority of Academy Award-nominated films were made in New York, but that's just the writing on the wall. Because Hollywood makes films for mass consumption, they have to. It's a big factory that has to turn out little Ford Pintos, and now it's the independents who are making the Jaguars and the Mercedes. I've always worked on the edges and the fringe, and I don't think it will be any other way.

Weren't you going to make a kind of sequel to Short Cuts *after* Cookie's Fortune?
Everyone was trying to make me do another *Short Cuts*, so I came up with this idea called *More Short Cuts*. It was taking some of the same characters in the original film, but in some cases the families had split. The two stories I had cut from *Short Cuts* I put back in, and we took another couple of Carver stories, as I owned the rights, and Anne worked on that script for about a

year, I guess. Then I remember she came to my house in California, and I said, 'Anne, let's just dump this. It's not going to work. I don't want to do it, it taints the original and I have no real passion for it.' But I asked her about a one- or two-page story she'd done about a gynaecologist in Dallas and suggested doing that. And that became *Dr T and the Women*. After that I stopped her contract, because I can't really make any more films set in the South!

Dr T and the Women

It's not your usual way to work with major Hollywood stars who bring a lot of their own persona to a film, so how did Richard Gere become involved?
When the script was finished, I sent it to Gere, whom I'd known for a while, though we'd never worked together, and with whom I'd discussed several projects. Now, you could have had an unknown actor play the doctor, but then I would have had to deal more with the reality of the character's behaviour. I felt I needed a movie star to make the character work for my idea, so that the audience would have a preconception of him. To be able to open up the movie showing the lady with her feet in the stirrups and a gynaecologist down there with his speculum, he looks up, and it turns out to be Richard Gere – I thought, 'That's what I want.' And Gere got it and said, 'I'll do this.' There were no big money discussions. He and I became partners, we made the film and we had control. Once I had Gere, I had no particular problems.

So for a change there were no agents working busily behind the scenes?
Agents will come in and tell actors, 'If you want to be a star and get the parts you want, you're going to have to listen to us,' and they make it almost impossible. Many times actors have been advised by their agents to misbehave and be difficult and make demands. It seems more recently that there is an ugliness in the business, people are mean rather than courteous and polite. It's as if what you're supposed to do is abuse people. And I couldn't last a day under those circumstances. This work is hard enough to start with, and if there isn't harmony and everybody isn't having a good time, I can't function. I guess others can, as many good films come out of adversity. But somehow, there now seems to be a feeling that if you're having a good time, you're not serving your art. I don't believe that for a second.

67 Richard Gere as gynaecologist Doctor Sullivan Travis at work between the
legs of a patient in *Dr T and the Women* (2000)

What attracted you to this subject?
I thought about this whole situation of gynaecology, where most women are
involved and the men don't know anything and don't choose to. Their attitude is, 'Oh, my wife's gone to the pussy doctor.' Then they ask her, 'Well,
who is this guy anyway?' 'Oh, he's this short Jewish man . . .' And then he
meets this guy at a cocktail party and he's about six foot three and black and
extremely handsome! So it's something not discussed between men and
women, and I felt that everybody has fantasies and questions about gynaecologists that are never answered. I thought there would be a curiosity to it,
and there is. The whole idea of all these guys who went to med school and
made the choice to be gynaecologists rather than brain surgeons – most of
them were kind of geeks, and it was really about pussy, about women.

Anne Rapp told me you even suggested simply calling the film Pussy.
Yes. I mean, I just took this guy who is totally immersed in a society of
women – that was what it was about. I thought Helen Hunt was great in it.
Her character Bree was probably bisexual. She wasn't married to anybody
and she felt his wife was there for good, so she didn't feel she was stealing
anybody's husband. She wasn't doing anything wrong that I could see. And
he made the assumption that because she went to bed with him, she loved
him. That shows the tight, socially opinionated, egocentric man he is – he

believes he loves women but he's been looking at them at the wrong end all his life!

At one point we were going to end the film with the marriage proposal, that he would take her out of her world and her golf, and she was saying, 'Why would I want that?' That was his problem at the beginning, that he had to take care of all these women, and here's one that didn't need taking care of. And that's when I thought of the ending. I said, 'That's it, we'll do the birth of a baby.' Women never see that, unless they're a nurse.

The storm was prepared for throughout, and it was supposed to be symbolic in a way, as he's been in a tornado of women all his life. He's been wrong about his life, and now he delivers a boy, it's something he can deal with. And I think the birth scene gave the movie its guts.

In spite of it being written by a woman, the film received quite a bit of criticism for its portrayal of the Dallas ladies with their perfect hair and obsession with clothes and accessories.
I'm crazy about the film, but a lot of women journalists, because of political correctness, couldn't praise it. They'd say, 'Wait a minute, is this a misogynistic film? Are you making fun of women?' I say, 'Go to Dallas or pick up *Vogue* and just thumb through it and tell me I'm satirizing women when they go shopping in Dallas, for this is the truth.' You'll see them there dressed to the nines. Rich women don't have anything else to *do* down there. And the women in the picture playing those women *were* those women. I had big sessions with them – twenty a day would come in – and they told me that's all they did, they tried to get their names in the paper, so they get invited to more parties. It's kind of a contest, and everybody does behave like that.

As far as the way we showed lesbianism in the film goes, I don't think there was anything stereotypical about that. Men and women see a different film in *Dr T*, and I think women got the film the most.

Notes

1 Altman and his son Stephen had spent over six months scouting locations in Italy for *Rossini, Rossini*, a biopic of the Italian composer of comic operas, most famously *The Barber of Seville*. The movie, with a script by prolific British television writer Andrew Davies, was to have been cast with Vittorio Gassman as old Rossini and Richard E. Grant as the young Rossini. After it was shut down and Altman fired, the project was revived shortly afterwards and made

by veteran Italian director Mario Monicelli, with Philippe Noiret as Rossini and Gassman playing Beethoven.

2 Raymond Carver (1938–88) wrote poetry and fiction and was first published in 1968, beginning respectively with *Near Klamath* (1968) and *Put Yourself in My Shoes* (1974). He struggled with alcoholism and an embattled first marriage, but for his last ten years lived in happier circumstances in Port Angeles, Washington, with the poet Tess Gallagher. In the 1980s he won a number of awards and was regularly published, with an anthology of his short stories appearing in the UK in 1985. He died from cancer at the age of fifty.

3 *La Ronde* (1950) was a star-studded adaptation directed by Max Ophüls of Arthur Schnitzler's play, set in nineteenth-century Vienna, comprising ten episodes in which one sexual partner links with the next to complete a circle.

4 *Tales of Manhattan* (1942), directed by Julien Duvivier, follows a dress tailcoat through five episodes featuring different characters, with a collection of Hollywood stars including Charles Boyer, Rita Hayworth, Henry Fonda, Ginger Rogers, Charles Laughton, Edward G. Robinson, Paul Robeson and George Sanders.

5 *Angels in America*, Tony Kushner's epic play about the effect of AIDS on the life of American homosexuals in the mid–1980s, won a Tony and the Pulitzer Prize in 1993 when first presented on stage. For the 2003 television version produced by HBO, directed by Mike Nichols and with a remarkable cast including Al Pacino and Meryl Streep, Kushner himself wrote the screenplay, cutting about ninety minutes from the original play and rewriting scenes to bring it down to six and a half hours.

6 Harvey Weinstein, together with his brother Bob, founded the independent distribution and subsequently production company Miramax in 1979. After scoring great successes with foreign-language films, supporting them with aggressive marketing campaigns, they did especially well with *sex, lies and videotape* (1989) and *The Crying Game* (1992), and branched into extensive production, with Harvey managing the art-house films and Bob forming Dimension films for more commercial fare, such as the *Scream* series. More recently, after becoming an autonomous subsidiary of Disney, their ambitions have grown with such costly epics as *Gangs of New York* (2002) and *Cold Mountain* (2004).

7 *Yesterday, Today and Tomorrow* (1963), directed by Vittorio de Sica, comprised three different stories within one film. The first and best segment was about a wife – Sophia Loren – who avoids imprisonment for black-marketeering by making sure that her husband – Marcello Mastroianni – keeps her constantly pregnant. By this stage in his career De Sica was a long way from the neo-realist films he made in the late 1940s and early 1950s, the most famous of which, *Bicycle Thieves* (1948), has often been cited by Altman as a great influence upon him.

8 *Insomnia* (2002) was an American remake of a Norwegian thriller of the same

title, in which two city cops arrive in Alaska, where there is continuous day-light, and attempt to solve a local murder. Starring Al Pacino, Robin Williams and Hilary Swank, it was the American début of young British director Christopher Nolan, previously responsible for *Following* (1998) and *Memento* (2000).

9 Frank Costello (1891–1973) was a famous Mafia boss who began his criminal career as part of Lucky Luciano's crew in New York and then expanded his own interests when Luciano was incarcerated in 1936. But he faced a danger-ous rival, Vito Genovese, and was caught out several times by the law, spending long stretches in prison in the 1950s. After a failed assassination attempt, Costello retired and died a peaceful death.

10 Boss Tom Prendergast, a Democrat politician, was famously corrupt and ran Kansas City as if Prohibition didn't apply to the city, keeping control of the racketeering by making sure that Town Hall, in effect, *was* the mob.

11 The three Bs refers to Bach, Beethoven and Brahms, considered to be the giants of the classical music tradition.

12 Harry Belafonte (b. 1927) grew up in poverty in Jamaica but became an actor in New York and in 1952 began singing ballads and popularizing the calypso beat. This career continued in parallel to occasional film roles, such as in *Carmen Jones* (1954), *Island in the Sun* (1957), *Odds Against Tomorrow* (1959) and *Uptown Saturday Night* (1974).

13 *Amos'n'Andy* was a hugely popular radio show which ran from 1928, featur-ing two white actors, Freeman Gosden and Charles Correll, who portrayed black characters using 'Negro dialect'. In 1951 the two men created a television show with the same characters but played by an all-black cast. However, after making seventy-eight episodes over two years, the show was cancelled follow-ing protests from people and organizations who now found the stereotypical characters unacceptable. Nevertheless, the show remained popular and was syndicated right up until 1966.

14 *Bird* (1988) was Clint Eastwood's deeply felt biopic of the great jazz saxo-phonist Charlie Parker (played by Forest Whitaker), who revolutionized jazz in the 1940s but was ultimately destroyed by his drug addiction. For the sound-track, Parker's own recordings were used, enhanced by a contemporary backing.

15 John Grisham (b. 1955) turned from being a successful lawyer to being a successful novelist with such books as *A Time to Kill*, *The Firm*, *The Pelican Brief*, *The Client* and *The Rainmaker*, all of which have been filmed by Holly-wood.

16 Kenneth Branagh (b. 1960) was born in Northern Ireland but began his acting career in London, making an impact on stage in *Another Country* and working in the Royal Shakespeare Company before he formed his own, the Renaissance Theatre Company. He made a great impact by following Olivier in directing himself in the lead role in a film of *Henry V* (1989), a tradition which

he continued with three other Shakespeare adaptations, *Much Ado About Nothing* (1993), *Hamlet* (1996) and *Love's Labour's Lost* (2000).

17 Chinese-born Changwei Gu was acclaimed for his cinematography for *Ju Dou* (1990) and *Farewell My Concubine* (1998), and after working with Altman in the US he shot *Autumn in New York* (2000). In 2005 his directorial début, *Peacock*, was unveiled at the Berlin Film Festival.

18 *Midnight in the Garden of Good and Evil* (1997) was Clint Eastwood's film adaptation of John Berendt's best-selling non-fiction book about a New York journalist arriving in Savannah and becoming caught up in a bizarre murder trial.

19 Flannery O'Connor and Eudora Welty, along with Carson McCullers, have been characterized as the trio of women writers who excelled in the style dubbed 'Southern Gothic'. O'Connor (1925–64) was born in Savannah and made an impact with her novel *Wise Blood* in 1952, which was subsequently filmed by John Huston. Welty (1909–2001) was born in Jackson, Mississippi, and published her first short story, *The Death of a Travelling Salesman*, in 1936, and it was this form for which she was most celebrated.

8

Gosford Park – The Company – Tanner on Tanner

Gosford Park

DAVID THOMPSON: *What brought you to England to do a period film?*
ROBERT ALTMAN: Bob Balaban[1] has been a friend of mine for years – he's sort of a Renaissance man, an actor, producer and director. And he said, 'Can't we do something together?' I said to him, 'I tell you what, I've never done a murder mystery, you know? A whodunnit set in a big house, *Ten Little Indians*, an Agatha Christie kind of murder mystery. I'd like to jump into that genre if we could find something.' So Bob read everything by Agatha Christie that hadn't been done and said, 'They're all exactly the same, there's nothing there.' So he started reading more obscure material from that period, but that all turned out to be similar stuff. So I said, 'Well, what we want isn't here. We want a house where everyone's invited, the whole thing.' And we went to Eileen Atkins and Jean Marsh, who had done *Upstairs, Downstairs*, neither of whom I knew, to see if they could come up with an outline. What they did was fine and excellent, but the exact opposite of what I wanted to do – it was rather sentimental. But they were very generous about it.

Then Bob came up with Julian Fellowes, who had been working with him on another project for Anthony Hopkins. And I literally hired Julian on the phone. I'd never met him nor read anything by him. He did a rather complete outline, and I got excited by it, so he came to California and we made some changes, changed some elements, and it kind of grew. I approached Eileen to play a role, thinking, 'Gee, she won't want to do this,' but she was thrilled. In fact, everybody who became involved in the project was very generous, and we encountered very little of the neuroses and paranoia you usually run into.

I knew we were going to have a lot of people in the cast, but by casting someone like Maggie Smith I knew we weren't going to have a problem with knowing who she was each time you saw her. It was very important to help the audience separate and keep track of who's who. Also, everyone liked the script, and actors were very keen to be part of it.

There was a lot of comment about how you required the actors to be available to you throughout the shoot.
Part of the deal. So many American actors will say, 'I'd love to be in your film, six days, hell, I'll be there.' And I'd say, 'No, this is ten weeks . . .' Then their agents come in, and they don't want them to do it. In *Gosford Park*, Alan Bates worked five days a week for the first six and half weeks of shooting, and I don't think he had five words to say – he was bubbling in the background there. But he was there all the time. I found that the philosophy of the English actors – and I think it's related to the theatre – was that they all were there and knew what they were doing. And I never saw an agent the whole time I was shooting. If I had had any American actors who would let their agents near us, they would have been out measuring trailers and saying, 'He has seventeen more steps to walk to the set than she does. I want my client's trailer moved closer.' And then everything falls apart.

Was tackling a period drama in a country foreign to you a worry?
I'm sort of an Anglophile. I think most Americans are. We share a language and a literature, so it's in our genes, I guess. I don't know who the American antecedents of this type of murder mystery are – perhaps Hawthorne. But we didn't say, 'Well, if we do it in England it'll be this kind of picture.' We just followed the arrow where it took us. Now, given the English setting, my problem was how do I get it right? So Julian, who is 'to the manor born', became our technical advisor as well and was on the set for just about every scene we shot. We also had a housemaid, a butler and a cook, all in their mid to late eighties, who had been in service in this period. They were available to the actors all the time. I said, 'I don't want to have any situations where the drama is more important than the truth.' I wanted the behaviour and manners to be right, as I knew I would be under scrutiny. I didn't want people saying, 'Oh, that's an American coming over and telling us how to clean our scullery.'

Why did you bring American characters into the piece – the movie producer and his young companion?
I needed a voice that in a way would be *my* voice, that could respond to the customs and behaviour that I would find surprising, so I needed a surrogate in the film. I think having this producer of Charlie Chan films took away the Merchant-Ivory/Jane Austen kind of approach to these things. It allowed me in the room. But I don't say that to be derogatory to Merchant-Ivory[2] – in fact, had they not done their films, *Gosford Park* wouldn't have been made,

as there wouldn't have been a reference. The first people I called were Ismail and Ruth to ask their advice, and they gave us a lot of help.

Did you ever feel in danger of creating what is often referred to in Britain as 'heritage cinema', Merchant-Ivory being the most famous example?
I didn't want to confuse the two. I didn't want to copy anything. I wanted to take the elements that the audience would be familiar with and present them properly, because most of the period films done about the 1920s and 1930s are not very accurate. We went through a few artisans in hiring our crew, who said they knew about these things, but we'd look at them and say, 'Well, they're simply wrong. I mean, they didn't use that fork, and they didn't put tablecloths on the table, and they didn't have breakfast served to them, and so on.'

I mean, we're in a cycle with movies in our lives, I don't think there is a policeman alive today who didn't learn his behaviour from looking at films. Nor a gangster . . . And when the World Trade Center was attacked, everybody said, 'What's going on? Are they making a movie?' So I was determined not to copy other movies that were wrong. And we had really good technical advice and looked into it very carefully.

There's no question that your camera style in Gosford Park *is very distinctive.*
I wanted to take the preciousness out of the period drama. The minute you go back in time, you have people talking more precisely, more slowly. That's how we think they behaved in those drawing rooms, and it simply isn't true. The only way I know it isn't true is that I lived at that time, and I saw my mother and my father and my aunt and my uncles and how they behaved, and everything wasn't that formal and precise. The way to take the formality out of it was in the camera shots. Normally the camera is very precise – I mean, *Brideshead Revisited*[3] and all of those things. There's a shot and everything is perfect; you cut in while the person says their line. I said, 'I don't want to do that.' And I decided to do what I had done in *The Long Goodbye*, that is, 'We're going to move the camera constantly, but arbitrarily, not in any rhythm that you would think belongs to the action.' If the snapper line was 'Did you love him?' followed by 'I hated him,' then instead of going for a close-up on the person who says that, they'd be on their way out of the door. It might even be off-screen. So you make the audience find the drama in the situation, rather than serve it up to them.

Do your editors find this difficult to deal with?
As Geri was doing something else at the time, my editor on this film was Tim

Squyres, who does all of Ang Lee's films. He was working on the material for four weeks in America while I was shooting in England and didn't know what to make of it at first, because this isn't the way it's supposed to be . . . But in the end he got it just fine. If somebody asked me why I did it this way, I'd say, 'The truth of the matter is I'm trying to make it sloppy and ragged. I'm trying to make it more difficult.' In my mind we serve the audience up most stuff. We put it in front of them, and we don't make them do any work. They fall asleep or they're just not that interested. But if I can make them move their body – and I sit in on screenings and look at the backs of people's heads – if I can see those heads bobbing, then I know I've got those people into the film.

How does it affect the lighting of your scenes?
Using more than one camera saves time. The cutting is easier, because the actors are always in the right place, and unless you are lighting for one shot to create a Vermeer, you simply light the arena and throw the actors into it. I'm not trying to make the kind of film where the close-up is lit quite differently from the two-shot to make the girl look radiant, and you can't move out of that light. Though they make it so it matches, it really changes totally.

Why did you choose Andrew Dunn as your cinematographer?
The reason I chose him was seeing *The Madness of King George* on video, and I couldn't figure out what it was that made it so compelling, except that there seemed to be a hot spot in every frame. There always was one place where there was kind of a blow-out, which gave depth to it. If you see white light in a frame of film, you can't see the details of what it's covering, and that means there's a mystery to it, there's more in there than your eye is getting.

From what I witnessed on set, your way of using cameras had a strong influence on the way the actors performed.
With the two cameras on tracks running around and moving, and the actors out there going through their stuff, they don't know whether they're on camera or not, they don't know if it's a close-up . . . So suddenly they're relieved of the responsibility of saying, 'Oh, this is my close-up. I'd better be good here.' They figure out, 'I'd better be good all the time because I don't know whether they're getting me or not.' I think that relieves them, in a way, but it also throws them back more into the theatre. Many of them were theatre actors, of course. In a case like this, all of these people became peers,

so there weren't three leads and six supporting actors and then the extras. Everybody was a peer and the behaviour was quite different. Also, when there's that many of them, they tend to police themselves, because nobody wants to be the bad boy, no one's going to throw a tantrum or become difficult or not come out of their dressing room.

In this film, the downstairs people were not allowed to have any make-up, except if they were putting it on to go out. I said, 'They didn't wear it.' And they might say, 'Well, don't you have to balance the lighting?' I'd say, 'No, don't worry about that.' Suddenly they're in the arena and their own behaviour becomes consistent with the behaviour of their character.

Gosford Park had a screenplay by Julian Fellowes, a man well steeped in the peculiar ways of the British aristocracy – his wife is Lady-in-Waiting to Princess Michael of Kent – which took into account the particular manners of the different classes in Britain and a period manner. Did you still allow the actors to improvise to some degree?
Well, if you have a dinner scene, with twelve or fourteen people at the table and five servants attending to them, there would be a linear progression in that. The scene might open with Maggie Smith saying, 'Anybody want to play bridge after dinner?' And it ends when somebody drops their teacup in the soup. So we'd start there, with everybody knowing who their character is, and we know when we get to the teacup we're going to stop. In the meantime, I just let them talk, and they're very good at it. And, of course, we had microphones on everybody. When we look at the dailies, we've got maybe three or four mikes mixed, because that's all the mixer can do at the time. But when we cut the film, we find things coming up in the dialogue that I never heard. So we fold these things in, and it makes the soufflé a lot tastier.

I noticed when you were shooting that you rarely referred to the script.
I wouldn't look at the script unless I had to check something. I had a person to do that for me. And I don't learn the script. I can't tell you the number of times we would do a scene, and I'd say, 'That's great, OK, let's move on.' And the script girl would say, 'But she didn't say anything about stealing the toilet water.' And I'd say, 'Well, that's the point of the scene, we're gonna do one more and get the toilet water bit back in.' It's because I'm not looking for that. I'm not trying to underscore the plot. I'm really interested in the behaviour of the people.

The one character who actually existed was Ivor Novello.[4] Why did you introduce him into the party?

68 Ivor Novello (Jeremy Northam) entertains visiting Hollywood producer
Morris Weissman (Bob Balaban) and the British aristocracy over
the weekend at *Gosford Park* (2001)

He is the only real person that we referred to and used in the film. I was sitting at my desk, and the room I look into is a library, where I keep all my thirty-five years' worth of research stuff. I was thinking about how to get indigenous music into the film, without having Georgie Stoll conducting an orchestra.[5] And I remembered research I had done over thirty years ago for the World War I project *The Chicken and the Hawk*, and on the shelves was all this stuff about Ivor Novello. So I pulled it out and started going through it, and it was exactly the same period. So we added Ivor as a character, and by having to be fairly accurate with the way we treated him, that gave credence to the fictional characters.

What's revealing is that not all the characters react to him in the same way.
Well, the posh people aren't into his form of entertainment. But all of the downstairs people were his real audience, and he probably had more work out there and was more popular than Noël Coward. So his character gave us what I call a real good clothes line to hang stuff on. He was not posh – his mother was a schoolteacher – but he was accepted into this group because he was an entertainer and a movie star. It was a bit like having Bobby Darin to dinner.

Like your other multi-cast films, did you plan to have a tour guide?
Our philosophy was that we would tell the story through below-stairs gossip. Kelly Macdonald becomes our tour guide. She's a maid to Maggie Smith and a novice. She's new to everything, so we're able to see things as she's told what is what, and any time I had to have something explained, I would have her there to have it explained to. She's the thread that takes us from the first to the last shot.

Do you see Gosford Park *as a portrait of a society in decline?*
The film was set during the hunting season in November 1932, the last shooting season before the fall of the Reichstag, which was also the end of that upstairs-downstairs world of indentured servitude. Society was opening up for women in particular; the social structure was changing. A lot of it had to do with increased communication and transportation. Previously, if a fourteen-year-old girl was born in small village, sleeping with four sisters in one bed, she couldn't really get an education or find a job anywhere, and if she wasn't going to get married she would have to go into service to be taken care of and live in safety. Otherwise she went to London and became a prostitute. There weren't any other options until after World War I, and then by the end of World War II this form of servitude had gone, though there are

echoes of it everywhere. We saw hundreds of stately homes, in each of which forty servants had worked indoors to handle a household of four people.

Before you began filming, one precedent for Gosford Park *used in the pre-publicity was Jean Renoir's 1939 classic* The Rules of the Game *(*La Règle du jeu*), which, of course, also dealt with class conflict over a weekend at a country house when a shooting party gathers together.*

Although we went in saying 'It's *Ten Little Indians*' I became more interested in it being like *The Rules of the Game*. It was like having the Iraqis and the Americans living in the same house. It was these two totally different societies, who had totally different opinions of each other. To me, that became the drama, what the film was about. The upstairs people who live by these particular rules, they're not very deep, they don't go past the surface much. There's much less of an infrastructure than below stairs. You could say the downstairs people are more stupid, because their hierarchy is more complex. But their lives are fuller.

I was constantly trying to underscore the plot, because I was more interested in the behaviour of the characters. I talked freely at the time of the film's release about the fact there's a murder taking place, because I didn't

69 Altman examines the hierarchies of the kitchen downstairs in *Gosford Park* (2001)

want people to spend the first hour of the picture wondering what's going to happen. If I take an audience of two hundred people, twenty of them would get it right off the bat. They would say, 'Oh, here's this guy, this is happening here, this is happening there . . .' I didn't go to great pains to disguise or hide anything.

I believe a significant change in the script was made when shooting was under way.
After six and a half weeks of shooting, I saw Helen Mirren and Eileen Atkins in the lunch hall together in costume for the first time. And I said, 'My God, these women look like sisters.' I had made a terrible mistake, because I had been very careful in the casting not to have any two people who looked alike. I think one of the big problems in films today is they cast them according to 'Oh, this guy is really hot now, and this guy is hot, let's put them in the same film.' And you dress them alike, they look alike, and you can't tell them apart. So I was very careful to separate everybody in the casting. It was a long process. And when I saw Eileen Atkins and Helen Mirren in mufti, they weren't at all alike. But with their wardrobe and wigs on, I thought I was in trouble.

Julian was at another table. I said right then, 'Let's make them sisters who hate each other.' And this whole thing was done over pudding! Without that change, I think we would have had an intellectual film of which people would have said, 'Hey, that's really nice.' But I don't think emotionally we would have had a catharsis. So having this scene at the end of the picture, which was not in the original script, allowed the audience to go 'Ooh!' because they were told something they didn't know before and they see the emotional response to that information.

Had I been obliged to go to a studio or to a producer and say, 'I'm going to change this after shooting six and a half weeks,' it would never have happened. So now if it was a mistake, it's my mistake, but I know it wasn't because it was indigenous to the material. It happened because it was right, and I had the power to allow it to happen.

The Company

Did the warm response to Gosford Park, *which was both a critical and a commercial success, help in the choices that followed?*
It takes a lot of money to make pictures, so I would say that most of the films that I have done have been what I *could* do. I don't know what I would have

done if they'd just said, 'Well, do what you want to do.' I probably would have made a lot of worse films than I have done. Basically, if someone says you can do a film as long as it's about an Irish woman, I'd say, 'Oh, I can do that!' You're trying to fill the time. If I have a year and I can't work during that whole year, I consider that year wasted if I'm not producing anything. For example, I went to Austria at the end of January 2003 for two days to shoot a commercial. Now I do it for the money, but no matter what, I learn something from it, or at least I can be sure I'd never do it again. I don't think we really have choices in what we do. If somebody offers me a job and I don't have anything else to do, I try usually to work that job out. There was a time when my whole thrust was to make a picture. And if somebody said, 'Well, it's got to be a Dracula picture,' I would say, 'OK, I can do that.' I don't sit around and think, 'Ah, this is what the muse tells me, so this is what I'm going to do now.' *Gosford Park* was the most unlikely project to come to fruition, other than maybe *The Company*. If you'd told me about either one of them before the fact, I would have gone, 'Really?' Even with *Gosford Park*, going into it, I never really thought it was going to happen. I just didn't see it occurring, neither for me nor as a film.

How did The Company *begin? Ballet had not featured on your radar before.*
After the *Scream* movies, Neve Campbell[6] became a hot property. She'd been a dancer at the National Ballet School of Canada when she was a kid. And having been a dancer, she went to Warner Bros, who wanted to keep her, and said, 'I want to do a dance movie.' So they developed two or three scenarios for her. And they were all the same – they were all about the poor little girl who struggles to become a ballerina and finally makes it. But she just wanted to make a film in which she was one of the dancers. So she went to Barbara Turner, who wrote *Georgia* and *Pollock*, and together they somehow picked the Joffrey Company in Chicago and spent three years with them. Barbara travelled around with them, took notes, made recordings and ended up with all this stuff that is the real thing.

They did a script and got it to Killer Films, a small production outfit, and they sent it to me, as Barbara knows me and I know her. I said, 'Barbara, I'll read it but I'm never going to do this, as I know nothing about dance and there's no point in me thinking about it.' So I read it and I couldn't see it at all. I just kept saying, 'I really can't do this.' But I was trying to accommodate her as much as possible. I was going to do a script about a bear with Paul Newman for Miramax, but then Harvey Weinstein came into the act. I'd hired Naomi Watts, and he said that would take $3 million away from the budget because she didn't mean anything. And I said, 'Well, you call her up and tell her because I've hired her!' Anyway, in the process of all this I quit, and decided instead to do the dance picture. I thought, 'Why not jump into the abyss? I didn't know anything about country music, but I made *Nashville.*'

It's really Neve's film, and she's the producer of it. I said to her, 'I'll do this but I really have just to go in and do it. And you'll just be one of the dancers, and I don't want to hear from you any more than anyone else in the company.' And so I did it.

Did mixing up performance and backstage life in The Company *have any connection with what you did on* Black and Blue?
Yes, I did a little bit of that there, and it certainly entered my mind, because that was my first real exposure to dance and the backstage stuff was the most compelling part of it. But on *The Company* there was all this discussion about hiring actors to play these people, and I said, 'Well, you can't teach actors to dance, and I can't teach dancers to act.' Then it occurred to me that these dancers spend their entire lives in front of a mirror looking at themselves, so they're not audience-shy. So it seemed to me I could work with them. And I found out that they're incredibly disciplined, because they're used to that. During the procedure that I set up before shooting, I would say, 'All right, everybody ready, stand by, and now action!' Now I don't usually do that in that manner, but I did here, because I told them that the minute you hear the word 'action', you are on stage in front of an audience until somebody says 'cut'. So, of course, they were there on time, they were prompt, they worked as a single unit. I was really moved and inspired by them.

We had forty-four dancers, and I spent a couple of months with them before shooting and spoke with each of them privately. If I would tell one dancer, 'When you come in, don't go any further than a foot back from where that mark is,' they would do that for the rest of their lives unless I changed it. I could not have done this with forty-four actors – by the time they would have the discipline to make the straight lines, a week would have gone by! As we got into this thing and started shooting it, I would start really testing them, saying, 'You say this and you say that, talk about how you hurt your ankle, or your boyfriend, or whatever you would say . . .' And I would put mikes on different people. We did a lot of dances at the beginning, so everybody got used to me, they got used to the system, and I got used to them. We kind of learned how to communicate, to the point where I hardly used any actors at all – just for parts like Malcolm McDowell's and a couple of Chicago actors doing non-dancing things. But all the dancers and dance masters, they're all themselves.

So once again you were mixing the faux *and the real, but blurring the distinction even further.*

That was the intention, and I think it's really going to influence what I do from now on. I really liked doing this, working with the dancers, crossing that reality line and being able to use them in that way – though it's dicey.

As you say, aside from Neve Campbell as the dancer Ry – who trained for six months and learned eight dances specially for the film – the only principal actors were Malcolm McDowell[7] as Alberto Antonelli, the director of the company, and James Franco as Ry's boyfriend. What led you to make those casting choices?

Well, I've known Malcolm for thirty years or more. He was the only person I ever thought of. I called him right away, and he said yes. Then when I wasn't going to do the picture, I called him again and said, 'Malcolm, I'm sorry, this isn't going to happen,' and he was very disappointed. And then I threw the Miramax film out for this and called him again. I don't think anybody else was discussed for this character. I think his performance came primarily from Gerald Arpino, who is the founder and director of the Joffrey Ballet of Chicago. It's not an imitation of him; he paraphrased him. We didn't write a

70 Dancer Ry (Neve Campbell) receives instruction from Alberto Antonelli (Malcolm McDowell), the director of *The Company* (2003)

lot for Malcolm. He hung out for two weeks with Gerry, who's probably more of a caricature than Malcolm. He's very out there. And Malcolm just got it.

I thought of James Franco. I don't know why, except I saw that James Dean film he did, and of course he knew me because of that documentary, *The James Dean Story*, which he'd seen about a billion times! It's how all these things work out; it's all about connections, whether they're real or imaginary, or something that you're familiar with.

I believe you knew the choreographer Robert Desrosiers, who created The Blue Snake ballet and gave a compelling performance as himself.
That's right. It was because Allan Nicholls had done a Leonard Cohen special in Canada many years ago and had used Desrosiers as one of the dancers. I thought he was very brave to allow himself to do that performance, because the character is who he is. A lot of people thought we'd brought in a comic actor.

The first reaction of most people to the film was that they felt the lack of a story.
Well, there was the 'Funny Valentine' episode, which was the obligatory story of one dancer being injured and another taking her place, and we put it at the front of the picture so we could serve that convention. But Ry never became a star, even in the storm – people were more distracted by the storm itself. There are stories in the film, things that happen to certain people, there are arcs in there. But I don't think there's a real story. There are relationships and hints of things that are never followed through, much like *Gosford Park*. Stories that don't become stories, just elements of stories that don't wind up, so to speak. The way we ended up doing it, it's like a ballet, so it has a happy ending, it's a positive kind of '*pas*'. The ho-hum of it is whether the lack of dramatic arc would play with an audience, and that was a concern for me.

That's not an unusual risk for you to take.
Yes, but I usually don't know I'm taking the risk! I think I'm definitely on the right track, usually. But my impression is that you really get to know these dancers as people.

From what you've intimated about your way of directing the dancers, you didn't adhere very closely to the script.
Barbara said of her script, 'Every word I wrote, I heard these people say.

There's nothing original in there.' I said, 'You heard them say it last year. This year it's different, and these people playing them aren't the same people. So it's not important that you heard someone walk by and say, "Oh my God, it's late, I've got to get home and feed the kids." I've got an actor who doesn't have any kids!' Barbara would say, 'But it was just so right.' And I'd say, 'You're stuck in your mind, you've got pictures there that you just can't get rid of.' I couldn't have done that twenty years ago. I'd have had a big fight with her and thrown her off the set and not allowed her in.

I wouldn't let any of the dancers see the script. I didn't use it. When they came in to do a scene, I'd be asked, 'Do you want to show them something?' I'd say, 'No, no, you say this, you say this, and you say this.' And I'd draw it out of them so fast that they couldn't repeat exactly what I said, so they were paraphrasing. An actor's more skilled at saying the exact words, because they're trained for that. I wouldn't give any of the dancers the script. I said, 'I don't want you to learn anything. I just want you to make it up as we go along.' Of course, I would tell them what the important point of any scene was.

As we edited the picture, I looked at the scenes we did very early on and I thought, 'Man, if I'd done that at the end of filming rather than the beginning, it would have been a different scene.' It would have had a different energy. And the scenes we did at the end are better. The other thing that helped was that I don't know that much about ballet, and I didn't consider these people as pros. At first I found myself thinking, 'I'm not doing the right thing here because I'm talking to these people like they're amateurs, and here are some of the best dancers on the planet.' I began to have more confidence in what they could do, and if I started this picture again today, I think it would be a different film. I don't know if it would be a *better* film. Probably not. You get to a point where you know too much. If you had a person who was a dancer like Bob Fosse or someone experienced in that world, they couldn't make the picture I would make, because their focus would be on the rights and wrongs and whys and wherefores of the dance. I don't have that eye.

Were the ballets you featured in the film already part of their repertory?
Yes and no. Some of them were, some of them they had to learn. We looked at hundreds of tapes of ballets, and Neve had this 'Funny Valentine' idea, but most of the selection process came through her, as I don't know this dance world. I mean, I could just look at these pieces and see whether they were different enough from each other to suggest the eclectic nature of their repertoire. I didn't want everything to look like *Swan Lake*. I'd never heard of

anyone doing a dance on the end of a noose, but I was entertained and moved by it, so I said, 'Let's do that.' Other times I'd say, 'I don't really care. What is it you want to do? Let me see it!' I tended to go towards things that were less about technique, so you didn't have to be a ballet buff or aficionado to like the dance. So there was a certain amount of stuff on point, and some it was just plain excitement, like the salsa dance.

To me, it's all sex – they're all emulating fucking! They all look like they're naked. The guys wear those tights that go right up the crack of their ass, so they're naked, and they've got pretty good bodies too, as they're all in shape. I'd walk into a room and there would be a girl lying on her back with her legs up in the air and spread apart, and she'd say, 'Oh, hi, Mr Altman!' And I'm looking . . . It's a different culture. And it's sad too, as these people work so hard and they really abdicate from the general paths of life. That's why they become so incestuous – they're always matching up with people who have the same disciplines that they do. And also that's why they don't last so long. At thirty-five, most of them are finished. Once they go on points, they're never without pain until they stop. So they learn to do all this stuff through pain; they're like athletes. Injuries are a big, big deal, and they happen often. We featured one where the girl snaps her Achilles tendon. Well, she's finished, of course. No more dancing.

The scene has a real sense of terror, because you sense that feeling but it's completely unspoken.
That's right. Everyone knew what happened, but they didn't want to face it. Then Neve hurts her shoulder, and Maia has a neck spasm, but all these are part of the fabric of their lives. They have to learn to work through them, and that's why there are usually double casts. In *The Blue Snake* dance they have to get the costume off Neve and on to Maia and still get her on stage in time. And these are all things which have actually happened. The storm in the outside venue is another example; that really happened once to the Joffrey company.

The Company was shot on High Definition Video, though on the big screen that's not so evident – the image is very beautiful and filmic. It looks as though you were using quite a few cameras simultaneously on this film.
Going into this new kind of territory was very exciting. I had three or four cameras – usually four, for all the dances. The rest was done sometimes with three, always with two cameras. You couldn't ask for a lot of takes from the dancers – they would have been exhausted! Rarely did we go for more than

one take for the actual dances. I had one take where we turned four cameras on and went for about thirty minutes before I called 'cut'. It was when the dancers have a Christmas party and a roast; they decorate the gym, and then the dancers do these parodies of different people and the dances in their repertory that we've seen. It was their chance to let off steam about their dance masters. The scene really humanizes the company in a way that I think is important.

The dance sequences are very beautiful to watch.
Generally, we placed the cameras were we could and filmed. The lighting is totally general. I think Andrew Dunn's contribution to the film is really big and looks glorious. But I think if you were to take twenty cameramen of his calibre, eighteen of them would not have taken this job, because why would they? They don't know about Hi Def. There are bad vibes around about it. Some people would say that using video makes it a cheap film, so you're doing it to save money, but that's not true. At least, *I* couldn't figure out how to save money. This was a whole new potion, and Andrew just dived in and loved every moment of it. We both walked into the fog. We had no idea where the cliff was. We just charged ahead and hoped we wouldn't fall off. He didn't, for sure, and I don't believe I did.

On the musical side, you used the 'Funny Valentine' theme, the Rodgers and Hart song, in various guises, just as you'd done with the song in The Long Goodbye.
We used it to score the little romantic story we had with Ry and Josh, so it was more of a *pas de deux* than a movie conceit. Just boy meets girl, boy dates girl, boy fucks girl, boy continues to see girl ... That's why we took out so much of their dialogue, to make it more like a dance. I brought in Van Dyke Parks, who'd worked for me on *Popeye* and was the piano player in the movie, to help with the music. He composed the entire score for the last ballet, *The Blue Snake*, which was a children's ballet. It had to be stronger than what was originally written, which was early 1980s minimalist stuff, which you get bored with rather quickly. I was worried what Desrosiers' reaction would be, but he loved it.

What kind of feedback did you get from the Joffrey Company?
Not much was negative. A lot of the Joffrey patrons felt there wasn't enough of the company in the performances, and the only bad review of the performance we got was from one of the leading patrons of the company, who said that we should have had Maia rather than Neve Campbell.

What about the cinema audience?
It did well; no one lost their money. Some people complained it was too soft and they would say, 'What's really happening here?' But it was exactly what I set out to do: a year in the working life of a ballet company. There was no story, really; just getting inside the conscience of that company and going about it in a very undramatic way. I think it's the most honest of the films that have been made on this subject. And it's taken me off in a new direction, which is, 'Why cater to the worst in the audience, rather than trying to bring the audience up to the best of what the performance is?' And logically, this is the last track I'm going to be on, so I'm going to ride it all down the rails to the next station!

Do you believe that in the future we will still be watching films on a big screen?
Oh, I think so, but I don't think that film will be the medium. It might be the medium for twenty years or so, because there are so many cinemas around the world with film projectors, and people are used to it. A film like *The Company* is a big wide-screen picture, and nobody's going to say, 'Oh, that was shot on tape.' They'll know about it but they couldn't spot it, mainly. But eventually they're not going to deal with sending reels of film into a theatre, having a projectionist put it up and focus it. This stuff is going to come from a central point and just be plugged in, picked up and projected in whatever the venue is. But then maybe you don't want something that big to be that sharp! In *McCabe & Mrs Miller*, I was putting all kinds of shit in front of the lens to get rid of this very sharp quality, trying to evoke a sense of period.

So that communal experience is still valid for you?
Oh, absolutely. I wouldn't have made *The Company* for HBO, because I think it would be ineffective on a small screen.

Of all the American directors, I feel your films – especially those of the 1970s – have suffered most on television, mainly because of your distinctive use of the scope (1:2.35) screen ratio created by using an anamorphic lens.
They do, because almost every one was done anamorphic, and I did use the frame. And on television much of it was lost. I stopped using the anamorphic process in the 1980s because most of the films I was making then I knew would ultimately be seen on smaller screens. But I liked the anamorphic image because that's the way I believe you see. Now I'm kind of blind on one side, but looking at you, I'm really seeing that shape.

Since your return to feature film-making in the 1990s, you appear to have enjoyed good relationships with your producers.
On the last few films I've had David Levy as producer, and his job, as he sees it, I think, is to make my job possible. So what he's doing is solving problems to give me the elbow room to make the film. I've rarely been a hired director, meaning that I've been hired on a film and consequently I could be fired. So I've not had the experience of working with a producer who would come on the set and say, 'Listen, you didn't get coverage of that scene. I want a close-up of that girl there.' And I'd say, 'I don't think she should be in the picture.' 'Well, shoot the goddamn thing anyway.' I've never had that. I've had it requested of me, and sometimes I've honoured that request. But there's no film-maker who has had a better shake than I've had. I know that most people work for a producer who wants his idea served, or a commercial consideration is uppermost. When I did work in television with producers like that, I found the best thing was to lie to them. These were benevolent lies, to my mind. My real thought process was, 'I'm going to help him, I'm going to give him something that's really good!'

Following The Company, *you had various projects in development, including* Mata Hari, *proposed as a three-hour biopic for television of the famous spy, to be played by Cate Blanchett. There was also* The Widow Claire, *about a recently bereaved wife defending herself against suitors in a southern town, with Kate Winslet discussed for the lead role. One film that looked particularly hopeful was* Voltage, *an ensemble piece about an engineering factory making small parts for airplanes in 1991, during the George Bush Sr era when it was decided not to pursue Saddam Hussein. With a script by Alan Rudolph from the novel by Robert Grossbach, the film at one point had a projected cast list including Joaquin Phoenix, Philip Seymour Hoffman, Harry Belafonte and Elliott Gould.*
Nobody would pay for it. I went too far with it, made assumptions, which I always do, and they're always wrong. The guy who put up the money for *The Company* tried to get *Voltage* done. But with a Bush as president, nobody would want me to do the picture.

In the meantime, you made commercials, and in March 2002 signed up to shoot five TV promos for E-channel to accompany The Academy Awards Countdown, *featuring famous actors recreating great scenes in film history, including Dustin Hoffman in* The Graduate, *Eric McCormack as Don Corleone in* The Godfather, *Minnie Driver as Hannibal Lecter in* Silence of the Lambs *and Ving Rhames as Travis Bickle in* Taxi Driver. *In late 2004 you made a sequence of commercials for Revlon with famous actresses. And throughout this time, you continued to plan making the film* Paint, *formerly known as* Ultraviolet, *a screenplay by Jeffrey Lewis. When it was first announced, Salma Hayek was set to play a documentary film-maker who, while making a film about a murdered artist, finds the art community to be more twisted than she thought. James Franco was cast as the victim's brother.*

It's set in the contemporary art world of New York, and it's a melodrama with a murder mystery. The main character is a video artist whose work is part of the texture of the piece. It's a project that refuses to die.

Tanner on Tanner

In 2004 you had the opportunity to return to a character you had created with Garry Trudeau, Congressman Jack Tanner. Hadn't you originally intended to follow Tanner's career immediately after he lost out for the presidency at the 1988 Democratic Convention?

At the end of the Convention in Atlanta in 1988, we were trying to get HBO to fund us to do four more episodes to continue right up to the election and to run Tanner as an independent. They finally backed out of that. But I hadn't given them a satisfactory ending to the series. I left it wide open so you didn't know what Tanner was going to do. The segue we made to the new series, it was not about the politics but about documentary film-making and reporting in the news.

I imagine you saw that continuing the story sixteen years on was possible when you recorded the introductions with the original cast of Michael Murphy, Pam Reed and Cynthia Nixon playing their characters reminiscing for the re-runs of Tanner '88 *on the Sundance Channel.*

It was just amazing. Sixteen years on! We didn't have long briefing sessions with them; they just came in and did it. And the same was true for the series. It was well performed and I'm very proud of it. The idea of making Alex Tanner a documentary film-maker came right out of doing those intro-ductions. It was Garry's idea. And when we did get the go-ahead from the Sundance Channel to go back into Tanner's world, we couldn't go the political route, because we had no particular political agenda we could get into. Although Jack Tanner was still in the Democratic Party, we now had him teaching at Michigan State University.

The documentary idea seemed definitely the way to go, and when we got to the Boston National Democratic Convention, my God, there were forty accredited film crews there, an average of five persons each on the floor. You couldn't go anywhere without another crew shooting you! So that really turned and worked in our favour. For our interview with Michael Moore, we had to get permission from him to use it after we shot it, because he didn't know we were there at the time. Our guys were just alongside all the others. We had shots when we were following Michael Murphy and Pam Reed through the Convention, and these people would come up and shake his hand and say, 'Hey, Jack, I remember you in '88!' We didn't know who they were. And the real politicians *had* to recognize him, because they had cameras on them.

You amplify the sense of cameras being everywhere by mixing up the work of at least three separate crews.
We had my crew, with two cameras, then Deke's crew, which had a camera a step down, and then the student Stewart's camera, which was a little $800 model. In fact, there wasn't so much difference in the final look, so we had to degrade Stewart's quite a bit.

The real coup, of course, is that while everyone assumes Stewart isn't to be taken seriously, his film about Alex has the most to say, as well as being far more inventive a piece of film-making than his subject's effort.
It outed her own ego in that she couldn't resist being the subject of a film, because she was not a very good film-maker. As Redford said, she was telling us things we already know.

In a way we were satirizing ourselves for what we'd done in '88, only this time we had the point of view of not trying to fool the audience but to let them know that everybody was fooling everybody else and that the process was the real subject of all these films. With film schools and cheap digital cameras everywhere, everybody's doing it, and there is now more film document than there is real life.

The key scene must be when both Alex Tanner and Alex Kerry, who really was making a film about her father, are both trying to interview Ronald Reagan Jr at the same time.
That was kind of staged, of course, but Alex and Cynthia were wonderful, getting into a real catfight. Cynthia has this great enthusiasm. I thought her performance was really good.

It's better when you view all four parts together as a movie, I think. It's quite surprising in that form, because you see how all our heroes fail. She fails to get her documentary, her father is a wimp, and it tells us about how these candidates have to treat themselves and cover all bases so they can't make enemies. Her father compromised, and it makes for a very sad piece.

It showed great cheek to have Kerry's speech written by Jack Tanner.
Then you see him deny it at the end, so everybody fails. If it was a very obviously pro-Kerry piece, then I think it could have done some damage. People would have seen it as one-sided in favour of the Democrats. I think it actually does him a favour, makes him more of a human being. We were clearly pro-Democrat in our slant; that's our position. But we weren't doing what Michael Moore did. We were making fiction out of these non-fictional people. I hope it has as long an impact as *Tanner '88* has had. I don't know anyone who's had the opportunity to take a cast of people, shoot them for a six-hour piece and then revisit the territory sixteen years later using the same cast as the same people.

Following Tanner on Tanner, *you went to Chicago to direct another opera, this time based on one of your own films –* A Wedding.
It was commissioned by the Chicago Lyric Opera for December 2004, their fiftieth anniversary, so they put more money than usual into it. The writer Arnold Weinstein and the composer William Bolcom did *A View from the Bridge* together, and then I collaborated with them on *McTeague*, directing it on stage. It was an opera from the novel, which I read, and I was familiar with the Von Stroheim movie, but it didn't have a big influence. When it was done for TV, I let Frank Barhydt mix scenes from the opera with clips from the movie, as I wouldn't let them film the opera straight from the stage. Since there's already a film of *A Wedding*, I don't have to worry about that again.

For *A Wedding*, Arnold and I did the libretto before Bill began composing the music. We had to bring the characters down a little bit, combining many of them. The drunk doctor, who was played by Howard Duff, we've combined him with the Pat McCormick part, the fat guy who makes the pass at Tulip. Snooks, the father of the bride, is combined with the Reverend, so he's now more of a Bush character who's found God. Dramaturgically, it stands up much better. And when you think about the story, it is very operatic, because all the incidents become emotionally very large. Robin Wagner did the set, which is gorgeous in its presentation.

In the film, there's the car crash at the end in which the wrong people get killed, and everyone soon forgets about them. I think that's truthful. I mean, it's the way you react. You think that your son and daughter-in-law have been killed in a car crash, and then you see them come down the stairs and you're so thrilled: 'Oh, my God, you're alive!' And somebody says, 'Who was in the car?' 'Oh, that must have been that other couple.' But you're still celebrating. There's something rather crass about that, but I think those are truthful human emotions. Everyone's thinking about themselves; it's very natural. I planned it so that for the opera, as you came into the lobby of the theatre, there was going to be this car with a big bow on it saying 'Just married' and tin cans and all that stuff. It would still be there in the intermission. But when you'd leave, you would see this burnt-out shell of a car, still steaming. I said to the people at the Lyric, 'This is part of the libretto. I think it's better than in the movie, because as you leave there would be this smouldering reminder of what really occurred, the fiery, terrible death of two people.' But the fire department wouldn't let me do it!

Following the opera, which received high praise from the critics and sold out every performance, your next project is A Prairie Home Companion, *based on the popular American radio variety show created and performed by Garrison Keillor,[8] which has been broadcast on National Public Radio since 1974.*

It's all to be done in the venue where he does his show: the Fitzgerald Theatre in St Paul, Minnesota. He does a radio show that's on for two hours once a week, and we're going to shoot it as a production of that show, and you'll see the sound effects man at work and so on. Then we're going to add to that the Johnson Sisters, who sing two numbers, and that'll be Meryl Streep and Lily Tomlin, the last of the Johnson Sisters Sextet. Then there'll be Woody Harrelson and John C. Reilly as two cowboy singers. A lot of the characters he talks about, like his private detective 'Guy Noir', you'll see the actors reading the parts. You'll also see a lot of the shenanigans going on backstage and find that Guy Noir is actually the guard at the back entrance. In the end, we fold all these elements back in so that you realize these are all part of Garrison's alter ego. I had a meeting with some money guys, and they said, 'Well, the ending in the script is a little weak.' And I said to them, 'What you read in the script will never be in the film! But I can't tell you what it will be, because it's something that's going to have to come out of this material.' Just as I didn't change the dances in *The Company*, so I wouldn't interfere with Keillor's humour. Basically, my film has to be what that show is. I have to keep its integrity. The core audience for this is Garrison Keillor's audience, who include the Bush people, so I think it has a chance!

*You've completed over thirty feature films and many hours of television.
Does it surprise you that you've achieved so much?*
If I look back at all my work, it all seems like yesterday. I can't imagine how
all this time got away. All of it is basically the same; none of it comes from
any brilliance. It comes from enthusiasm, a little bit of ego and tenacity. It's
been such a gift to do any of this.

Notes

1 Bob Balaban (b. 1945) has had an extensive career on stage, television and film,
   both as an actor and director, notably of *Parents* (1989). His acting credits
   include *Midnight Cowboy* (1969), *Close Encounters of the Third Kind* (1977),
   Prince of the City (1981), *Alice* (1990), *Bob Roberts* (1992), *Deconstructing
   Harry* (1997), *Ghost World* (2000) and *A Mighty Wind* (2003).
2 The partnership of producer Ismail Merchant and director James Ivory was
   formed in India in the early 1960s, beginning with *Shakespeare Wallah* (1965),
   in collaboration with the German-born novelist and screenwriter Ruth Prawer
   Jhabvala. Their great success began with a series of elegant literary adaptations:
   of Henry James with *The Europeans* (1979) and *The Bostonians* (1984), and of
   E. M. Forster with *A Room with a View* (1986) and *Howard's End* (1992),
   the latter pair proving very successful and consolidating the Merchant-Ivory
   tradition as the model for British period drama.
3 *Brideshead Revisited*, an eleven-episode adaptation of Evelyn Waugh's novel
   first shown on British television in 1981, perfectly exemplified the 'white flannel'
   tradition of tasteful literary adaptations that have remained popular in British
   film and television. Dealing with the decline of the aristocracy in the period
   between the wars, the saga is imbued with a heavy nostalgia for the lost world of
   Edwardian England.
4 Ivor Novello (1893–1951) was a Welsh-born matinee idol of the British stage
   and screen who also created many musicals and popular songs, including the
   immortal 'Keep the Home Fires Burning'. Especially memorable was his mysterious role in Hitchcock's *The Lodger* (1926), which was remade in sound with
   him in Hollywood in 1932 to lesser effect, as is commented upon in *Gosford
   Park*.
5 Georgie Stoll (1905–85), a music director and conductor famous on radio,
   worked extensively on the soundtracks of many MGM musicals from the 1930s
   to the 1960s, winning an Academy Award for *Anchors Aweigh* in 1945.
6 Neve Campbell (b. 1973) was born and raised in Canada, and after abandoning
   her ambitions as a ballet dancer, she turned to acting and became famous as
   teenager Julia Salinger in the TV series *Party of Five* (1994–2001). Moving on to
   the cinema, she played the lead role of Sidney Prescott in the horror hit *Scream*

(1996) and its two sequels, which placed her in the high-earning league of screen actresses.

7 Malcolm McDowell (b. 1943) was working in minor roles in the theatre when he auditioned for Lindsay Anderson's film *If . . .* (1968) and won the lead role. He subsequently made a great impact as the malevolent thug Alex in Stanley Kubrick's *A Clockwork Orange* (1971), though few of his subsequent roles have used him as well. In 1980 Altman had hoped to make *The Smith County Widow* with Malcolm McDowell and his then wife, Mary Steenburgen.

8 Garrison Keillor (b. 1942) was born in Anoka, Minnesota, and began his radio career as a student of the University of Minnesota. In 1969 he began writing for *The New Yorker* magazine, and an article about the Grand Ole Opry inspired him to create a live variety show on radio. The first show entitled *A Prairie Home Companion* took place on 6 July 1974 in a St Paul college theatre before twelve people, but its popularity quickly grew. After relocating to New York for four seasons, he returned to Minnesota in 1993 to continue the show in its proper Midwestern setting, with its fictional town of Lake Wobegon. Keillor has also published books for adults and children, written poetry and made several recordings.

Filmography

Early Film Credits

1947

Christmas Eve

Mathilda Reid has a greedy nephew who wants her judged incompetent so that he can take control of her fortune. The only way she can save herself is to bring her three adopted sons together for a reunion at Christmas – Michael, a penniless playboy, Mario, who has become embroiled with a Nazi war criminal, and Jonathan, a hard-drinking rodeo rider.

Director: Edward L. Marin
Production Company: United Artists
Producer: Benedict Bogeaus
Screenplay: Laurence Stallings, from a story by Laurence Stallings, Richard H. Landau and (uncredited) Robert Altman
Cast: George Raft, George Brent, Randolph Scott, Joan Blondell, Virginia Field, Ann Harding, Reginald Denny
90 mins

1948

Bodyguard

A tough but straight Los Angeles policeman is suspended from the force for insubordination and becomes bodyguard to a rich widow, the owner of a meat-packing plant. While investigating threats made against her, he starts to uncover the truth behind the murder of a meat inspector at the plant. But this leads him to be framed for the murder of his former supervisor in the police, for which he has to call on his fiancée, a police clerk, to access files to help him clear his name.

Director: Richard Fleischer
Production Company: RKO Radio Pictures
Producer: Sid Rogell
Screenplay: Fred Niblo Jr, Harry Essex, from a story by Robert Altman, George W. George
Cast: Lawrence Tierney, Priscilla Lane, Philip Reed, June Clayworth, Steve Brodie, Frank Fenton, Charles Crane, Elisabeth Risdon
62 mins

1951
Corn's A-Poppin'

An unscrupulous press agent arranges sponsorship for a tacky television show in order to help sales of rival popcorn companies. But the success of a new country-and-western performer on the show, and the discovery of a new and better popcorn, foil his plan.

Director: Robert Woodburn
Production Company: Crest
Screenplay: Robert Altman, Robert Woodburn
Cast: Jerry Wallace, Pat McReynolds, James Lantz, Dora Wells, Keith Painton, Noralee Benedict, Little Cora Weiss, Hobie Shepp and the Cowtown Wranglers
62 mins

Films as Director

1957
The Delinquents
(filmed in 1955)

Scotty, a young man, falls in love with Janice, but her father believes her too young at sixteen to be 'going steady'. Although Scotty's mother objects to the idea, his father gives his son the keys to his car. At a drive-in movie, Scotty meets Cholly and his gang. Cholly offers to date Janice and bring her to Scotty, and sets about persuading her parents that he's really wanting to get ahead by working on the stock market. They all meet at a party in a mansion which is raided by the cops. Scotty is blamed for raising the alarm, and in retaliation Cholly kidnaps Janice. Scotty rescues her and beats up Cholly.

Distribution: United Artists
Producer: Robert Altman
Screenplay: Robert Altman
Cinematography (b/w): Charles Paddock
Sound: Bob Post
Editor: Helene Turner
Music: Bill Nolan Quintet Minus Two
Song: 'The Dirty Rock Boogie' (Julia Lee)
Production Design: Chet Allen
Cast: Tom Laughlin (*Scotty*), Peter Miller (*Cholly*), Rosemary Howard (*Janice*), Richard Bakalyan (*Eddy*), Helene Hawley (*Mrs White*), Leonard Belove (*Mr White*), Lotus Corelli (*Mrs Wilson*), James Lantz (*Mr Wilson*), Christine Altman (*Sissy*), George Kuhn (*Jay*), Pat Stedman (*Meg*), Norman Zands (*Chizzy*), James

Leria (*Steve*), Jet Pinkston (*Molly*), Kermit Echols (*Barman*), Joe Adleman (*Station Attendant*)
71 mins

The James Dean Story

A documentary, mostly using actuality and photographs, evoking the short life and death by automobile accident of the actor James Dean (1931–55), whose three major films were *East of Eden* (Elia Kazan, 1955), *Rebel Without a Cause* (Nicholas Ray, 1955) and *Giant* (George Stevens, 1956). The documentary includes interviews with family and friends of the actor, examining his background in Fairmount, Indiana, and rise to fame in New York and Los Angeles. Those featured include Marcus and Ortense Winslow (his uncle and aunt), Markie Winslow (his cousin), Mr and Mrs Dean (his grandparents), Adeline Hall (his teacher), his friends Bing Traster, Mr Carter, Jerry Luce, Louie De Liso, Arnie Langer, Arline Sax, Chris White, George Ross, Robert Jewett, John Kalin, Lew Bracker, Glenn Kramer, Patsy D'Amore, Billy Karen, Lillie Kardell, and highway cop Sergeant Nelson.

Distribution: Warner Brothers
Producers: Robert Altman, George W. George
Screenplay: Stewart Stern
Cinematography (b/w): Louis Lombardo
Photographs: Dennis Stock, Roy Schatt, Frank Worth, Weegee, Edward Martin, Dick Miller, Peter Basch, Carlyle Blackwell Jr, Tom Caffrey, Jack Delano, Murray Garrett, Paul Gilliam, Fred Jordan, Russ Meyer, Don Ornitz, Paul Popesil, Charles Robinson, Jack Stager, Phil Stern, William Veercamp
Sound: Cathey Burrow, Bert Schoenfeld, James Nelson, Jack Kirschner
Editors: Robert Altman, George W. George
Music: Leith Stevens
Song: 'Let Me Be Loved' (Tommy Sands)
Production Design: Louis Clyde Stoumen
Narrator: Martin Gabel
82 mins

1964

Nightmare in Chicago
(*expanded version of TV film* Once Upon a Savage Night)

Over Christmas, an emotionally unbalanced man who is dubbed 'Georgie Porgie' murders several women throughout the Midwest but always manages to escape the police. On the O'Hare Turnpike outside Chicago, he kidnaps a waitress, who has to listen to his tales of an overbearing mother. When the cops try to block the whole area over a three-day period, the killer steals a truck and joins an army convoy carrying explosives along the main highway to evade them. Eventually the police

221

learn that the killer suffers from oversensitive sight and arrest him by shining spotlights into his eyes.

Production Company: Roncom/Universal
Producer: Robert Altman
Screenplay: Donald Moessinger, from the novel *Death on the Turnpike* by William P. McGivern
Cinematography: Bud Thackery
Sound: Ed Somers
Editors: Danford B. Greene, Larry D. Lester
Music: John Williams
Cast: Charles McGraw (*Harry Brockman*), Robert Ridgely (*Dan McVea*), Ted Knight (*Commissioner Lombardo*), Barbara Turner (*Bernadette Wells*), Philip Abbott (*Myron Ellis*), Douglas A. Alleman (*Ralph*), Charlene Lee (*Wynnette*), Arlene Kieta (*The Blonde*), Robert C. Harris (*Officer Newman*), John Alonzo (*Officer Miller*)
81 mins

1968

Countdown

The American space team, knowing that the Russians have launched a spacecraft taking a man to the moon, decide to bring forward their attempt using the Mercury capsule. Astronaut Lee Stegler is selected over his colleague Chiz Stewart, whose military status is considered a political problem. The more experienced Chiz makes it clear to everybody he doesn't believe Lee is up to the task. Despite pressure from his family to reconsider, Lee takes off and, after a series of technical problems, makes a successful voyage to the moon. Although he is unable to see the beacon signals of a shelter essential to his survival, Chiz disobeys orders and lands regardless, losing contact with Earth, where it is assumed he is dead. On the moon he finds the wreckage of the Russian ship and its crew all dead, and just as his oxygen is about to run out, he finally discovers the shelter.

Production Company: William Conrad Productions for Warner Brothers
Producers: James Lydon, William Conrad
Screenplay: Loring Mandel, based on the novel *The Pilgrim Project* by Hank Searls
Cinematography (Panavision): William W. Spencer
Sound: Everett A. Hughes
Editor: Gene Milford
Music: Leonard Rosenman
Production Design: Jack Poplin
Cast: James Caan (*Lee Stegler*), Robert Duvall (*Colonel 'Chiz' Stewart*), Joanna Moore (*Mickey Stegler*), Barbara Baxley (*Jean Stewart*), Charles Aidman (*Gus, the doctor*), Steve Ihnat (*Ross*), Michael Murphy (*Rick*), Ted Knight (*Larson*), Stephen

Colt (*Ehrman*), John Rayner (*Dunc*), Charles Irving (*Seidel*), Bobby Riha Jr (*Stevie Stegler*)
101 mins
(cut to 73 mins for UK distribution)

1969
That Cold Day in the Park
Frances Austen, thirty-two and unmarried, lives alone in a large apartment in Vancouver. Finding an unkempt young man alone in a nearby park on a rainy day, she takes him home and suggests he stay. The boy never speaks, and taking him to be mute, Frances talks continuously to him, believing they have a growing relationship. When Frances is out, the boy invites his sister to the apartment, and after some incestuous games together, they both leave. Frances, having turned down a pass made by a doctor considerably older than her, returns and goes into the boy's bedroom offering herself to him, only to discover she has been talking to a dummy. On his return, Frances keeps the boy prisoner in the apartment, bringing in a prostitute, Sylvie, to keep him happy. While they are making love, a jealous Frances bursts in and murders her. While the boy hopes to escape, a deluded Frances tries to persuade him all is going to be fine again.

Production Company: Factor-Altman-Mirell Films Ltd/Commonwealth International
Producers: Donald Factor, Leon Mirell
Screenplay: Gillian Freeman, based on the novel by Richard Miles
Cinematography: Laszlo Kovacs
Sound: John Gusselle
Editor: Danford B. Greene
Music: Johnny Mandel
Production Design: Leon Ericksen
Cast: Sandy Dennis (*Frances Austen*), Michael Burns (*Boy*), Susanne Benton (*Nina*), John Garfield Jr (*Nick*), Luana Anders (*Sylvia*), Edward Greenhalgh (*Dr Stevenson*), Doris Buckingham (*Mrs Ebury*), Alicia Ammon (*Mrs Pitt*), Lloyd Berry (*Mr Pitt*), Michael Murphy (*The Rounder*), Linda Sorenson (*The Prostitute*), Rae Brown (*Mrs Parnell*)
110 mins
(cut to 105 mins for UK distribution)

1970
M*A*S*H
At the 4077th Mobile Army Surgical Hospital in Korea, the need constantly to operate on wounded men brings together surgeons Hawkeye Pierce, Duke Forrest and Trapper John McIntyre, who sustain their work through drink, revelry and the pursuit of women. A new senior nurse, whom they nickname Hot Lips, supports

the overtly religious Major Burns in condemning the behaviour of the men, who retaliate with a series of practical jokes on the pair that lead Burns to be taken away as a mental patient. When the dental officer known as Painless Pole decides to commit suicide because he believes he has homosexual tendencies, the men collaborate on staging a 'last supper' in which they pretend to administer Painless with a suicide pill and then bring him to his senses by persuading a nurse to make love to him. After Trapper John and Hawkeye Pierce make a trip to Tokyo to perform an emergency operation on a senator's son, the unit becomes involved in a football game which they rig so as to win an easy victory. Eventually Hawkeye and Duke receive their orders to return home, leaving Trapper John to continue with a new team.

Production Company: Aspen/20th Century Fox
Producer: Ingo Preminger
Screenplay: Ring Lardner Jr, based on the novel by Richard Hooker
Cinematography (Panavision): Harold E. Stine
Sound: Bernard Freericks, John Stack
Editor: Danford B. Greene
Music: Johnny Mandel
Song: 'Suicide Is Painless' (Ahmad Jamal)
Production Design: Jack Martin Smith, Arthur Lonegan
Cast: Donald Sutherland (*Hawkeye Pierce*), Elliott Gould (*Trapper John McIntyre*), Tom Skerritt (*Duke Forrest*), Sally Kellerman (*Major Hot Lips*), Robert Duvall (*Major Frank Burns*), Jo Ann Pflug (*Lt Dish*), Rene Auberjonois (*Dago Red*), Roger Bowen (*Col Henry Blake*), Gary Burghoff (*Radar O'Reilly*), David Arkin (*Sgt Major Vollmer*), Fred Williamson (*Spearchucker*), Michael Murphy (*Me Lay*), Kim Atwood (*Ho-Jon*), Tim Brown (*Corporal Judson*), Indus Arthur (*Lt Leslie*), John Schuck (*Painless Pole*), Ken Prymus (*Pfc Seidman*), Dawne Damon (*Capt Storch*), Carl Gottlieb (*Ugly John*), Tamara Horrocks (*Capt Knocko*), G. Wood (*General Hammond*), Bobby Troup (*Sgt Gorman*), Bud Cort (*Private Boone*), Danny Goldman (*Capt Murrhardt*), Corey Fischer (*Capt Bandini*), J. B. Douglas (*Colonel Wallace C. Merrill*), Yoko Young (*Japanese servant*), Ben Davidson, Fran Tarkenton, Howard Williams, Jack Concannon, John Myers, Tom Woodeschick, Tommy Brown, Buck Buchanan, Nolan Smith (*football players*)
116 mins

Brewster McCloud

Brewster McCloud lives undetected in a fallout shelter beneath the Houston Astrodome, working on the construction of a winged apparatus to enable him to fly. In his project he is supported by a teenage girl, Hope, and a mysterious guardian angel who may have been a bird in a former life, Louise. To further his research, Brewster works as chauffeur to Abraham, the hundred-and-twenty-year-old surviving Wright brother. Investigating the deaths of two prominent citizens, Captain Crandall is assisted by top San Francisco cop Frank Shaft. A key clue is provided by the corpse of the third victim, a corrupt narcotics agent, which is found covered in bird droppings. Against Louise's advice, Brewster sleeps with Astrodome guide Suzanne. After pursuing Brewster and Louise in a car chase, Shaft drives off the road into a lake and he commits suicide. When Brewster claims responsibility for the murders to Suzanne, she reports him to the aide of a homosexual politician, Haskell Weeks. Weeks becomes the fourth victim, and the police close in on Brewster, who finally launches himself on a maiden flight in the Astrodome but crashes to his death.

Production Company: An Adler-Phillips/Lion's Gate production for MGM
Producer: Lou Adler
Screenplay: Doran William Cannon
Cinematography (Panavision): Lamar Boren, Jordan Cronenworth
Sound: Harry W. Tetrick, William McCaughey
Editor: Lou Lombardo
Music: Gene Page
Songs: 'Brewster McCloud'; 'Lift Every Voice and Sing', 'White Feather Wings' (Merry Clayton); 'Last of the Unnatural Acts', 'The First and Last Thing You Do', 'I Promise Not to Tell' (John Phillips)
Production Design: Preston Ames, George W. David
Cast: Bud Cort (*Brewster McCloud*), Sally Kellerman (*Louise*), Michael Murphy (*Frank Shaft*), William Windom (*Haskel Weeks*), Shelley Duvall (*Suzanne Davis*), Rene Auberjonois (*Lecturer*), Stacey Keach (*Abraham Wright*), John Schuck (*Lt Alvin Johnson*), Margaret Hamilton (*Daphne Heap*), Jennifer Salt (*Hope*), Corey Fischer (*Lt Hines*), G. Wood (*Capt Crandall*), Bert Remsen (*Douglas Breen*), Angelina Johnson (*Mrs Breen*), William Baldwin (*Bernard*), William Henry Bennet (*Band Conductor*), Gary Wayne Chason (*Camera Store Clerk*), Ellis Gilbert (*Butler*), Verdie Henshaw (*Feathered Nest Sanatorium Manager*), Robert Warner (*Camera Store Assistant Manager*), Keith V. Erickson (*Professor Aggnout*), Thomas Danko (*Color Lab Man*), Dean Goss (*Eugene Ledbetter*), W. E. Terry Jr (*Police Chaplain*), Ronnie Cammack (*Wendell*), Dixie M. Taylor (*Nursing Home Manager*), Pearl Coffey Chason (*Nursing Home Attendant*), Amelia Parker (*Nursing Home Manageress*), David Welch (*Breen's son*)
105 mins

1971
McCabe & Mrs Miller
In Presbyterian Church, a north-western mining town at the turn of the century, a wandering gambler called John McCabe makes a big impression and sets up Sheehan's saloon. He then starts a prostitution business with girls from the local town of Bear Paw, but this develops into a large brothel when he is joined by an ambitious English whore, Constance Miller, to whom McCabe becomes deeply attracted. A large mining company based in Bear Paw send representatives to try to

buy McCabe out, but in spite of warnings from Constance that matters could turn bloody, McCabe refuses their offer. Three hired gunmen arrive next and callously shoot a young innocent cowboy as a demonstration of their ruthlessness. During a snowstorm, McCabe succeeds in killing the gunmen but is mortally wounded and is left to die while the townspeople try to put out a fire at the church. Constance, whose pleas for McCabe to leave town went unheeded, loses herself in an opium reverie.

Production Company: An Altman-Foster Production for Warner Brothers
Producers: David Foster, Mitchell Brower
Screenplay: Robert Altman, Brian McKay, based on the novel *McCabe* by Edmund Naughton
Cinematography (Panavision): Vilmos Zsigmond
Sound: John W. Gusselle, William A. Thompson
Editor: Louis Lombardo
Songs: 'Sisters of Mercy', 'The Stranger Song', 'Winter Lady' (Leonard Cohen)
Production Design: Leon Ericksen
Cast: Warren Beatty (*John Q. McCabe*), Julie Christie (*Mrs Constance Miller*), Rene Auberjonois (*Patrick Sheehan*), Hugh Millais (*Dog Butler*), Shelley Duvall (*Ida Coyle*), Michael Murphy (*Eugene Sears*), John Schuck (*Smalley*), Corey Fischer (*Mr Elliott, the Preacher*), William Devane (*Clement Samuels, the Lawyer*), Bert Remsen (*Bart Coyle*), Keith Carradine (*Cowboy*), Jace Vander Veen (*Bread*), Manfred Schulz (*Kid*), Jackie Crossland (*Lily*), Elizabeth Murphy (*Kate*), Linda Sorenson (*Blanche*), Elizabeth Knight (*Birdie*), Maysie Hoy (*Maysie*), Linda Kupecek (*Ruth*), Janet Wright (*Eunice*), Carey Lee McKenzie (*Alma*), Anthony Holland (*Ernie Hollander*), Tom Hill (*Archer*), Berg J. Newson (*Jeremy Berg*), Wayne Robson (*Sheehan's Bartender*), Wayne Grace (*McCabe's Bartender*), Jack Riley (*Riley Quinn*), Robert Fortier (*Town Drunk*), Wesley Taylor (*Shorty Dunn*), Anne Cameron (*Mrs Dunn*), Graeme Campbell (*Bill Cubbs*), J. S. Johnson (*J.J.*), Joe Clarke (*Joe Shortreed*), Harry Frazier (*Andy Anderson*), Edwin Collier (*Gilchrist*), Terence Kelly (*Quigley*), Brantley F. Kearns (*Fiddler*), Don Francks (*Buffalo*), Rodney Gage (*Sumner Washington*), Lili Francks (*Mrs Washington*)
121 mins

1972

Images

Alone in her luxurious apartment, Cathryn is working on a fairy-tale story called 'In Search of Unicorns' when she receives a phone call informing her that her husband Hugh is with another woman. When Hugh returns, she is thrown into a panic by his apparent transformation into Rene, a former lover who is now dead. To comfort Cathryn, Hugh takes her to their isolated house in the country. But there she begins seeing herself from afar, and Rene reappears to her. Her anxieties mount when Hugh is joined by Marcel, another former lover of Cathryn and whose daughter Susannah reminds her of her younger self. Left alone by Hugh, Cathryn's confusion of identities mounts, and she believes herself to have shot Rene and stabbed Marcel. Driving home to meet Hugh, she again encounters herself on the road and sees that her next victim is herself.

Production Company: Lion's Gate Productions (Dublin) for the Hemdale Group
Producer: Tommy Thompson
Screenplay: Robert Altman
Cinematography (Panavision): Vilmos Zsigmond
Sound: Liam Saurin
Editor: Graeme Clifford
Music: John Williams, Stomu Yamash'ta
Production Design: Leon Ericksen
Cast: Susannah York (*Cathryn*), Rene Auberjonois (*Hugh*), Marcel Bozzuffi (*Rene*), Hugh Millais (*Marcel*), Cathryn Harrison (*Susannah*), John Morley (*Old Man*)
101 mins

1973
The Long Goodbye

Philip Marlowe, a bumbling private detective who has trouble with his cat demanding a certain brand of food, is visited one night by his old buddy Terry Lennox, who has quarrelled with his wife Sylvia. Marlowe drives Terry to Tijuana airport, and on his return the police inform him that Sylvia has been murdered and arrest him as an accessory. Marlowe says nothing and is released when they hear Lennox has confessed and committed suicide. Then Eileen Wade hires Marlowe to find her alcoholic husband Roger, who has fallen into the hands of a creepy therapist, Dr Verringer. Marlowe is threatened by racketeer Marty Augustine, who is furious that Lennox disappeared with $350,000 belonging to him. Visiting the Wades, Marlowe is witness to Roger committing suicide by wandering into the ocean, and when the police arrive, Eileen tells them that Roger killed Sylvia. Marlowe is again apprehended by Marty Augustine but released when the money is suddenly returned to him. Hearing that Eileen has vanished, Marlowe travels to Mexico and finds that the local police faked Terry's death. He visits Terry, who is waiting for Eileen to join him in his retreat, and realizing that Terry had killed Sylvia after she had discovered his affair, Marlowe shoots him dead.

Production Company: Lion's Gate Films for United Artists
Producer: Jerry Bick
Screenplay: Leigh Brackett, based on the novel *The Long Goodbye* by Raymond Chandler
Cinematography (Panavision): Vilmos Zsigmond
Sound: John V. Speak
Editor: Lou Lombardo

Music: John Williams
Song: 'The Long Goodbye' (The Dave Grusin Trio, Jack Sheldon, Clydie King, Jack Riley, Morgan Ames' Aluminium Band, The Tepotzlan Municipal Band)
Cast: Elliott Gould (*Philip Marlowe*), Nina Van Pallandt (*Eileen Wade*), Sterling Hayden (*Roger Wade*), Mark Rydell (*Marty Augustine*), Henry Gibson (*Dr Verringer*), David Arkin (*Harry*), Jim Bouton (*Terry Lennox*), Warren Berlinger (*Morgan*), Jo Ann Brody (*Jo Ann Eggenweiler*), Steve Coit (*Detective Farmer*), Jack Knight (*Mabel*), Pepe Callahan (*Pepe*), Vince Palmieri (*Vince*), Pancho Cordoba (*Doctor*), Enrique Lucero (*Jefe*), Rutanya Alda (*Rutanya Sweet*), Tammy Shaw (*Dancer*), Jack Riley (*Piano Player*), Ken Samson (*Colony Guard*), Jerry Jones (*Detective Green*), John Davies (*Detective Dayton*), Rodney Moss (*Supermarket Clerk*), Sybil Scotford (*Real Estate Lady*), Herb Kerns (*Herbie*), Danny Goldman (*Bartender*), Kate Murtagh (*Nurse*), David Carradine (*Prisoner*), Arnold Strong/ Schwarzenegger (*Hood*)
111 mins

1974
Thieves Like Us
During the Depression in the Deep South three escaped convicts – known as T-Dub, Chicamaw and Bowie – take shelter with a relative of Chicamaw's, Dee Mobley, whose daughter Keechie becomes attracted to the youthful Bowie. The three men resume their life as bank robbers and for safety move in with T-Dub's sister-in-law Mattie. T-Dub falls for Mattie's sister, Lulu, while Chicamaw drinks heavily. Preparing for another hold-up, Bowie is injured in a road accident, and Chicamaw rescues him, shooting two policemen to make their escape. Bowie takes refuge in an old shack close by Dee Mobley's, where he and Keechie become lovers. The three robbers hold up another bank, but a bank clerk is shot and the men split up. After making his getaway, Bowie hears that T-Dub was killed and Chicamaw arrested. Bowie and Keechie move into a motel run by Mattie, and then, posing as a sheriff, he smuggles Chicamaw out of prison. But when Chicamaw callously kills a hostage, Bowie dumps him on the side of the road. Returning to Keechie, who informs him she's pregnant, Bowie is shopped to the police by Mattie and is killed when they fire on his cabin.

Production Company: A Jerry Bick-George Litto Production for United Artists
Producer: Jerry Bick
Screenplay: Joan Tewkesbury, Robert Altman, Calder Willingham, based on the novel by Edward Anderson
Cinematography: Jean Boffety
Sound: Don Matthews
Editor: Lou Lombardo
Songs: 'Massah's in the Cold, Cold Ground', 'Just a Song at Twilight', 'I Love You Truly', 'Deep River', 'It's Somebody's Birthday Today', 'In the Five and Ten Cents

Store', 'Baby, Take a Bow', 'She'll Be Coming Round the Mountain When She Comes'
Visual Consultants: Jack DeGovia, Scott Bushnell
Cast: Keith Carradine (*Bowie Bowers*), Shelley Duvall (*Keechie*), John Schuck ('*Chicamaw' Elmo Mobley*), Bert Remsen ('*T-Dub' T. W. Masefield*), Louise Fletcher (*Mattie*), Ann Latham (*Lula*), Tom Skerritt (*Dee Mobley*), Al Scott (*Capt Stammers*), John Roper (*Jasbo*), Mary Waits (*Noel*), Rodney Lee Jr (*James Mattingley*), William Watters (*Alvin*), Joan Tewkesbury (*Lady in Train Station*), Dr Edward Fisher, Josephine Bennett, Howard Warner (*Bank Hostages*), Eleanor Matthews (*Mrs Stammers*), Pam Warner (*Woman in Accident*), Suzanne Majure (*Coca-Cola Girl*), Walter Cooper and Lloyd Jones (*Sheriffs*)
123 mins

California Split

In a casino near Los Angeles, Charlie Waters wins at poker and then is accused by Lew, a bad loser, of collaborating with the dealer, Bill Denny. Bill and Charlie become friends over a few drinks but then are beaten up by Lew and his mob, who take their money. Bill is invited by Charlie to stay in his house, where he lives with two prostitutes, Barbara and Susan. Bill and Charlie do well at the racetrack based on Charlie's lucky hunch. Wanting to celebrate with the girls, they pose as policemen to scare off their transvestite client, Helen. Back at the racetrack, Charlie beats up Lew and recovers his money. Bill is heavily in debt to his bookie Sparkie and decides to go gambling in Reno to make some serious money, and is joined by Charlie. Bill follows his intuition and wins at poker, blackjack and roulette, making $82,000. He splits the money with Charlie, but says he's through with gambling, as he no longer feels the sensation of a winning streak.

Production Company: Won World for Columbia Pictures
Producers: Robert Altman, Joseph Walsh
Screenplay: Joseph Walsh
Cinematography (Panavision): Paul Lohmann
Sound: Chris McLaughlin, George Wycoff, Jim Webb
Editor: Lou Lombardo
Songs: Phyllis Shotwell
Production Design: Leon Ericksen
Cast: Elliott Gould (*Charlie Waters*), George Segal (*Bill Denny*), Ann Prentiss (*Barbara Miller*), Gwen Welles (*Susan Peters*), Edward Walsh (*Lew*), Joseph Walsh (*Sparkie*), Bert Remsen ('*Helen Brown*'), Barbara London (*Lady on the Bus*), Barbara Ruick (*Reno Barmaid*), Jay Fletcher (*Robber*), Jeff Goldblum (*Lloyd Harris*), Barbara Colby (*Receptionist*), Vince Palmieri (*First Bartender*), Alyce Passman (*Go-Go Girl*), Joanne Strauss (*Mother*), Jack Riley (*Second Bartender*), Sierra Bandit (*Woman at Bar*), John Considine (*Man at Bar*), Eugene Troobnik (*Harvey*), Richard Kennedy (*Used Car Salesman*), John Winston (*Tenor*), Bill Duffy

(*Kenny*), Mike Greene (*Reno Dealer*), Tom Signorelli (*Nugie*), Sharon Compton (*Nugie's Wife*)
109 mins

1975
Nashville

In Nashville, home to country-and-western music, aspiring and successful musicians gather, all to the background of a political campaign for the Replacement Party, whose invisible presidential candidate Hal Philip Walker delivers his speech from a touring van, while John Triplette and local supporter Delbert Reese organize events and sponsorship for him. The main stars approached are seasoned star Haven Hamilton and the popular Barbara Jean, who is recovering from a recent collapse on her arrival at the airport. Visitors to Nashville include runaway Kenny Fraiser and dizzy Albuquerque, as well as Opal, an overinsistent English radio journalist claiming to work for the BBC. At the Grand Ole Opry, black singer Tommy Brown is followed on stage by the recovering Barbara Jean's talented rival, Connie White. Also in the sidelines are a singing trio, Bill, Tom and Mary. While Bill and Mary bicker over their marriage, Tom plays the stud and sleeps with many of the women he encounters, including the groupie Martha and even Delbert's wife Linnea, who sings in a local gospel choir. Meanwhile, Delbert hires the talentless waitress Sueleen Gay for a fund-raising party; when her singing fails to please, she is obliged to strip for the men. After Barbara Jean suffers a breakdown at her comeback concert, her manager and husband Barnett agrees to her participating in a big rally for Walker, a free event. But after she has finished her songs there, Kenny takes a gun from his violin case and shoots her. In the confusion that follows, the microphone is passed to Albuquerque, who seizes her opportunity and raises the spirits of the crowd.

Production Company: American Broadcasting Corporation for Paramount
Producer: Robert Altman
Screenplay: Joan Tewkesbury
Cinematography (Panavision): Paul Lohmann
Sound: Jim Webb, Chris McLaughlin
Editors: Sidney Levin, Dennis Hill
Music Supervision: Richard Baskin
Songs: '200 Years', 'For the Sake of the Children', 'Keep-a-Goin'' (Henry Gibson); 'Yes, I Do' (Lily Tomlin); 'Down to the River' (Smokey Mountain Laurel); 'Let Me Be the One', 'I Never Get Enough' (Gwen Welles); 'Sing a Song' (Lily Tomlin, James Dan Calvert, Donna Denton); 'The Heart of a Gentle Woman' (Dave Peel); 'Bluebird' (Timothy Brown); 'The Day I Looked Jesus in the Eye', 'Memphis', 'Rolling Stone', 'I Don't Know if i Found it in You' (Karen Black); 'Tapedeck in His Tractor (The Cowboy Song)', 'My Idaho Home', 'Dues' (Ronee Blakley); 'Old Man Mississippi' (Misty Mountain Boys); 'One, I Love You' (Henry Gibson, Ronee

Blakley); 'I'm Easy', 'Honey' (Keith Carradine); 'It Don't Worry Me' (Barbara Harris); 'Since You've Gone', 'Trouble in the USA', 'Swing Low, Sweet Chariot', 'Rose's Café', 'My Baby's Cookin' in Another Man's Pan'
Cast: David Arkin (Norman), Barbara Baxley (Lady Pearl), Ned Beatty (Delbert Reese), Karen Black (Connie White), Ronee Blakley (Barbara Jean), Timothy Brown (Tommy Brown), Keith Carradine (Tom Frank), Geraldine Chaplin (Opal), Robert DoQui (Wade), Shelley Duvall (L.A. Joan [Martha]), Allen Garfield (Barnett), Henry Gibson (Haven Hamilton), Scott Glenn (Pfc Glenn Kelly), Jeff Goldblum (Tricycle Man), Barbara Harris (Albuquerque) David Hayward (Kenny Fraiser), Michael Murphy (John Triplette), Allan Nicholls (Bill), Dave Peel (Brad Hamilton), Cristina Raines (Mary), Bert Remsen (Star), Lily Tomlin (Linnea Reese), Gwen Welles (Sueleen Gay), Keenan Wynn (Mr Green), James Dan Calvert (Jimmy Reese), Donna Denton (Diana Reese), Merle Kilgore (Trout), Carol McGinnis (Jewel), Sheila Bailey and Patti Bryant (Smokey Mountain Laurel), Richard Baskin (Frog), Jonnie Barnett, Vassar Clements, Misty Mountain Boys, Sue Barton, Elliott Gould and Julie Christie (Themselves)
161 mins

1976
Buffalo Bill and the Indians, or Sitting Bull's History Lesson
In 1885 Buffalo Bill Cody presents his Wild West Show, employing genuine Indians in fake skirmishes. To his irritation, Ned Buntline, the popular writer who created the Buffalo Bill myth, pays a visit. Meanwhile, Sitting Bull, a political prisoner represented by Indian William Halsey, agrees to participate in the show in return for being allowed to settle nearby with his entourage and be paid six weeks' salary in advance. Then Sitting Bull insists that the recreation of Custer's Last Stand be rendered closer to history, showing how the Sioux were brutally betrayed, and Cody fires him. But he has to hire him back when his star turn, sharpshooter Annie Oakley, objects. When Sitting Bull rides into the arena, he eventually wins the audience over to his side, and Cody feels humiliated. Word arrives that President Grover Cleveland and his wife Frances Folsom plan to visit the show during their honeymoon. Sitting Bull, who has dreamed of meeting the President, has his request denied. He disappears, and Cody hears that he has been shot dead at Standing Rock. But Cody has a sleepless night in which he imagines trying to justify himself to Sitting Bull. The show goes on with Halsey now playing Sitting Bull and accepting defeat at Cody's hands.
Production Company: Dino de Laurentiis Corporation/Lion's Gate Films/Talent Associates-Norton Simon
Producer: Robert Altman
Screenplay: Alan Rudolph, Robert Altman, suggested by the play Indians by Arthur Kopit
Cinematography (Panavision): Paul Lohmann

Sound: Jim Webb, Chris McLaughlin
Editors: Peter Appleton, Dennis Hill
Music: Richard Baskin
Production Design: Tony Masters
Cast: Paul Newman (*William F. Cody, 'Buffalo Bill'*) Joel Grey (*Nate Salisbury*), Burt Lancaster (*Ned Buntline*), Kevin McCarthy (*Major John Burke*), Harvey Keitel (*Ed Goodman*), Allan Nicholls (*Colonel Prentiss Ingraham*), Geraldine Chaplin (*Annie Oakley*), John Considine (*Frank Butler*), Robert DoQui (*Oswald Dart*), Mike Kaplan (*Jules Keen*), Bert Remsen (*Crutch*), Bonnie Leaders (*Margaret*), Noelle Rogers (*Lucille Du Charme*), Evelyn Lear (*Nina Cavalini*), Denver Pyle (*McLaughlin*), Frank Kaquitts (*Sitting Bull*), Will Sampson (*William Halsey*), Ken Krossa (*Johnny Baker*), Fred N. Larsen (*Buck Taylor*), Jerry Duce and Joy Duce (*Trick Riders*), Alex Green and Gary MacKenzie (*Munoz and Manuel, Mexican Whip and Fast Draw Act*), Humphrey Gratz (*Old Soldier*), Pat McCormick (*Grover Cleveland*), Shelley Duvall (*Frances Folsom*), E. L. Doctorow (*O. W. Fizician*), Helen Doctorow (*Aunt Ruth*), Lois Smith (*Mrs Fizician*), Thomas Hal Phillips (*General Benjamin*), John Bianchi (*Captain De Long*), Arlene Donovan (*Huntse Widoe*), Bernard Drew (*Max*), Bruce Lohmann (*Brewster*), Bob Eberle (*Guard*), Patricia Resnick (*Florence Viva*), Monty Westmore (*Make-Up Man*), Joyce Rudolph (*Joyce*)
123 mins
(Cut to 104 mins for European distribution)

1977

3 Women

Texas-born Pinky Rose begins work as a therapist at the Desert Springs Geriatric and Rehabilitation Centre in California. Millie Lammoreaux, also from Texas, becomes her tutor, pretending to a sophistication she clearly lacks and endlessly talking about her ideas of domestic styling. The immature Pinky, devoted to Millie, becomes her room-mate in the Purple Sage Apartments. Millie introduces her to a nearby ranch called Dodge City, owned by former stuntman Edgar Hart and his pregnant wife Willie, who maintains a reserved distance and decorates the place with murals involving strange mythical creatures. When the guests fail to turn up for her party, an angry Millie brings Edgar back to the apartment, and when Pinky is required to leave, she throws herself into the swimming pool. Recovering in hospital, Pinky becomes more assertive and prickly. When Millie brings along an old couple who say they are Pinky's parents, Pinky refuses to recognize them. Edgar arrives one night to say Willie is having her baby, and the two women rush to her aid. Pinky watches as Millie helps deliver a stillborn child. While Edgar dies in mysterious circumstances, the three women set up home together.

Production Company: Lion's Gate Films for 20th Century Fox.
Producer: Robert Altman.

Screenplay: Robert Altman
Cinematography (Panavision): Charles Rosher
Sound: Jim Webb, Chris McLaughlin
Editor: Dennis Hill
Music: Gerald Busby
Visual Consultant: J. Allen Highfill
Cast: Shelley Duvall (*Millie Lammoreaux*), Sissy Spacek (*Pinky Rose*), Janice Rule (*Willie Hart*), Robert Fortier (*Edgar Hart*), Ruth Nelson (*Mrs Rose*), John Cromwell (*Mr Rose*), Sierra Pecheur (*Ms Bunweill*), Craig Richard Nelson (*Dr Maas*), Maysie Hoy (*Doris*), Benito Moreno (*Alcira*), Leslie Ann Hudson (*Polly*), Patricia Ann Hudson (*Peggy*), Beverly Ross (*Deidre Black*), John Davey (*Dr Norton*)
123 mins

1978
A Wedding
At a grand wedding ceremony presided over by the doddery Bishop Martin, Muffin Brenner is married to Dino Corelli. The two families converge at the Corellis' grand mansion on their Midwest estate just as their elderly matriarch, Nettie Sloan, is dying in her bedroom. The family doctor Jules Meecham keeps quiet about it to help Dino's fragile and morphine-addicted mother, Regina, whose husband, Luigi Corelli, once a restaurateur in Italy, is regarded socially as beneath the Sloans. The *nouveau riche* manners of the Breen family pose great problems for wedding co-ordinator Rita Billingsley, especially as none of the invited guests arrive. Mackenzie Goddard, husband to another Sloan sister, Antoinette, takes the opportunity to declare his love for Tulip, the bride's mother. Following more misbehaviour, including the unveiling of a nude portrait of the bride by Nettie's sister, the Brenners are aghast to discover that Buffy, Muffin's silent sister, is pregnant by Dino, though there are other possible fathers among his military academy. In the early hours of the morning, the Brenners leave in disgust but return after coming upon a fatal traffic accident apparently involving the bride and groom. A slanging match between both families follows until Muffin and Dino emerge from upstairs, and it turns out the victims were a friend and ex-girlfriend of the groom. With Nettie's death now known to everyone, Luigi announces that he had made a pact with her that, since he was only a waiter, he would never allow his family to visit the Sloan estate. Having previously been disturbed by the arrival of his brother Dino I, Luigi now feels himself to be a free man.

Production Company: Lion's Gate Films for 20th Century Fox
Producer: Robert Altman
Screenplay: John Considine, Patricia Resnick, Allan Nicholls, Robert Altman, from a story by John Considine and Robert Altman
Cinematography (Panavision): Charles Rosher

Sound: Jim Webb, Chris McLaughlin, Jim Bourgeois, Jim Stuebe
Editor: Tony Lombardo
Music: John Hotchkis, Tom Walls
Cast: Carol Burnett (*Tulip Brenner, mother of the bride*), Paul Dooley (*Snooks Brenner, father of the bride*), Amy Stryker (*Muffin Brenner, the bride*), Mia Farrow (*Buffy Brenner, the bride's sister*), Dennis Christopher (*Hughie Brenner, the bride's brother*), Gerald Busby (*Rev David Ruteledge, Tulip's brother*), Peggy Ann Garner (*Candice Ruteledge, David's wife*), Mark R. Deming (*Matthew Ruteledge, son of David and Candace*), Mary Siebel (*Aunt Marge Spar, Snooks's sister*), Margaret Ladd (*Ruby Spar, Aunt Marge's daughter*), Lesley Rogers (*Rosie Bean, a bridesmaid*), Timothy Thomerson (*Russell Bean, Rosie's husband, a trucker*), Marta Heflin (*Shelby Munker, a bridesmaid*), David Brand, Chris Brand, Amy Brand, Jenny Brand, Jeffrey Jones, Jay D. Jones, Courtney MacArthur and Paul D. Keller III (*The Ruteledge Children*), Lillian Gish (*Nettie Sloan, the groom's grandmother*), Nina Van Pallandt (*Regina Corelli, the groom's mother*), Vittorio Gassman (*Luigi Corelli, the groom's father*), Desi Arnaz Jr (*Dino Corelli, the groom*), Belita Moreno (*Daphne Corelli, the groom's twin sister*), Dina Merrill (*Antoinette Goddard, the groom's aunt*), Pat McCormick (*Mackenzie Goddard, art collector, groom's uncle*), Virginia Vestoff (*Clarice Sloan, the groom's aunt*), Howard Duff (*Dr Jules Meecham, the Corelli family doctor*), Ruth Nelson (*Aunt Beatrice Sloan Cory, Nettie's sister*), Ann Ryerson (*Victoria Cory, Beatrice's granddaughter*), Craig Richard Nelson (*Capt Reedley Roots, faculty member of the groom's military school*), Jeffrey S. Perry (*Bunky Lemay, groom's friend, an usher*), John Cromwell (*Bishop Martin*), Luigi Proietti (*Dino Corelli I, Luigi Corelli's brother*), Geraldine Chaplin (*Rita Billingsley, wedding co-ordinator*), John Considine (*Jeff Kuykendall, chief of security*), Lauren Hutton (*Florence Farmer, the film producer*), Allan Nicholls (*Jake Jacobs, the cameraman*), Maysie Hoy (*Casey, soundperson*), Viveca Lindfors (*Ingrid Hellstrom, the caterer*), Mona Abboud (*Melba Lear, Rita's assistant*), Beverly Ross (*Nurse Janet Schulman*), Harold C. Johnson (*Oscar Edwards, the chef*), Alexander Sopenar (*Victor, the wedding photographer*), Patricia Resnick (*Redford, female security guard*), Dennis Franz (*Koons, male security guard*), Margery Bond (*Lombardo, female security guard*), Cedric Scott (*Randolph, the houseman*), Robert Fortier (*Jim Habor, the gardener*), Maureen Steindler (*Libby Clinton, the cook*), David Fitzgerald (*Kevin Clinton, son of the Corelli cook*), Susan Kendall Newman (*Chris Clinton, Kevin's bride*), Pamela Dawber (*Tracey Farrell, the groom's ex-girlfriend*), Gavan O'Herlihy (*Wilson Briggs, the groom's ex-room-mate*), Bert Remsen (*William Williamson, the only guest*)
125 mins

1979

Quintet

With the planet overwhelmed by a new ice age, and finding no more seals to hunt, Essex returns with his pregnant partner Vivia to the city he left ten years before. Outside, dogs feed on the carcases of the old and sick; inside, the population are absorbed by a board game called Quintet in which the object is to kill one's opponents. Essex's brother Francha takes him to a game which is interrupted by a deadly bomb blast. Essex survives and hunts down the man responsible, Redstone, only to find someone has already killed him. In the pockets of the corpse are the Quintet tokens belonging to Francha and a list of six names – Redstone, Francha, Deuca, Goldstar, St Christopher and Ambrosia. Assumed to be Redstone, Essex visits the Hotel Electra and finds a game in progress but being played for real. Goldstar and Deuca are the next victims, and in spite of Essex's protestations, Ambrosia refuses to give up her role as 'sixth man', the person who arranges the killing order in the game. She in turn fails to dissuade St Christopher from trying to kill Essex, who ignores her warnings. But St Christopher dies in a natural disaster, and Essex kills Ambrosia before she can make her move. In spite of Grigor suggesting that he might make a great player, Essex leaves the city, following the trail of the wild geese.

Production Company: Lion's Gate Films for 20th Century Fox
Producer: Robert Altman
Screenplay: Frank Barhydt, Robert Altman, Patricia Resnick, from a story by Robert Altman, Lionel Chetwynd, Patricia Resnick
Cinematography (Panavision): Jean Boffety
Sound: Robert Gravenor
Editor: Dennis M. Hill
Music: Tom Pierson
Production Design: Leon Ericksen
Cast: Paul Newman (*Essex*), Vittorio Gassman (*St Christopher*), Fernando Rey (*Grigor*), Bibi Andersson (*Ambrosia*), Brigitte Fossey (*Vivia*), Nina Van Pallandt (*Deuca*), David Langton (*Goldstar*), Tom Hill (*Francha*), Monique Mercure (*Redstone's Mate*), Craig Richard Nelson (*Redstone*), Maruska Stankova (*Jaspera*), Anne Gerety (*Aeon*), Michel Maillot (*Obelus*), Max Fleck (*Wood Supplier*), Françoise Berd (*Charity House Woman*)
118 mins

A Perfect Couple

An audio-visual dating agency, 'Great Expectations', brings together Alex Theodopoulos and Sheila Shea at a concert at the Hollywood Bowl. Alex comes from a proud Greek family of classical musicians ruled by his father, Panos, and he is afraid to introduce Sheila to them. She in turn makes excuses to hide her role as a singer in a pop group, Keepin' 'Em Off the Streets. Sheila attempts to find another date, but Alex intervenes and finds out her true identity. But the communal house she lives in, which includes a lesbian couple, proves too much of a distraction for Alex and he smuggles Sheila into the Theodopoulos mansion, with disastrous results. Alex attempts to date someone else without success, and now in love with Sheila, he joins her on tour and becomes a groupie with the band. Still unable to cope with the lifestyle of the younger generation, Alex returns home to find his sister has died from a weak heart after an attempt to break away from the family. Angry at his unforgiving father, Alex leaves home and finds Sheila once again at the Hollywood Bowl, where the group are performing.

Production Company: Lion's Gate Films for 20th Century-Fox
Producer: Robert Altman
Screenplay: Robert Altman, Allan Nicholls
Cinematography (Panavision): Edmond L. Koons
Sound: Robert Gravenor, Don Merritt
Editor: Tony Lombardo
Music: Tom Pierson, Tony Berg, Allan Nicholls
Songs: 'Somp'ins Got a Hold on Me' (Tomi-Lee Bradley, Steven Sharp); 'Hurricane' (Ted Neeley and Keepin' 'Em Off the Streets band); 'Week-End Holiday' (Ted Neeley); 'Won't Somebody Care', 'Lonely Millionaire' (Marta Heflin, Steven Sharp); 'Love is All There is' (Heather McRae); 'Searchin' for the Light' (Tomi-Lee Bradley); 'Fantasy' (Heather McRae and Keepin' 'Em Off the Streets band); 'Don't Take Forever' (Tomi-Lee Bradley and Keepin' 'Em Off the Streets band); 'Let the Music Play' (Keepin' 'Em Off the Streets band); 'Goodbye Friends' (Keepin' 'Em Off the Streets band, including Renn Woods)
Production Design: Leon Ericksen
Cast: Paul Dooley (*Alex Theodopoulos*), Marta Heflin (*Sheila Shea*), Titos Vandis (*Panos Theodopoulos*), Belita Moreno (*Eleousa Theodopoulos*), Henry Gibson (*Fred Bott*), Dimitra Arliss (*Athena*), Allan Nicholls (*Dana '115'*), Ann Ryerson (*Skye '147'*), Poppy Lagos (*Melpomeni Bott*), Dennis Franz (*Costa*), Margery Bond (*Wilma*), Mona Golabek (*Mona*), Terry Wills (*Ben*), Susan Blakeman (*Penelope Bott*), Melanie Bishop (*Star*), Fred Bier and Jette Seear (*The Imperfect Couple*), Ted Neeley (*Teddy*), Heather McRae (*Mary*), Tomi-Lee Bradley (*Sydney-Ray*), Steven Sharp (*Bobbi*), Tom Pierson (*Conductor*), Tony Berg, Craig Doerge, Jeff Eyrich, David Luell, Butch Sandford, Art Wood, Renn Woods (*Keepin' 'Em Off the Streets*)
112 mins

1980
Health (H.E.A.L.T.H.)
A convention of the National H.E.A.L.T.H. ('Happiness, Energy And Longevity Through Health') organization is held in a luxury hotel in St Petersburg, Florida, and two candidates are running for presidency: Esther Brill, an eighty-three-year-old virgin with a tendency to fall into a catatonic state, and Isabella Garnell, an

intellectual reformist. Dick Cavett hosts an aborted television debate with both candidates and White House advisor Gloria Burbank. While trying to maintain fairness, Burbank finds herself besieged by both parties. She is, however, annoyed by Brill's public-relations agent, Harry Wolff, to whom she was once married, and is more impressed by the high-minded Garnell. The next morning the body of an independent candidate, Harold Gainey, is discovered in the hotel swimming pool, but miraculously he comes back to life. Burbank continues to favour Garnell until she meets a strange-looking woman who informs her both she and Garnell had sex-change operations. After she is insulted by a hotel guest calling himself Colonel Cody, Burbank seeks comfort from Harry Wolff and spends the night with him. The following day Gainey is again found at the bottom of the swimming pool. Cavett attempts to tape his show a second time, but it is interrupted by the announcement that Brill has won the election. An argument with the Colonel reveals the strange-looking woman to be political hustler Bobby Hammer in disguise. Wolff explains to Burbank that the Colonel is actually Brill's younger brother Lester, who believes himself to be Buffalo Bill. Feeling that Wolff has taken advantage of her, Burbank leaves the convention in a rage, and while Lester Brill throws a tantrum in the lobby, a departing Cavett encounters Dinah Shore, arriving to cover a hypnotists' convention.

Production Company: Lion's Gate Films for 20th Century Fox
Producer: Robert Altman
Screenplay: Frank Barhydt, Robert Altman, Paul Dooley
Cinematography: Edmond L. Koons
Sound: Robert Gravenor, Don Merritt
Editors: Tony Lombardo, Dennis M. Hill, Tom Benko
Music: Joseph Byrd, Allan Nicholls
Songs: 'Exercise the Right to Vote', 'Health' (The Steinettes), 'Chick and Thin'
Production Design: Robert Quinn
Cast: Glenda Jackson (*Isabella Garnell*), Lauren Bacall (*Esther Brill*), Carol Burnett (*Gloria Burbank*), James Garner (*Harry Wolff*), Dick Cavett (*Himself*), Paul Dooley (*Harold Gainey*), Donald Moffatt (*Colonel Cody*), Henry Gibson (*Bobby Hammer*), Diane Stilwell (*Willow Wertz*), MacIntyre Dixon (*Fred Munson*), Alfre Woodard (*Sally Benbow*), Ann Ryerson (*Dr Ruth-Ann Jackle*), Allan Nicholls (*Jake Jacobs*), Margery Bond (*Daisy Bell*), Georgann Johnson (*Lily Bell*), Mina Kolb (*Iris Bell*), Bob Fortier (*Henderson*), Nancy Foster (*Gilda*), Julie Janney, Diane Shaffer, Nathalie Blossom, Patty Katz (*The Steinettes*)
96 mins

Popeye

Popeye, after surviving a shipwreck, rows in his dingy into the harbour town of Sweethaven and is immediately subject to the taxes demanded from everybody by the mysterious Commodore. Refusing to be discouraged by the antipathy shown towards him by the townspeople, Popeye rents a room from the Oyls, whose daughter Olive is engaged to the unpleasant Captain Bluto. At the Roughhouse Café, Popeye explains to Wimpy that he is trying to find his long lost father, who he believes is still alive. One night Popeye encounters Olive Oyl, who is no longer so keen on Bluto. Someone switches her hamper and in the replacement they discover a baby boy, whom they decide to take in. An angry Bluto destroys the Oyl house and threatens further trouble. Wimpy takes the baby, now named Swee'pea, to the local racetrack, where he reveals an ability to pick winners. Bluto forces Wimpy to kidnap Swee'pea so that the baby can help him find the secret treasure of the Commodore, who turns out to be Popeye's father, held prisoner by Bluto. Popeye rescues his 'pappy' and goes in pursuit of Bluto, who has taken Olive and Swee'pea to Scab Island, where the treasure is located. The treasure turns out to be Popeye's childhood possessions, and when he eats the spinach he once refused, his extraordinary strength helps him defeat Bluto and become a local hero.

Production Company: Paramount/Walt Disney
Producer: Robert Evans
Screenplay: Jules Feiffer, based on characters created by E. C. Segar
Cinematography: Giuseppe Rotunno
Sound: Robert Gravenor
Editors: Tony Lombardo, John W. Holmes, David Simmons
Music: Harry Nilsson, Van Dyke Parks, Tom Pierson
Songs: 'I'm Popeye the Sailor Man', 'I Yam What I Yam', 'He Needs Me', 'Swee'pea's Lullaby', 'Sweethaven', 'Blow Me Down', 'Everything is Food', 'Sailin'', 'It's Not Easy Being Me', 'He's Large', 'I'm Mean', 'Kids'
Production Design: Wolf Kroeger
Cast: Robin Williams (*Popeye*), Shelley Duvall (*Olive Oyl*), Ray Walston (*Poopdeck Pappy*), Paul Dooley (*Wimpy*), Paul L. Smith (*Bluto*), Richard Libertini (*Geezil*), Donald Moffat (*Taxman*), MacIntyre Dixon (*Cole Oyl*), Roberta Maxwell (*Nana Oyl*), Donovan Scott (*Castor Oyl*), Allan Nicholls (*Roughhouse*), Wesley Ivan Hurt (*Swee'pea*), Bill Irwin (*Ham Gravy, the Old Boyfriend*), Robert Fortier (*Bill Barnacle, the Town Drunk*), David McCharen (*Harry Hotcash, the Gambler*), Sharon Kinney (*Cherry, his Moll*), Peter Bray (*Oxblood Oxheart, the Fighter*), Linda Hunt (*Mrs Oxheart, his Mom*), Geoff Hoyle (*Scoop, the Reporter*), Wayne Robson (*Chizzelflint, the Pawnbroker*), Larry Pisoni (*Chico, the Dishwasher*), Carlo Pellegrini (*Swifty, the Cook*), Susan Kingsley (*La Verne, the Waitress*), Michael Christensen (*Splatz, the Janitor*), Ray Cooper (*Preacher*), Noel Parenti (*Slick, the Milkman*), Karen McCormick (*Rosie, the Milkmaid*), John Bristol (*Bear, the Hermit*), Dennis Franz (*Spike*), Carlos Brown (*Slug*), Ned Dowd (*Butch*), Hovey Burgess (*Mort*), Roberto Messina (*Gozo*), Pietro Torrisi (*Bolo*), Margery Bond (*Daisy*), Judy Burgess (*Petunia*), Sandra MacDonald (*Violet*), Eva Knoller (*Min*), Peggy Pisoni (*Pickelina*), Barbara Zegler (*Daphne*), Paul Zegler (*Mayor Stonefeller, the Official*), Pamela Burrell (*Mrs Stonefeller*), David Arkin (*Mailman/Policeman*)

114 mins
(cut to 96 mins for European release by Disney. With Altman's approval, three songs were omitted – 'Sailin' ', sung by Popeye and Olive Oyl, and 'It's Not Easy Being Me' and 'Kids', sung by Poopdeck Pappy)

1982
Come Back to the Five and Dime, Jimmy Dean, Jimmy Dean
McCarthy, Texas, 1975. A twentieth anniversary reunion of the Disciples of James Dean fan club is in preparation at the local Woolworth's five and dime store. Sissy, who still works there, welcomes back Stella Mae, now married to a millionaire, Edna Louise, pregnant for the seventh time, and Mona, the leader of the group. In flashbacks to twenty years before, it is revealed that Joe, an effeminate boy who once swept out the store, was raped by the town bully, Lester T. A strange and sophisticated woman calling herself Joanne turns up and surprises them all by announcing that she is in fact Joe after a sex change. Mona recalls how she once went with Joe to be an extra on *Giant* and spent a night with James Dean, resulting in her son Jimmy, whom she believes is retarded. But Joanne reveals it was she who Mona slept with when she was Joe, and that Sissy married Lester T., who left her after she had a mastectomy. Before the Disciples part again, Mona and Sissy do a McGuire Sisters number with Joanne, just as they did twenty years before with Joe.

Production Company: A Sandcastle 5/A Mark Goodson presentation in association with Viacom
Producer: Scott Bushnell
Screenplay: Ed Graczyk, based on his own play
Cinematography: Pierre Mignon
Sound: Franklin Stettner, Keith Gardner
Editor: Jason Rosenfield
Songs: 'Sincerely', 'If it's a Dream', 'Seems Like Old Times', 'It May Sound Silly', 'You'll Never Know Till Monday', 'Are You Looking for a Sweetheart?', 'I'm in the Mood for Love', 'The Last Dance', 'Miss You', 'Answer Me My Love', 'Kid's Stuff', 'Moon Love'; 'Melody of Love' (The McGuire Sisters); 'Keep on Walkin' ' (Jo Ann Harris); 'How Long Has it Been?' (The Statesmen Quartet); 'Must Jesus Bear the Cross Alone?' (Allan Nicholls)
Production Design: David Gropman
Cast: Sandy Dennis (*Mona*), Cher (*Sissy*), Karen Black (*Joanne*), Sudie Bond (*Juanita*), Kathy Bates (*Stella Mae*), Marta Heflin (*Edna Louise*), Mark Patton (*Joe*), Caroline Aaron (*Martha*), Ruth Miller (*Clarissa*), Gena Ramsel (*Sue Ellen*), Ann Risley (*Phyllis Marie*), Dianne Turley Travis (*Alice Ann*)
110 mins

1983

Streamers

A barracks at the training camp of the 83rd Airborne Division finds a group of young recruits uneasy at being thrown together: the vain, taunting Richie, the oversensitive Billy and the laid-back Roger. Billy is irritated by Richie's homosexual horseplay. Another recruit, Martin, has attempted suicide and been discharged. Carlyle, a black recruit from another barracks, feels oppressed by the army life and the predominance of whites and turns to fellow black Roger for support. Two sergeants, Rooney and Cokes, frequently drunk, regale the younger men with stories about warfare and parachuting. Roger and Carlyle go on a trip to Washington, and Billy joins them, mainly to annoy Richie. When they return, Carlyle responds to Richie's taunts by saying he's his 'punk' and orders the other two to leave the barracks. When Billy refuses a row breaks out, ending in Billy being fatally stabbed. When a drunk Rooney intervenes, he is also stabbed to death. After the bodies have been removed and the MPs arrest Carlyle, Cokes comes looking for Rooney and in his melancholy state expresses sympathy for Richie being homosexual.

Production Company: Streamers International Distributors
Producers: Robert Altman, Nick J. Mileti
Screenplay: David Rabe, based on his own play
Cinematography: Pierre Mignot
Sound: John Pritchett
Editor: Norman Smith
Songs: 'Boy from New York City' (The Ad Libs); 'Boys in the Attic' (Ellie Greenwich); 'What a Guy', 'Let's Go Together', 'The Kind of Boy You Can Forget' (The Raindrops); 'I'm Gonna Make You Mine' (Alan Braunstein)
Production Design: Wolf Kroeger
Cast: Matthew Modine (*William 'Billy' Wilson*), Michael Wright (*Carlyle*), Mitchell Lichtenstein (*Richard 'Richie' Douglas*), David Alan Grier (*Roger Hicks*), Guy Boyd (*Sergeant Rooney*), George Dzundza (*Sergeant Cokes*), Albert Macklin (*Martin*), B. J. Cleveland (*Pfc Bush*), Bill Allen (*Lieutenant Townsend*), Paul Lazar (*MP Lieutenant*), Phil Ward (*MP Sergeant Kilick*), Terry McIlvain (*Orderly*), Todd Savell (*MP Sergeant Savio*), Mark Fickert (*Dr Banes*), Dustye Winniford (*Staff Sergeant*), Robert S. Reed (*MP*)
118 mins

1984

Secret Honor

Richard Milhous Nixon returns to his office late one night, and after setting up his tape recorder, begins his rambling justification of the Watergate affair that caused him to resign the presidency. He is thrown back to his early life, when after a stint as a fairground barker in Arizona his family moved to California. Reading from his memoirs, he talks about his belief in the American Dream, how he was badly treated by Eisenhower, and the Committee of a Hundred who set him up for a political career. Political opponents J. F. Kennedy and Helen Gahagan Douglas are recalled, but his most painful memories are about his domineering mother and Henry Kissinger, who was praised as a peacemaker at his expense. Finally he declares that his position as President became impossible when the Committee of a Hundred were obliging him to continue the Vietnam War to serve their business interests and that the Watergate scandal was a cover for his deeper treason. But after taking up a gun and contemplating suicide, he instead directs his rage towards all his enemies, declaring 'Fuck 'em.'

Production Company: Sandcastle 5. In co-operation with the University of Michigan (Department of Communication), Los Angeles Actors' Theatre
Producer: Robert Altman
Screenplay: Donald Freed, Arthur M. Stone, based on their own play
Cinematography: Pierre Mignot
Sound: Andy Aaron
Editor: Juliet Weber
Music: George Burt
Production Design: Stephen Altman
Cast: Philip Baker Hall (Richard Milhous Nixon)
85 mins

1985

Fool for Love

At the El Royale motel by the Mojave desert, the owner May is disturbed by the arrival of Eddie. He claims he has come to take care of her, while she accuses him of seeing other women, in particular The Countess. As their mutual attraction manifests itself, a family of a father, mother and young daughter arrive at the motel. The father leaves, and May retreats to her cabin to wash and change clothes, provoking Eddie to leave, accusing her of waiting for another man. The father of the family returns, and when the little girl is accidentally locked out, May comforts her. The family then leave, while an old man living in a nearby trailer recalls an incident when he drove his wife and daughter through southern Utah; this then happens to the family, who appear to be an incarnation of the young May and her parents. Eddie returns and taunts May with some rope tricks, but his horseplay is disturbed by a visit from The Countess, who shoots up the motel before driving off. Martin, evidently May's date, turns up, which provokes Eddie to explain that he and May are in a sexual relationship, while being half-brother and -sister. He claims their father lived with two separate families, but one day took Eddie to meet the other family, when he met and fell in love with May. May reveals that it was revealing their love to Eddie's mother which led to her suicide. The old man protests that these stories are distortions of the truth. The Countess reappears and begins a fire with her shooting; Eddie drives off after her, May walks away with her bags, and the old man disappears into his blazing trailer.

Production Company: Cannon
Producers: Menahem Golan, Yoram Globus
Screenplay: Sam Shepard, based on his own play
Cinematography: Pierre Mignot
Sound: Daniel Brisseau
Editors: Luce Grunenwaldt, Steve Dunn
Music: George Burt
Songs: 'Let's Ride', 'It Comes and Goes', 'Go Rosa', 'You Lied Your Way', 'Call Me Up', 'Love Shy', 'First and Last Reel Cowboy', 'Why Wyoming' (Sandy Rogers); 'Honky Tonk Heroes', 'Black Rose' (Waylon Jennings)
Production Design: Stephen Altman
Cast: Sam Shepard (*Eddie*), Kim Basinger (*May*), Harry Dean Stanton (*Old Man*), Randy Quaid (*Martin*), Martha Crawford (*May's Mother*), Louise Egolf (*Eddie's Mother*), Sura Cox (*Teenage May*), Jonathan Skinner (*Young Eddie*), April Russell (*Young May*), Deborah McNaughton (*The Countess*), Lon Hill (*Mr Valdes*)
108 mins

1987
O.C. and Stiggs
(filmed in 1983)
In Phoenix, Arizona, Oliver Cromwell Ogilvy, known as 'O.C.', joins his best friend Mark Stiggs in one of a series of raids on the property of insurance salesman Randall Schwab and his alcoholic wife Elinore, daughter Lenore and her Chinese husband Frankie Tang, and son Randall Jr. They buy an Uzi machine gun from Sponson, a crazed Vietnam veteran, as a present for Lenore and Frankie's wedding. At the wedding, O.C. falls for Michelle and for a while is distracted from his usual wild jinks with Stiggs. But then they go on a trip with their school friend Barney to Flora, Mexico, and there sign up King Sunny Ade and his African Beats to perform at their school concert. After skinny-dipping in the Schwabs' pool with two girl-friends, O.C. and Stiggs meet Pat Coletti, who makes outsize women's clothes. O.C.'s affair with Michelle is not helped by her encounter with his grandfather Gramps, a former policeman who delights in telling bloodthirsty stories. Stiggs decides to raise money for him by staging a benefit for addicts and drunks at the Schwabs' house. But when Randall Schwab returns home, the boys take cover and call in Sponson, who arrives in a helicopter and takes Schwab for a ride. O.C. gets back together with Michelle, and Paul Coletti sends them a cheque to save Gramps from going to an old folks' home.

Production Company: Sand River Productions for MGM/UA
Producers: Robert Altman, Peter Newman

Screenplay: Donald Cantrell, Ted Mann, based on a story by Tod Carroll, Ted Mann
Cinematography: Pierre Mignot
Sound: John Pritchett
Editor: Elizabeth Kling
Music: King Sunny Ade and his African Beats
Production Design: Scott Bushnell
Cast: Daniel H. Jenkins (*Oliver Cromwell Ogilvy, 'O.C.'*), Neill Barry (*Mark Stiggs*), Jane Curtin (*Elinore Schwab*), Paul Dooley (*Randall Schwab*), Jon Cryer (*Randall Schwab Jr*), Laura Urstein (*Lenore Schwab*), Victor Ho (*Frankie Tang*), Ray Walston (*Gramps*), Donald May (*Jack Stiggs*), Carla Borelli (*Stella Stiggs*), Stephanie Elfrink (*Missie Stiggs*), Amanda Hull (*Debbie Stiggs*), James Gilsenan (*Barney Beaugereaux*), Tina Louise (*Florence Beaugereaux*), Cynthia Nixon (*Michelle*), Greg Wangler (*Jefferson Washington*), Dennis Hopper (*Sponson*), Alan Autry (*Goon*), Louis Nye (*Garin Sloan*), Dan Ziskie (*Rusty Galloway*), Martin Mull (*Pat Coletti*), Melvin Van Peebles (*Wino Bob*), Tiffany Helm (*Charlotte*), Dana Anderson (*Robin*), Bob Uecker (*Bob Uecker*), Margery Bond (*Mrs Bunny*), Jeannine Ann Cole (*Nancy Pearson*), Nina Van Pallandt (*Clare Dejavue*), Thomas Hal Phillips (*Hal Phillip Walker*)
109 mins

Beyond Therapy

At Les Bouchons, a French restaurant in New York, Bruce looks forward to a romantic dinner with Prudence, who has answered his lonely-hearts ad. But her nervous state is not helped by his guileless revelation that he is bisexual and living with a man. Both take off for their therapists, Charlotte and Stuart; Bruce sees Charlotte, who treats her patients like children; and Prudence finds herself the subject of Stuart's libidinous advances. The offices of the two therapists are conveniently side by side, and they frequently visit each other for sex. Prudence answers another ad, and though it turns out to be Bruce again, this time a romance ensues. Bruce invites her to his home, but his lover Bob has been tipped off by his mother Zizi as to Bruce's intentions and refuses to leave. Bruce persuades Bob to see Charlotte. Prudence accepts an invitation from Bruce to dine at Les Bouchons, and Charlotte encourages Bob to go as well, as her son Andrew works there as a waiter and is looking for a flat-mate. Stuart masquerades as a waiter in the hope of winning over Prudence. Bob expresses his anger by firing off a gun, but it turns out to be loaded with blanks. Bruce and Prudence realize they love each other and decide to honeymoon in Paris. Bob takes up with Andrew and placates Zizi, while Stuart and Charlotte find refuge once again in sex.

Production Company: New World Pictures/Sandcastle 5
Producers: Roger Berlind, Steven Haft
Screenplay: Christopher Durang, Robert Altman, based on the play by Christopher Durang

Cinematography: Pierre Mignot
Sound: Philippe Lioret, Daniel Belanger
Editors: Steve Dunn, Jennifer Ague
Music: Gabriel Yared
Song: 'Someone to Watch Over Me' (Yves Montand)
Production Design: Stephen Altman
Cast: Julie Hagerty (*Prudence*), Jeff Goldblum (*Bruce*), Glenda Jackson (*Charlotte*), Tom Conti (*Stuart*), Christopher Guest (*Bob*), Geneviève Page (*Zizi*), Cris Campion (*Andrew*), Sandrine Dumas (*Cindy*), Bertrand Bonvoisin (*Manager*), Nicole Evans (*Cashier*), Louise-Marie Taillefer (*Chef*), Matthew Lesniak (*Mr Bean*), Laure Killing (*Charlie*), Gilbert Blin and Vincent Longuemare (*Waiters*)
93 mins

Aria
(Compilation film, with other episodes directed by Nicolas Roeg, Charles Sturridge, Jean-Luc Godard, Julien Temple, Bruce Beresford, Franc Roddam, Ken Russell, Derek Jarman, Bill Bryden)

Les Boréades
In the late eighteenth century, a boisterous, unruly audience, among them whores and lunatics, misbehave at a performance of Rameau's opera *Les Borèades*.

Production Company: Boyd's Co. Film Productions for Lightyear Entertainment, Virgin Vision
Producer: Don Boyd
Screenplay: Robert Altman
Cinematography: Pierre Mignot
Sound: Neil Walwer
Editor: Jennifer Auge
Music: 'Lieux desoles', 'Suite des vents', 'Jouissons! Jouissons!' from Rameau's *Les Borèades*, performed by Jennifer Smith, Anne-Marie Rodde, Philip Langridge, Monteverdi Choir and English Baroque Soloists conducted by John Eliot Gardiner
Production Design: Scott Bushnell, John Hay
Cast: Bertrand Beauvoisin, Cris Campion, Anne Canovas, Sandrine Dumas, Jody Goelb, Julie Hagerty, Philipine Leroy-Beaulieu, Geneviève Page, Delphine Rich, Louis-Marie Taillefer
89 mins (complete film)

1990
Vincent & Theo
1880. Vincent Van Gogh lives by choice in a poor Belgian mining community. After forsaking the church, he declares to his younger brother Theo that he will devote himself to art. Theo works as an assistant in his uncle's art gallery in Paris and supports Vincent, in return for which his brother sends all his paintings to him.

Vincent moves to the Hague to study under Anton Mauve, while Theo opens a new gallery in Montmartre to promote more modern art. Vincent marries his model Sien Hoornik, a prostitute who has become pregnant, and they move to Paris, where Sien finds the poverty of their life unbearable and leaves him. Theo, despairing over a bout of syphilis which delays his marriage to Jo Bonger, proves unable to sell anything by Vincent, who moves to Provence. Theo is disturbed by the paintings that emanate from Arles and pays for Gauguin to join his brother. But Gauguin shows no feeling for the work produced by Vincent, who becomes more and more unbalanced, mutilates his ear and enters an asylum. Dr Gachet, a noted lover of Impressionist art, is persuaded by Theo to help cure Vincent. But after a period of tranquillity, Vincent overhears Gachet warning his daughter Marguerite, who is attracted to the artist, that he is still mad. Vincent commits suicide. Theo is struck with guilt, and in spite of his lack of success, turns his gallery over to Vincent's work. A year later Theo himself succumbs to insanity and dies.

Production Company: Belbo Films (Paris), Central Films (London)
Producers: Ludi Boeken, David Conroy, Emma Hayter
Screenplay: Julian Mitchell
Cinematography: Jean Lepine
Sound: Alain Curvelier
Editors: Françoise Coispeau, Geraldine Peroni
Music: Gabriel Yared
Production Design: Stephen Altman
Cast: Tim Roth (*Vincent Van Gogh*), Paul Rhys (*Theo Van Gogh*), Johanna ter Steege (*Jo Bonger*), Wladimir Yordanoff (*Paul Gaugin*), Jip Wijngaarden (*Sien Hoornik*), Anne Canovas (*Marie*), Hans Kesting (*Andries Bonger*), Adrian Brine (*Uncle Cent*), Jean-François Perrier (*Léon Boussod*), Vincent Vallier (*Rene Valadon*), Peter Tuinman (*Anton Mauve*), Marie-Louise Stheins (*Jet Mauve*), Oda Spelbos (*Ida*), Jean-Denis Monory (*Emile Bernard*), Jean-Pierre Castaldi ('*Pere*' *Tanguy*), Annie Chaplin (*1st Painter*), Humbert Camerlo (*2nd Painter*), Louise Boisvert (*Mme Ginoux*), Sarah Bentham (*Marie Hoornik*), Vincent Souliac (*Paul Millet*), Klaus Stoeber (*Zouave*), Florence Muller (*Rachel*), Viviane Fauny Camerlo (*Mme Viviane*), Alain Vergne (*Dr Rey*), Feodor Atkine (*Dr Peyron*), Jean-Pierre Gos (*Trabuc*), Jean-Pierre Cassel (*Dr Paul Gachet*), Bernadette Giraud (*Marguerite Gachet*), Mogan Mehlem (*M. Ravoux*), Thérèse Crémieux (*Mme Ravoux*)
140 mins
(TV version: 200 mins)

1992
The Player
Griffin Mill, an ambitious young executive at a Hollywood studio, is not only worried by the arrival of another hungry executive, Larry Levy, but also by a series of unsigned postcards threatening his life because of his bad treatment of

a screenwriter. Mill's girlfriend, story editor Bonnie Sherow, suggests that a five-month period is long enough for someone to be so disturbed as to take such action, and looking through his list of unreturned calls, Mill finds the name David Kahane. Tracking down Kahane, Mill first sees his girlfriend June Gudmundsdottir, a painter, at work, and then contrives to run into the writer at a revival movie theatre. They argue, Mill strikes Kahane and accidentally kills him. At the studio the next day Mill is told the police know he was the last person to see Kahane. But another anonymous message arrives, and a worried Mill goes to Kahane's funeral, where he meets and takes home June. In response to another card, Mill goes to the St James Club, where he encounters producer Andy Civella and English director Tom Oakley, who pitch him a dark anti-death penalty drama called *Habeas Corpus*. Mill lets Levy take over the project, which he believes bound for failure. While the police keep the pressure on him about Kahane's murder, Mill pursues June, who puts him off until they go to a desert spa in Mexico. After Mill is not identified by an eyewitness to the murder, he becomes the studio head and makes *Habeas Corpus* into a corny romantic thriller. Bonnie protests and is fired, and as Mill makes his way home to a pregnant June, now his wife, he receives a phone call offering him a script about a producer who gets away with murdering a screenwriter.

Production Company: Avenue Entertainment
Producers: David Brown, Michael Tolkin, Nick Wechsler
Screenplay: Michael Tolkin, based on his own novel
Cinematography: Jean Lepine
Sound: Rich Gooch, John Pritchett
Editor: Geraldine Peroni
Music: Thomas Newman
Songs: 'Snake', 'Drums of Kyoto' (Kurt Newman), 'Precious' (Les Hooper), 'Tema Para Jobin' (Joyce, Milton Nascimento)
Production Design: Stephen Altman
Cast: Tim Robbins (*Griffin Mill*), Greta Scacchi (*June Gudmundsdottir*), Fred Ward (*Walter Stuckel*), Whoopi Goldberg (*Detective Susan Avery*), Peter Gallagher (*Larry Levy*), Brion James (*Joel Levison*), Cynthia Stevenson (*Bonnie Sherow*), Vincent D'Onofrio (*David Kahane*), Dean Stockwell (*Andy Civella*), Richard E. Grant (*Tom Oakley*), Sydney Pollack (*Dick Mellen*), Lyle Lovett (*Detective DeLongpre*), Dina Merrill (*Celia*), Angela Hall (*Jan*), Leah Ayres (*Sandy*), Paul Hewitt (*Jimmy Chase*), Randall Batinkoff (*Reg Goldman*), Jeremy Piven (*Steve Reeves*), Gina Gershon (*Whitney Gersh*), Frank Barhydt (*Frank Murphy*), Mike E. Kaplan (*Marty Grossman*), Kevin Scannell (*Gar Girard*), Margery Bond (*Witness*), Susan Emshwiller (*Detective Broom*), Brian Brophy (*Phil*), Michael Tolkin (*Eric Schecter*), Stephen Tolkin (*Carl Schecter*)
124 mins

1993
Short Cuts

In the suburbs of Los Angeles, helicopters spray for medfly. At a concert given by young cellist Zoe Trainer, Dr Ralph Wyman and his wife Marian make friends with Claire and Stuart Kane. At home, young mother Lois Kaiser earns money by answering sex calls, to the irritation of her husband Jerry. Policeman Gene Shepard argues with his wife Sherri, and goes off to see his mistress, Betty Weathers. Earl Piggot, a chauffeur, drops in at a nightclub where Tess Trainer, Zoe's mother, performs jazz songs. The next day Bill and Honey Bush say goodbye to their neighbours, promising to look after their tropical fish. Earl drops in on his wife Doreen, a waitress at a diner. Stuart Kane and his friends Gordon and Vern stop by on their way to a day out fishing. Helicopter pilot Stormy Weathers finishes his shift and contacts his estranged wife Betty, who is in bed with Gene Shepard. Ann Finnigan calls in at Andy Bitkower's bakery to order a cake for her son Casey's birthday. Doreen is driving home when Casey, on his way to school, steps in front of her and is knocked down. The boy picks himself up and refuses Doreen's help, but later Anne finds him slumped unconscious at home, and on her TV broadcaster husband Howard's advice, takes him to hospital. The fishing party come across the dead body of a woman, but they decide not to let it spoil their trip but report it later. Jerry Kaiser is called by his friend Bill Bush, who proposes they have dinner together with their wives at the neighbours' apartment. Gene makes his weak excuses to his wife before going off on his motorbike, secretly taking the dog with him. After letting the dog go in another neighbourhood, he stops Claire the clown, supposedly for driving too slowly but as an excuse to get her phone number. She drives on to work at the same hospital where Casey was admitted. Dr Wyman tells Anne and Howard not to worry about their comatose son, while Paul, Howard's long-lost father, turns up and explains the reasons for his estrangement. Andy Bitkower disturbs Anne and Howard with abusive calls for not picking up the birthday cake. Back home, Doreen finds Earl unsympathetic to her story, and she is advised by her daughter Honey Bush to leave him. When Zoe fails to get her mother Tess to talk about her dead father, she reacts by slashing her hands and arms with broken glass. In the afternoon, Sherri Shepard is visited by her sister, Marian Wyman, who paints her nude. Gene takes Betty for a birthday meal, suggesting they might be more serious about each other. Back from his fishing trip, Stuart makes love to Claire, but she is disturbed when he tells her how they didn't report the dead body at once. Stormy Weathers, after finding about Betty's affair with Gene, breaks into her home and takes a chainsaw to the furniture. Casey emerges from his coma but dies shortly afterwards. Zoe, shocked by the grief of Casey's parents, seeks solace from her mother Tess, but she is too busy rehearsing her show to care. Zoe locks herself in the garage, waiting for the car exhaust fumes to kill her. Later in the week, Claire and Stuart turn up for a barbecue with Ralph and Marian. Gene returns home to Sherri and the kids and finds their missing dog.

Anne and Howard confront Andy Bitkower, who is filled with remorse. Tess is deeply shocked to find Zoe's body. Doreen and Earl make up their differences. The Bush family join up with the Kaisers for a picnic in the park. Bill and Jerry go their own way in pursuit of two young women cyclists. Jerry suddenly assaults one of them when an earthquake hits the city.

Production Company: Spelling Films International in association with Fine Line Pictures, Avenue Pictures
Producer: Cary Brokaw
Screenplay: Robert Altman, Frank Barhydt, based on the writings by Raymond Carver
Cinematography (Panavision): Walt Loyd
Sound: John Pritchett
Editor: Geraldine Peroni
Music: Mark Isham
Songs: Cello Concerto No. 2 by A. Dvorak, Cello Suite No. 5 by J. S. Bach, 'Schelomo' by E. Bloch, 'Berceuse' from 'The Firebird' by I. Stravinsky (Lori Singer and others); 'I Don't Want to Cry Anymore', 'Punishing Kiss', 'I Don't Know You', 'Conversation on a Bar Stool', 'I'm Gonna Go Fishin' ' (Annie Ross and The Low Note Quintet); 'Blue', 'Nothing Can Stop Me Now', 'Full Moon', 'These Blues', 'Those Blues', 'Imitation of a Kiss' (The Low Note Quintet)
Production Design: Stephen Altman
Cast: Andie MacDowell (*Ann Finnigan*), Bruce Davison (*Howard Finnigan*), Jack Lemmon (*Paul Finnigan*), Zane Cassidy (*Casey Finnigan*), Julianne Moore (*Marian Wyman*), Matthew Modine (*Doctor Ralph Wyman*), Anne Archer (*Claire Kane*), Fred Ward (*Stuart Kane*), Jennifer Jason Leigh (*Lois Kaiser*), Chris Penn (*Jerry Kaiser*), Joseph C. Hopkins (*Joe Kaiser*), Josette Maccario (*Josette Kaiser*), Lili Tyler (*Honey Bush*), Robert Downey Jr (*Bill Bush*), Madeleine Stowe (*Sherri Shepard*), Tim Robbins (*Gene Shepard*), Cassie Friel (*Sandy Shepard*), Dustin Friel (*Will Shepard*), Austin Friel (*Austin Shepard*), Lily Tomlin (*Doreen Piggot*), Tom Waits (*Earl Piggot*), Frances McDormand (*Betty Weathers*), Peter Gallagher (*Stormy Weathers*), Jarrett Lemmon (*Chad Weathers*), Annie Ross (*Tess Trainer*), Lori Singer (*Zoe Trainer*), Lyle Lovett (*Andy Bitkower*), Buck Henry (*Gordon Johnson*), Huey Lewis (*Vern Miller*), Danny Darst (*Aubrey Bell*), Margerie Bond (*Dora Willis*), Robert DoQui (*Knute Willis*), Darnell Williams (*Joe Robbins*)
188 mins

1994

Prêt-à-porter (Ready to Wear)

Paris, the week of the *prêt-à-porter* fashion shows. Olivier de la Fontaine, head of the French Fashion Council, receives a tie in the post with a letter from Sergei, an Italian resident in Moscow. After arguing with his wife Isabella, he puts on the tie and leaves, paying a visit to his lover, fashion designer Simone Lowenthal. At the airport, reporter for an American television fashion channel Kitty Potter interviews various celebrities. They include Regina Krumm of *Elle*, Sissy Wanamaker of *Harper's Bazaar* and Nina Scant of British *Vogue*. Fashion buyer Major Hamilton is ignored by Potter, but his wife Louise Hamilton encounters a *Houston Chronicle* reporter, Abbe Eisenhower, who has left the US without her bags. De La Fontaine meets Sergei, wearing an identical tie, but on their journey into Paris, de la Fontaine chokes to death on a ham sandwich, and Sergei panics and jumps out of the car. At the Grand Hotel, Eisenhower is obliged to share a room with *Washington Post* sportswriter Joe Flynn, who is supposed to follow up the 'murder' of de la Fontaine. Initial animosity between them develops into a sexual fling. English designer Cort Romney with his wife Violetta, and 'street' designer Cy Bianco and his lover and assistant Reggie prepare for their shows, at the same time as the House of Dior, Issey Miyake, Sonia Rykiel and Christian Lacroix. The three highly competitive fashion editors in turn pursue 'hot' photographer Milo O'Brannigan, who manages to humiliate all of them. He is actually working for Jack, Simone Lowenthal's son, who though married to the supermodel Dane, is actually having an affair with her sister Kiki. Sergei and Isabella meet and replay their romance from the time they married forty-two years before in Italy. Both Romney and Bianco have successful shows, but the events are coloured by the revelations that each is cheating with the other's partner. The three editors have their revenge on O'Brannigan when Wanamaker steals his negatives. The 'murder' is shown by the autopsy to have been an accident. Simone shocks everyone by staging her climactic show with all the models entirely nude. Kitty Potter is finally rendered speechless.

Production Company: Miramax Film International
Producer: Robert Altman
Screenplay: Robert Altman, Barbara Shulgasser
Cinematography: Pierre Mignot, Jean Lepine
Sound: Alain Curvelier
Editor: Geraldine Peroni
Music: Michel Legrand
Songs: 'Here Comes the Hotstepper' (Ini Kamoze), 'Here We Come' (Salt'N'Pepa), '70s Love Groove' (Janet Jackson), 'These Boots are Made for Walking' (Sam Phillips), 'Martha' (Eric Mouquet, Michel Sanchez), 'Keep Givin' Me Your Love' (Cece Peniston), 'Supermodel Sandwich' (Terence Trent d'Arby), 'Style is Coming Back in Style' (John Pizzarelli), 'I'm Too Sexy' (Right Said Fred), 'My Girl Josephine' (Supercat), 'Natural Thing' (M People), 'Jump on Top of Me' (The Rolling Stones), 'Pretty' (The Cranberries), 'Close to You' (The Brand New Heavies), 'Get Wild' (NPG), 'Lemon' (U2), 'I Like Your Style' (Tower of Power), 'I Got the Bull By the Horns' (k.d. lang), 'Dopest Ethiopian' (Asante), 'Ruby Baby' (Bjork), 'Be Thankful for What You Got' (William DeVaughn), 'Addicted to Love' (Robert Palmer), 'Unchained Melody' (The Righteous Brothers), 'Blackjack' (Donald Byrd), 'As' (Dag), 'Abat-jour' (Henry Wright), 'Twiggy, Twiggy' (Pizzicato

5), 'Raga' (Jah Wobble), 'How Long Dub' (Soul II Soul), 'Reste sur moi' (Patricia Kass), 'Third Time Lucky' (Basia), 'Same Brown Earth' (Latin Players), 'Violent and Funky' (Infectious Grooves), 'Swamp Thing' (The Groove), 'L'accordeoniste', 'La Coulante du pauvre Jean' (Edith Piaf), 'Transit Ride' (Guru), 'Here We Go' (Stakka Bo), 'La Vie en rose' (Grace Jones); Concerto for Trumpet and Strings by Torelli, Bacarolle by Offenbach, 'The Pirates of Penzance' by Gilbert and Sullivan
Production Design: Stephen Altman
Cast: Danny Aiello (*Major Hamilton*), Anouk Aimée (*Simone Lowenthal*), Lauren Bacall (*Slim Chrysler*), Kim Basinger (*Kitty Potter*), Michel Blanc (*Inspector Forget*), Anne Canovas (*Violetta Romney*), Jean-Pierre Cassel (*Olivier de la Fontaine*), François Cluzet (*Jean-Pierre*), Roissy de Palma (*Pilar*), Rupert Everett (*Jack Lowenthal*), Kasia Figura (*Vivienne*), Teri Garr (*Louise Hamilton*), Richard E. Grant (*Cort Romney*), Linda Hunt (*Regina Krumm*), Sally Kellerman (*Sissy Wanamaker*), Ute Lemper (*Albertine*), Tara Leon (*Kiki Simpson*), Sophia Loren (*Isabelle de la Fontaine*), Lyle Lovett (*Clint Lammeraux*), Chiara Mastroianni (*Sophie Choiset*), Marcello Mastroianni (*Sergei/Sergio*), Tom Novembre (*Reggie*), Stephen Rea (*Milo O'Brannigan*), Sam Robards (*Craig*), Tim Robbins (*Joe Flynn*), Georgianna Robertson (*Dane Simpson*), Julia Roberts (*Anne Eisenhower*), Jean Rochefort (*Inspector Tantpis*), Lili Taylor (*Fiona Ulrich*), Tracey Ullman (*Nina Scant*), Tapa Sudana (*Kerut*), Forest Whitaker (*Cy Bianco*)
133 mins

1996

Kansas City

Kansas City, 1934. The day of the mayoral elections, telegraph operator Blondie O'Hara kidnaps Carolyn Stilton, the wife of presidential advisor Henry Stilton. Blondie needs her to negotiate the return of her husband, Johnny, who is being held by the all-powerful black gangster Seldom Seen. Earlier in the day, Johnny, in connivance with cab driver Blue Green, robbed wealthy black government contractor Sheepshan Red on his way to gamble in Seldom Seen's Hey Hey Club. Johnny wore burnt cork to pose as black, but Seldom discovered the residue on Red's coat and had him captured and brought to the club. Blondie contacts Henry Stilton and tells him to use his connections to ensure Johnny's release or she will shoot his wife. Henry, worried about upsetting the balance of power favouring the Democrats, nevertheless contacts Boss Prendergast for his help. While the musicians play through the night in the club, backstage Seldom Seen taunts Johnny and Blue and eventually has Blue beaten to death in an alley. Blondie, inspired by another viewing of Jean Harlow's latest film, has Carolyn – whose addiction to laudanum has kept her docile and obedient – help her dye her hair once again. The next morning, Johnny returns to Blondie but collapses to reveal his stomach has been cut open. While Blondie weeps over his body, Carolyn picks up her gun, shoots Blondie and walks outside to join Henry in his car.

Production Company: Ciby 2000/Sandcastle 5
Producer: Robert Altman
Screenplay: Robert Altman, Frank Barhydt
Cinematography: Oliver Stapleton
Sound: John Pritchett
Editor: Geraldine Peroni
Music: Hal Willner, Steven Bernstein
Songs: 'Hosts of Freedom' (The Lincoln College Preparatory Academy Band), 'Indiana', 'Blues in the Dark', 'Pagin' the Devil', 'Froggy Bottom', 'Lullaby of the Leaves', 'Queer Notions', 'Tickle Toe', 'Moten Swing', 'I Surrender Dear', 'I Left My Baby', 'Yeah Man', 'Lafayette', 'Solitude' (musicians of The Hey-Hey Club)
Production Design: Stephen Altman
Cast: Jennifer Jason Leigh (*Blondie O'Hara*), Miranda Richardson (*Carolyn Stilton*), Harry Belafonte (*Seldom Seen*), Michael Murphy (*Henry Stilton*), Dermot Mulroney (*Johnny O'Hara*), Steve Buscemi (*Johnny Flynn*), Brooke Smith (*Babe Flynn*), Jane Adams (*Nettie Bolt*), Jeff Feringa (*Addie Parker*), A. C. Smith (*Sheepshan Red*), Martin Martin (*'Blue' Green*), Albert J. Burnes (*Charlie Parker*), Ajia Mignon Johnson (*Pearl Cummings*), Tim Snay (*Rally Speaker*), Tawanna Benbow (*Rose*), Cal Pritner (*Governor Parker*), Jerry Fornelli (*Tom Prendergast*), Michael Ornstein (*Jackie Giro*), Michael Carozzo (*Charlie Gargotta*), Joe Dirgirolamo (*John Lazia*)
The Hey Hey Club musicians: James Carter, Craig Handy, David Murray, Joshua Redman (tenor saxophones), Jesse Davis, David 'Fathead' Newman Jr (alto saxophones), Don Byron (clarinet/baritone saxophone), Olu Dara, Nicholas Payton, James Zollar (trumpet), Curtis Fowlkes, Clark Gayton (trombone), Victor Lewis (drums), Geri Allen, Cyrus Chestnut (piano), Ron Carter, Tyrone Clark, Christian McBride (bass), Russell Malone, Mark Whitfield (guitar), Kevin Mahogany (vocalist)
115 mins

1998
The Gingerbread Man
In Savannah, Georgia, successful local attorney Rick Magruder gives a lift home after a party to Mallory, a waitress. He sleeps with her and the next day discovers she is being stalked by her father, Dixon Doss, who has organized a cult around him. Dixon is arrested, and a judge commits him for psychiatric evaluation. When his followers break into the asylum and release their leader, Magruder hires private detective Clyde Pell to protect Mallory. Magruder then takes his two children out of school and joins Mallory in a hotel, but the children are kidnapped. He persuades Mallory to take him to Dixon's hiding place, where in defending himself he shoots Dixon dead. The children are found safe, but Magruder is arrested for murder. Preparing his defence, Magruder finds out that Mallory is not, as she

claims, divorced from her husband Pete. He tricks Mallory by lying about how much Dixon has left her in his will and tracks her to a rendezvous with her husband. Magruder discovers that Clyde Pell has been murdered, and when he fights with Pete in a storm, Mallory kills her husband with a flare gun. Magruder disarms her before she can kill him, and she is arrested, but his career is in ruins.

Production Company: Polygram Filmed Entertainment presents an Island Pictures/ Enchanter Entertainment production
Producer: Jeremy Tannenbaum
Screenplay: Al Hayes, based on an original story by John Grisham
Cinematography: Changwei Gu
Sound: John Pritchett
Editor: Geraldine Peroni
Music: Mark Isham
Production Design: Stephen Altman
Cast: Kenneth Branagh (*Rick Magruder*), Embeth Davidtz (*Mallory Doss*), Robert Downey Jr (*Clyde Pell*), Daryl Hannah (*Lois Harlan*), Robert Duvall (*Dixon Doss*), Tom Berenger (*Pete Randle*), Famke Janssen (*Leeanne*), Clyde Hayes (*Carl Alden*), Mae Whitman (*Libby*), Jesse James (*Jeff*), Troy Beyer (*Konnie Dugan*), Julia R. Perce (*Cassandra*), Danny Darst (*Sheriff Hope*), Sonny Seiler (*Phillip Dunson*), Walter Hartridge (*Edmund Hess*), Vernon E. Jordan Jr (*Larry Benjamin*), Lori Beth Sikes (*Betty*), Rosemary Newcott (*Dr Bernice Sampson*), Wilbur T. Fitzgerald (*Judge Russo*), David Hirsberg (*Tom Cherry*), Paul Garden (*Judge Cooper*)
114 mins

1999
Cookie's Fortune

Jewel Mae 'Cookie' Orcutt lives alone in a mansion house in the Deep South, lamenting her dead husband Buck. Her only real friend is Willis, a middle-aged black man who does odd jobs for her. She is in dispute with her two nieces, Camille Dixon and Cora Duvall, but dotes on Cora's daughter Emma, who has returned to town to work for the local catfish supplier and is in love with a local young cop. But before she and Cookie can meet again, the old lady shoots herself. Camille and Cora, busy with the local Easter pageant play, a free version of Oscar Wilde's play *Salome*, come by the house, and to avoid scandal, Camille eats the suicide note and makes Cookie's death look like a murder. Willis, the only suspect, is arrested and placed in jail, even though no one believes him capable of such an act. Following a protracted investigation, blood marks are found at the crime scene that only correspond to Camille's group, and she is arrested. Cookie's will is read out, and everything goes to Willis, who turns out in fact to be her closest relative. Meanwhile, Emma learns that Camille is her real mother. Only Cora can prove Camille's innocence, but she seems determined to follow her sister's previous instructions not to suggest it was anything but a murder. Willis is released, and Camille is imprisoned, where she has a mental breakdown.

Production Company: October Films presents a Sandcastle 5 and Elysian Dreams production
Producers: Robert Altman, Etchie Stroh
Screenplay: Anne Rapp
Cinematography: Toyomichi Kurita
Sound: Mark Weingarten
Editor: Abraham Lim
Music: David A. Stewart
Production Design: Stephen Altman
Cast: Glenn Close (*Camille Dixon*), Julianne Moore (*Cora Duvall*), Liv Tyler (*Emma Duvall*), Chris O'Donnell (*Jason Brown*), Charles S. Dutton (*Willis Richland*), Patricia Neal (*Jewel Mae 'Cookie' Orcutt*), Ned Beatty (*Lester Boyle*), Courtney B. Vance (*Otis Tucker*), Donald Moffat (*Jack Palmer*), Lyle Lovett (*Manny Hood*), Danny Darst (*Billy Cox*), Matt Malloy (*Eddie 'The Expert' Pitts*), Niecy Nash (*Wanda Carter*), Randle Mell (*Patrick Freeman*), Rufus Thomas (*Theo Johnson*), Ruby Wilson (*Josie Martin*), Preston Strobel (*Ronnie Freeman*)
118 mins

2000
Dr T and the Women
Dallas, Texas. Dr Sullivan Travis – or Dr T, as he's called by everyone – is the top gynaecologist in the city, his waiting room always bursting with eager patients, keeping his chief nurse Carolyn very busy. But Dr T's wife Kate is slipping into madness, his sister-in-law Peggy has moved in with her three young daughters, and his younger daughter Dee Dee is about to get married. His chief form of relaxation is with his male friends on shooting expeditions or at the golf club, where he meets the new pro, Bree Davis. After Kate strips naked in a shipping mall, she is committed to a home. Dr T begins an affair with Bree, enchanted by her casual attitude to life. A friend of Dee Dee's from college, Marilyn, arrives to be maid of honour and earns the dislike of Dr T's elder daughter Connie, a conspiracy theorist obsessed with the Kennedy assassination. Dr T learns that Kate wants a divorce, while Connie reveals to him that Marilyn and Dee Dee are ex-lovers. Confused by everything happening around him, Dr T's befuddlement leads Carolyn to make an unsuccessful pass at him. At the wedding, a storm brews up, and at the crucial moment Dee Dee decides to run off with Marilyn. Dr T turns to Bree to start afresh with him, but it seems she has already begun an affair with one of his hunting pals. He drives off into the heart of the storm, and when his car is sucked up by a tornado, he finds himself in a desert near a Mexican village, where he is called upon to deliver a baby boy.

Production Company: Initial Entertainment Group presents a Sandcastle 5 production
Producers: Robert Altman, James McLindon
Screenplay: Anne Rapp
Cinematography: Jan Kiesser
Sound: John Pritchett
Editor: Geraldine Peroni
Music: Lyle Lovett
Songs: 'You've Been So Good up to Now', 'She's Already Made Up Her Mind', 'Ain't It Something' (Lyle Lovett)
Production Design: Stephen Altman
Cast: Richard Gere (*Dr Sullivan 'Dr T' Travis*), Helen Hunt (*Bree Davis*), Farrah Fawcett (*Kate Travis*), Laura Dern (*Peggy*), Shelley Long (*Carolyn*), Tara Reid (*Connie Travis*), Kate Hudson (*Dee Dee Travis*), Liv Tyler (*Marilyn*), Robert Hays (*Harlan*), Matt Malloy (*Bill*), Andy Richter (*Eli*), Lee Grant (*Dr Harper*), Janine Turner (*Dorothy Chambliss*), Holly Pelham-Davis (*Joanne*), Jeanne Evans (*First Exam Patient*), Ramsey Williams (*Menopausal Patient*), Dorothy Deavers (*Patient with Cane*)
122 mins

2001

Gosford Park

Southern England, 1932. A large group of landed gentry and their servants arrive for a shooting party at Gosford Park, the country estate of Sir William McCordle and his wife Lady Sylvia. Aside from relatives, the guests include the popular composer and singer Ivor Novello and Hollywood film producer Morris Weissman, who is planning a Charlie Chan movie set in England. Many of the party resent Sir William as a self-made man rather than a true aristocrat. Downstairs, the regular servants are suspicious of Weissman's young American valet Henry Denton, who is in fact an actor researching a role and is happy to dispense sexual favours, which are welcomed by Lady Sylvia. While out shooting, Sir William is nearly injured in a shotgun blast. At dinner that night, Lt Commander Anthony Meredith, Lady Sylvia's brother-in-law, is annoyed that Sir William has backed out of a business venture. The Hon. Freddie Nesbitt is blackmailing Sir William's daughter Isobel to secure himself a job. The housemaid Elsie, who had an affair with Sir William, becomes incensed at their taunts and intervenes, which leads to her being instantly sacked. Tired of being insulted by his wife, Sir William retires to his study and is found murdered. Inspector Thompson arrives on the scene and finds out that he was murdered twice, since he was stabbed after being poisoned. One of the visiting maids, Mary Maceachran, discovers that one of the valets, Robert Parks, is in fact the illegitimate son of Sir William and the housekeeper, Mrs Wilson, from the time she worked in one of his factories. It also turns out that Mrs Croft, the cook, is the sister of Mrs Wilson, though the two remained distant for many years. Unlike the Inspector, Mary deduces that Mrs Wilson poisoned Sir William, knowing that Parks intended to kill him, and that it was Parks who stabbed the corpse. With most of the guests unaware of what has really transpired, they leave the estate.

Production Company: Capitol Films and The Film Council present in association with USA Films a Sandcastle 5 production in association with Chicagofilms and Medusa Film
Producers: Robert Altman, Bob Balaban, David Levy
Screenplay: Julian Fellowes, based on an idea by Robert Altman, Bob Balaban
Cinematography: Andrew Dunn
Sound: Peter Glossop
Editor: Tim Squyres
Music: Patrick Doyle
Songs: 'What a Duke Should Be', 'Nuts in May', 'The Land of Might-Have-Been', 'And Her Mother Came Too', 'I Can Give You the Starlight', 'Why Isn't it You?', 'Keep the Home Fires Burning' (Jeremy Northam as Ivor Novello); 'Waltz of My Heart', 'Glamorous Night' (Christopher Northam); 'The Way it's Meant to Be' (Abigail Doyle)
Production Design: Stephen Altman
Cast: Above Stairs – Maggie Smith (*Constance Trentham*), Michael Gambon (*William McCordle*), Kristin Scott Thomas (*Sylvia McCordle*), Camilla Rutherford (*Isobel McCordle*), Charles Dance (*Raymond Stockbridge*), Geraldine Somerville (*Louisa Stockbridge*), Tom Hollander (*Lt Commander Anthony Meredith*), Jeremy Northam (*Ivor Novello*), Bob Balaban (*Morris Weissman*), James Wilby (*Freddie Nesbitt*), Claudie Blakley (*Mabel Nesbitt*), Laurence Fox (*Rupert Standish*), Trent Ford (*Jeremy Blond*), Ryan Phillippe (*Henry Denton*); *Visitors* – Stephen Fry (*Inspector Thompson*), Ron Webster (*Constable Dexter*); *Below Stairs* – Kelly Macdonald (*Mary Maceachran*), Clive Owen (*Robert Parks*), Helen Mirren (*Mrs Wilson*), Eileen Atkins (*Mrs Croft*), Emily Watson (*Elsie*), Alan Bates (*Jennings*), Derek Jacobi (*Probert*), Richard E. Grant (*George*), Jeremy Swift (*Arthur*), Sophie Thompson (*Dorothy*), Meg Wynn Owen (*Lewis*), Adrian Scarborough (*Barnes*), Frances Low (*Sarah*), Joanna Maude (*Renee*), Teresa Churcher (*Bertha*), Sarah Flind (*Ellen*), Finty Williams (*Janet*), Emma Buckley (*May*), Lucy Cohu (*Lottie*), Laura Harling (*Ethel*), Tilly Gerrard (*Maud*), Will Beer (*Albert*), Leo Bill (*Jim*), Gregor Henderson Begg (*Fred*), John Atterbury (*Merriman*), Frank Thornton (*Mr Burkett*), Ron Puttock (*Strutt*)
137 mins

2003

The Company
One of the Joffrey Ballet company in Chicago is Ry, a young, up-and-coming dancer who has just broken up with her boyfriend and moonlights as a waitress in a

bar. The company is run by the flamboyant director Alberto Antonelli, who pushes everyone to extremes in search of excellence. At an outdoor performance, Ry bravely dances on during a storm in a *pas de deux* with male lead Domingo Rubio and is acclaimed for it. She begins a romance with a young chef, Josh, though their time together is limited. During the many rehearsals for an epic fantasy ballet 'The Blue Snake', there are recriminations and injuries, but Ry does well until the opening night, when an accident forces her to abandon the performance. The show goes on, and Ry is consoled by Josh in the wings.

Production Company: Capitol Films presents in association with CP Medien a Killer Films/John Wells production in association with First Snow Productions and Sandcastle 5 Productions
Producers: David Levy, Joshua Astrachan, Neve Campbell, Robert Altman, Christine Vachon, Pamela Koffer
Screenplay: Barbara Turner, from a story by Barbara Turner and Neve Campbell
Cinematography: Andrew Dunn
Sound: Peter Glossop
Editor: Geraldine Peroni
Production Design: Gary Baugh
Music: Van Dyke Parks
Song: 'My Funny Valentine' (Elvis Costello, Lee Wiley, Chet Baker, Kronos Quartet)
Ballets: 'Tensile Involvement' (Alwin Nikolais), 'Suite Saint-Saens' (Gerald Arpino), 'Trinity' (Gerald Arpino), 'Light Rain' (Gerald Arpino), 'My Funny Valentine' (Lar Lubovitch), 'Creative Force' (Laura Dean), 'La vivandi e re pas de six' (Arthur Saint-Leon), 'White Widow' (Moses Pendleton), 'Strange Prisoners' (Davis Robertson), 'The Blue Snake' (Robert Desrosiers)
Cast: Neve Campbell (*Ry*), Malcolm McDowell (*Alberto Antonelli*), James Franco (*Josh*), Barbara Robertson (*Harriet*), William Dick (*Edouard*), Susie Cusack (*Susie*), Marilyn Dodds Frank (*Ry's mother*), John Lordan (*Ry's father*), Mariann Mayberry (*Stepmother*), Roderick Peeples (*Stepfather*), Yasen Peyankov (*Justin's Mentor*), The Joffrey Dancers – David Robertson (*Alec*), Deborah Dawn (*Deborah*), John Gluckman (*John*), David Gombert (*Justin*), Suzanne L. Prisco (*Suzanne*), Domingo Rubio (*Domingo*), Emily Patterson (*Noel*), Maia Wilkins (*Maia*), Sam Franke (*Frankie*), Trinity Hamilton (*Trinity*), Julianne Kepley (*Julianne*), Valerie Robin (*Veronica*), Deanne Brown (*Dana*), Michael Smith (*Michael*), Michael Roy Prescott, Lar Lubovitch, Robert Desrosiers (*The Choreographers*), Charthel Arthur, Cameron Basden (*The Ballet Mistresses*), Mark Goldweber, Peter Lockett, Adam Sklute (*The Ballet Masters*)
112 mins

Films as Producer

1977
Welcome to L.A.
Director: Alan Rudolph
Producer: Robert Altman
Production Company: Lions Gate Films Inc
Screenplay: Alan Rudolph, based on the musical suite *City of the One-Night Stands* by Richard Baskin
Cinematography: Dave Myers
Sound: Jim Webb, Chris McLaughlin
Editors: William A. Sawyer, Tom Walls
Music: Richard Baskin
Cast: Keith Carradine, Sally Kellerman, Geraldine Chaplin, Harvey Keitel, Lauren Hutton, Viveca Lindfors, Sissy Spacek, Denver Pyle, John Considine, Richard Baskin, Allan Nicholls, Cedric Scott, Mike Kaplan, Diahann Abbott
106 mins

The Late Show
Director: Robert Benton
Production Company: Lions Gate Films Inc/Warner Bros
Producer: Robert Altman
Screenplay: Robert Benton
Cinematography: Charles Rosher
Sound: Jim Webb, Chris McLaughlin
Editors: Lou Lombardo, Peter Appleton
Music: Ken Wannberg
Production Design: J. Allen Highfill
Cast: Art Carney, Lily Tomlin, Bill Macy, Eugene Roche, Joanna Cassidy, John Considine, Ruth Nelson, John Davey, Howard Duff, Lynn Zuckerman
93 mins

1978
Remember My Name
Director: Alan Rudolph
Production Company: Lions Gate Films Inc
Producer: Robert Altman
Screenplay: Alan Rudolph
Cinematography: Tak Fujimoto
Sound: Robert Gravenor, Chris McLaughlin
Editor: Thomas Walls, William A. Sawyer
Music: Alberta Hunter
Cast: Geraldine Chaplin, Anthony Perkins, Moses Gunn, Berry Berenson, Jeff

257

Goldblum, Timothy Thomerson, Alfre Woodard, Marilyn Coleman, Jeffrey S. Perry, Carlos Brown, Dennis Franz
94 mins

Rich Kids
Director: Robert M. Young
Production Company: Lions Gate Films Inc
Producer: Robert Altman
Screenplay: Judith Ross
Cinematography: Ralf Bode
Sound: Robert Gravenor
Editor: Edward Beyer
Music: Craig Doerge, Allan Nicholls
Production Design: David Mitchell
Cast: Trini Alvarado, Jeremy Levy, Kathryn Walker, John Lithgow, Terry Kiser, David Selby, Roberta Maxwell, Paul Dooley, Irene Worth, Kathryn Grody, Diane Stilwell, Diane Kirksey, Beatrice Winde, Jill Eikenberry, Olympia Dukakis, Patti Hansen
101 mins

1994
Mrs Parker and the Vicious Circle
Director: Alan Rudolph
Production Company: Miramax International in association with Fine Line Pictures
Producer: Robert Altman
Screenplay: Alan Rudolph, Randy Sue Coburn
Cinematography: Jan Kiesser
Sound: Richard Nicol
Editor: Suzy Elmiger
Music: Mark Isham
Production Design: François Seguin
Cast: Jennifer Jason Leigh, Campbell Scott, Matthew Broderick, Andrew McCarthy, Tim McGowan, Nick Cassavetes, Gary Basaraba, Jake Johannsen, Chip Zien, Matt Malloy, Sam Robards, Martha Plimpton, Jane Adams, David Thornton, Leni Parker, Rebecca Miller, David Gow, Gwyneth Paltrow, James LeGros, Heather Graham, Amelia Campbell, Lili Taylor, Jennifer Beals, Gabriel Gascon, Peter Gallagher, Jean-Michael Henry, Wallace Shawn, Malcolm Gets, Keith Carradine, Stephen Baldwin, Peter Benchley, Mina Badie, Jon Favreau, Randy Lowell
124 mins

1997

Afterglow
Director: Alan Rudolph
Production Company: Moonstone Entertainment presents a Sandcastle 5 and Elysian Dreams production
Producer: Robert Altman
Screenplay: Alan Rudolph
Cinematography: Toyomichi Kurita
Sound: Claude La Haye
Editor: Suzy Elmiger
Music: Mark Isham
Production Design: François Seguin
Cast: Nick Nolte, Julie Christie, Lara Flynn Boyle, Jonny Lee Miller, Jay Underwood, Domini Blythe, Yves Corbeil, Alan Fawcett, Michelle-Barbara Pelletier, France Castel, Geneviève Bissonnette, Claudia Besco
114 mins

1998

Liv
Director: Edoardo Ponti
Production Company: E-Squared Films
Producer: Edoardo Ponti
Executive Producers: Robert Altman, Michelangelo Antonioni, Carlo Ponti
Screenplay: Edoardo Ponti
Cinematography: Rogalio Gonzalez-Abraldes
Sound: Ian Melchinger
Editor: Sabine El Chamaa
Music: Zbigniew Priesner
Production Design: Brooks Rawlins
Cast: Elizabeth Guber, Sandra Seacat, Raymond J. Barry, Elaine Kagan, Mil Nicholson, Vanessa Roth
38 mins

2000

Roads and Bridges
Director: Abraham Lim
Production Company: Celestial Entertainment
Producers: Marc H. Glick, Abraham Lim
Executive Producer: Robert Altman
Screenplay: Abraham Lim
Cinematography: Diego Quemada, Robert Learner, Denis Maloney

Sound: Frank Bradley
Editor: Abraham Lim
Music: Bradford Athey, Adam Gorgoni
Production Design: Abraham Lim, Daryl Locke
Cast: Emmet Brennan, Abraham Lim, Carter Williams, Gregory Sullivan, Soon-Teck Oh, Jim Arman, Joe Michaelski
105 mins

Trixie
Director: Alan Rudolph
Production Company: Pandora and Sony Pictures Classics present a Sandcastle 5 production
Producer: Robert Altman
Screenplay: Alan Rudolph, from a story by Alan Rudolph and John Binder
Cinematography: Jan Kiesser
Sound: Rick Patton
Editor: Michael Ruscio
Music: Mark Isham, Roger Neill
Production Design: Richard Paris, Linda Del Rosario
Cast: Emily Watson, Nick Nolte, Dermot Mulroney, Nathan Lane, Brittany Murphy, Lesley Ann Warren, Will Patton, Stephen Lang, Mark Acheson
111 mins

The Calvin Films

Of an estimated sixty short films Robert Altman made during his time at the Calvin Company, the following have achieved note.

Modern Football (1951)
Advice and illustration of how American football should be played, complete with a dream sequence.

The Sound of Bells (1952)
One Christmas, Santa Claus drives into a gas station, and discovering he is low on cash, instead promises the attendant many new customers – and his promise comes true, providing many examples of how best to run such a business.

King Basketball (1952)
Practical advice on how to play better basketball, prefaced by a visit to a game from a film director – Altman himself.

The Last Mile (1953)
A condemned murderer walks 'the last mile' to the electric chair, intercut with car crashes that cause many more deaths on the public highway.

Modern Baseball (1953)

Instruction on baseball techniques, with contributions from famous players such as Ford Frick, Connie Mack, Lou Boudreau, Casey Stengel, Smokey Burgess and Roy Campanella.

The Dirty Look (1954)

Sponsored by Gulf Oil and featuring an over-talkative barber played by William Frawley.

The Builders (1954)

Sponsored by the Southern Pine Association.

Better Football (1954)

William Frawley appears as a coach always ready with a quip.

The Perfect Crime (1955)

A vivid comparison is drawn between the murder of a mother and child during the robbery of a grocery store, when the killer is apprehended, with a crash caused by reckless driver that causes the deaths of his own wife and child. Sponsored by Caterpillar and the National Safety Council.

The Magic Bond (1956)

Made for the Veterans of Foreign Wars, and featuring their parade, this is a hymn of praise to the military spirit and criticism of the neglect of war veterans. The opening scene is a recreation of an army squadron under siege.

Television – First Period 1953–68

1953

Pulse of the City (plus co-creator, co-producer)

An anthology series comprising fifteen-minute dramas filmed in Kansas City, on which Altman shared production and direction with Robert Woodburn and used local talent, mainly from Calvin productions. Shown on the local WABD (DuMont) station.

1957

Suspicion

'Heartbeat' (production consultant only)

Episode of anthology series produced by Alfred Hitchcock on which Altman served as a production consultant and second-unit director on location in New York City. 'Heartbeat', directed by Robert Stevens, featured David Wayne as a man with a heart condition on a fatal wild weekend after his doctor has told him all is well. In supporting roles were Barbara Turner and Warren Beatty. Shown on CBS.

1957–8
Alfred Hitchcock Presents
'The Young One'; 'Together'

Notable show that ran for seven years, produced and presented by the famously rotund director and delivering stories of a macabre, suspenseful nature, always with a sting in their tail, and directed by such luminaries as William Friedkin, Arthur Hiller, Stuart Rosenberg, Sydney Pollack and the master himself. Shown on CBS.

1958
M Squad
'Lovers' Lane Killing'

Half-hour crime show featuring Lee Marvin as a tough plainclothes homicide detective in Chicago. Shown on NBC.

1958–9
Whirlybirds
'The Story of Sister Bridget (Teenage Robber)'; 'The Midnight Show'; 'Act of Fate (Witnesses)'; 'Road Block (Bank Robber)'; 'Rest in Peace (Merger)'; 'Guilty of Old Age'; 'A Matter of Trust'; 'Experiment X-74'; 'Christmas in June'; 'Time Limit'; 'The Big Lie (Billy and the Whirlybirds)'; 'Till Death Do Us Part'; 'The Perfect Crime (Confession of Murder)'; 'The Unknown Soldier (M.I.A.)'; 'Two of a Kind'; 'In Ways Mysterious'; 'The Black Maria'; 'The Sitting Duck'

Popular series produced at Desilu, often described as 'a Western with helicopters', in which two Californian pilots played by Kenneth Tobey and Craig Hill are involved in rescue missions and the pursuit of criminals. Syndicated.

The Millionaire
'The Dan Howell Story'; 'Millionaire Pete Hopper (Afraid of the Dark)'; 'Millionaire Hank Butler (Baby)'; 'Millionaire Angela Temple (Study in Terror)'; 'Millionaire Alicia Osante (Beauty and the Sailor)' (co-scripted only); 'Millionaire Henry Banning (The Show Off)' (co-scripted only); 'Millionaire Karl Miller (The Search)'; 'Millionaire Lorraine Daggett (The Beach Story)' (story only); 'Millionaire Doctor Joseph Frye (The Doctor's Dilemma)'; 'Millionaire Maureen Reynolds (Return . . . Deceased)'; 'Millionaire Sergeant Matthew Brogan (The Richest Sergeant in the World)'; 'Millionaire Andrew C. Cooley (Andy and Clara)' (plus script); 'Millionaire Jackson Greene (Beatnik)'; 'Millionaire Timothy MacKail (Taxi!)'

Hour-long shows produced independently by Don Fedderson which always began with the shadowy figure of John Beresford Tipton offering a cheque for a million dollars to an individual whose fate – comic or tragic – would then be followed. Shown on CBS.

1959
Hawaiian Eye
'Three Tickets to Lani'

One-hour show made at Warner Bros about a detective agency, Hawaiian Eye Private Investigations, based in a Honolulu hotel and featuring Bob Conrad and Anthony Eisley as the two slick detectives and Connie Stevens as a scatty nightclub singer and photographer. Shown on ABC.

1959–60
The Troubleshooters
'Liquid Death'; 'Disaster (The Law and the Profits)'; 'Trouble at Elbow End'; 'Lower Depths'; 'Tiger Culhane'; 'Moment of Terror'; 'Gino' (plus co-script); 'Swing Shift (Trouble at the Orphanage)'; 'Harry Maur'; 'The Town That Wouldn't Die'; 'Senorita'; 'Fire in the Hole'; 'No Stone Unturned'; 'The Carnival (The Cat-Skinner)' (plus co-script)

Half-hour dramas produced by Fredrick Ziv and United Artists and starring Keenan Wynn and Bob Mathias as the leaders of a construction gang tackling difficult and dangerous jobs involving dams, roads, bridges and canals. The cast also included Robert Fortier and Chet Allen. Shown on NBC.

U.S. Marshall (Sheriff of Conchise)
'The Third Miracle'; 'Sweepstake Charlie'; 'Tarnished Star'; 'Paper Bullets'; 'Triple Cross'; 'Dead End'; 'Rest in Peace'; 'The High Fence'; 'All's Not Gold That Glitters'; 'Death and Taxes'; 'Kill or Be Killed'; 'Special Delivery'; 'Backfire'; 'Assignment Crime'; 'Tapes for Murder'

Half-hour series produced at Desilu featuring John Bromfield as Frank Morgan, a contemporary Federal Marshal in Conchise County, Arizona. Syndicated.

Sugarfoot
'Apollo with a Gun'; 'The Highbinder'

Western series made at Warner Bros starring Will Hutchins as a correspondence-school law graduate known as 'Sugarfoot', journeying round the West seeking his fortune. Shown on ABC.

1960
The Man from Blackhawk
'The Hundred Thousand Dollar Policy'

Half-hour series starring Robert Rockwell as Sam Logan, an investigator for the Blackhawk Insurance Co in the Old West. Shown on ABC.

The Gale Storm Show (Oh! Susannah)
'It's Magic'
Half-hour comedy show produced by Desilu starring Gale Storm as a cruise director on a ship travelling the world. Her companion was played by former silent-film star Zazu Pitts. Shown on ABC.

Bronco
'The Mustangers'
Hour-long Western series produced at Warner Bros featuring Ty Hardin as Bronco Layne, a drifter in Texas following the Civil War. Shown on ABC.

Maverick
'Bolt from the Blue' (plus script)
Classic television Western series made at Warner Bros starring James Garner and Jack Kelly as two brothers who are ace card players and inveterate women-chasers. Altman's episode featured Roger Moore as their cousin Beauregard, and it was photographed by Harold E. Stine. Shown on ABC.

Westinghouse Desilu Playhouse
'The Sound of Murder'; 'Death of a Dream'
Shown on CBS. See *Kraft Mystery Theatre* below.

1960–1

The Roaring 20s
'The Prairie Flower'; 'Brother's Keeper'; 'White Carnation'; 'Dance Marathon'; 'Two a Day'; 'Right Off the Boat' (2 parts); 'Royal Tour'; 'Standing Room Only' (plus script)
Hour-long crime dramas made at Warner Bros, very loosely based on the 1939 movie starring Humphrey Bogart and James Cagney and set in New York during Prohibition, with the main characters working in a newspaper office. The regular cast included Dorothy Provine, Donald May, Rex Reason, John Dehner, Mike Road, Gary Vinson and James Flavin. Shown on ABC.

Bonanza
'Silent Thunder'; 'Bank Run'; 'The Duke'; 'The Rival'; 'The Secret'; 'The Dream Riders'; 'Sam Hill'; 'The Many Faces of Gideon Flinch'
The most celebrated of television Western series, created by David Dortort, hour-long shows in colour about the Cartwright family living on the Ponderosa ranch near Virginia City. The main stars were Lorne Greene, Dan Blocker, Michael Landon and Pernell Roberts. Altman's episodes were in the second season. Originally shown on NBC, *Bonanza* was in production up until 1973, and the shows are still syndicated internationally.

1961

Lawman
'The Robbery'
Half-hour Western series made at Warner Bros, starring John Russell as Marshall Dan Troop of Laramie, Wyoming, and as his deputy, Peter Brown. Altman's episode featured Robert Ridgely among the cast. Shown on ABC.

Surfside 6
'Thieves Among Honor (A Touch of Larceny)' (plus co-script)
Warner Bros series in which Troy Donohue, Van Williams and Lee Patterson played three detectives operating from a houseboat in Miami, Florida. Shown on ABC.

Peter Gunn
'Murder Bond'
Private-eye series starring Mark Stevens and produced by writer and director Blake Edwards. Shown on ABC.

Route 66
'Some of the People, Some of the Time'
Martin Milner and George Maharis played two drifters crossing the country in a series created by writer Sterling Silliphant. Altman's episode featured Keenan Wynn. Shown on CBS.

1961–2

Bus Stop
'The Covering Darkness'; 'Accessory by Consent'; 'A Lion Walks Among Us'; 'And the Pursuit of Evil'; 'Summer Lightning'; 'Door Without a Key' (plus co-story); 'County General'
Anthology hour-long series made at 20th Century Fox, loosely based on the William Inge play filmed with Marilyn Monroe in 1956. Basing the action in the small town of Sunrise in the Rocky Mountains assured a cast of regular characters alongside the people passing through on the interstate bus route. Altman's episodes featured Robert Redford, Barbara Baxley, Keenan Wynn, James McArthur and Howard Duff. Shown on ABC.

1962

Cain's Hundred
'The Left Side of Canada'
Hour-long series in which Peter Mark Richman played Nicholas 'Nick' Cain, a former underworld lawyer acting for the Federal Government to bring to justice one hundred top criminals. Shown on NBC.

The Gallant Men

'The Gallant Men (Battle Zone)'
A two-hour pilot for Warner Bros, a World War II drama about the American Fifth Army in Italy through the eyes of a war correspondent, played by Robert McQueeney. Shown on ABC.

1962–3

Kraft Mystery Theatre

'Death of a Dream'; 'Sound of Murder'; 'The Image Merchants' (plus producer)
One-hour anthology drama series comprising mystery and suspense films made in England and the US. Altman's episodes, 'Death of a Dream', featuring Robert Vaughn and Dianne Foster, and 'The Sound of Murder', featuring Alex Davison and Liam Redmond, were previously shown in the Westinghouse Desilu Playhouse on CBS. In 'The Image Merchants', a pilot for a series that never was, his cast included Melvyn Douglas, MacDonald Carey, Geraldine Brooks and Dianne Foster. Shown on NBC.

Combat!

'Forgotten Front'; 'Rear Echelon Commandos'; 'Any Second Now'; 'Escape to Nowhere'; 'Cat and Mouse' (also producer and script); 'I Swear by Apollo' (also producer); 'The Prisoner'; 'The Volunteer' (also producer); 'Off Limits' (also producer); 'Survival' (also producer)
Superior hour-long war adventure series about a US platoon in Europe in World War II, with Rick Jason and Vic Morrow as the regular leads. Altman directed about half of the first season, originally shown on ABC.

1963–4

Kraft Suspense Theatre

'The Long, Lost Life of Edward Smalley' (plus story); 'The Hunt' (co-story only); 'Once Upon a Savage Night (Nightmare in Chicago)'
One-hour anthology drama series produced by Roy Huggins at Universal. 'The Hunt', which Altman did not direct, boasted an impressive cast list that included Bruce Dern, James Caan and Mickey Rooney. See above for details of 'Once Upon a Savage Night', which was expanded into a feature film and retitled *Nightmare in Chicago*. Shown on NBC.

1964

The Long, Hot Summer

Hour-long pilot episode for series derived from the film of the same title made by Martin Ritt in 1958, which was based on William Faulkner's short story *The Hamlet*. The central characters, living in a fictional southern town called Frenchman's Bend, were played by Edmond O'Brien, Roy Thinnes, Dan O'Herlihy and Nancy Malone. Never transmitted.

1968

A Walk in the Night (plus co-producer, story and co-script)
Two-hour pilot episode for an unsold series called either *Night Watch* or *Chicago, Chicago*, written by Altman associates Brian McKay and Robert Eggenweiler and produced by Ray Wagner. Carol O'Connor and Andrew Duggan starred as detectives operating throughout the Great Lakes area. Shown on CBS.

Television – Second Period, from 1982

1982

Two by South: Precious Blood and Rattlesnake in a Cooler
In *Precious Blood*, two parallel actions take place in the same small Missouri home: a white man and a black nurse describe their respective childhoods, oblivious to each other, though their lives appear linked by the memory of a rape. In *Rattlesnake in a Cooler*, the setting is a sparsely furnished wooden cabin. To the occasional accompaniment of country-and-western songs, a macho cowboy recounts colourful tales protesting his strength and purpose and reveals his part in killing a cop.

Production Company: Alpha Repertory Television Service
Producers: Scott Bushnell, Joseph Butt
Screenplay: Frank South, from his own plays
Cinematography (video): Lloyd Freidus
Sound: John Hampton
Editors: Gary Princz, Max K. Curtis
Music: Danny Darst
Production Design: John Kavelin
Cast: *Precious Blood* – Guy Boyd, Alfre Woodard; *Rattlesnake in a Cooler* – Leo Burmeister, Danny Darst
Precious Blood: 60 mins. *Rattlesnake in a Cooler*: 57 mins

1985

Laundromat
Two lonely women, Alberta and DeeDee, meet at a laundromat at midnight, and while the attendant dozes, they reveal their lives to each other, bemoaning their absent husbands and lack of children. Shooter, a young black man, comes in with his laundry and invites them to join him next door in a bar where he plays pool, but they stay in the laundromat. Alberta suggests DeeDee leave her husband, and after a bitter argument, Alberta is made to confess she was recently widowed. DeeDee

returns home to her husband, and Alberta finally brings herself to wash the soiled shirt her husband died in.

Production Company: A Byck/Lancaster production of a Sandcastle 5 film
Producers: Dann Byck, David Lancaster
Screenplay: Marsha Norman, from her own play
Cinematography: Pierre Mignot
Sound: Daniel Brisseau
Editor: Luce Grunenwaldt
Songs: 'Common Folk', 'Somebody's Daddy', 'Can't Make a Livin'' on the Road' (Danny Durst); 'Downhearted Blues', 'Some Sweet Day', 'I'm Having a Good Time', 'Black Man', 'The Love I Have for You', 'My Castle's Rockin'', 'I Cried for You', 'My Handy Man Ain't Handy No More' (Alberta Hunter)
Production Design: David Gropman
Cast: Carol Burnett (Alberta Johnson), Amy Madigan (DeeDee Johnson), Michael Wright (Shooter Stevens)
57 mins

1987
The Dumb Waiter
On a wintry day, two hitmen, Ben and Gus, arrive by car at an isolated, deserted building and settle in the dingy basement to await news of their next assignment. They argue about how they spend their spare time and recent football matches until their attention is diverted by the mysterious arrival of an envelope under the door above. Gus opens it and finds inside some matches but no message. After getting out his gun, Gus checks outside but sees no one. He uses the matches to light the gas to boil the kettle, but after further bickering with Ben, he finds the supply has run out. The dumb waiter suddenly descends with a slip of paper, but it is just an order for food and drink. Ben points out there used to be a café upstairs. Another order turns up, and Ben suggests sending something in return, making Gus put all their provisions in the dumb waiter. The waiter keeps returning what they send, accompanied by further orders, the dishes becoming more exotic each time. They find a speaking tube, and Ben reports they have no more food to supply. He rehearses with Gus their working procedure, and their anxiety mounts as Gus accidentally allows his gun to go up in the waiter. Gus goes outside, Ben receives a message through the speaker tube that their victim will be with them soon, and then Gus comes through the door. Outside, a gun shot is heard, Ben leaves alone, and a van marked 'Compleat Cleaning Service' turns up.

Production Company: Secret Castle Productions/ABC
Producer: Robert Altman
Screenplay: Harold Pinter, from his own play
Cinematography: Pierre Mignot
Sound: Serge Beauchemin

Editor: Jennifer Auge
Music: Judith Gruber-Stitzer
Production Design: Violette Daneau
Cast: John Travolta (Ben), Tom Conti (Gus)
60 mins

The Room

After Rose Hudd speculates to her silent husband about who occupies the basement beneath their room, they have a visit from their landlord, Mr Kidd, ostensibly
checking out the pipes. He reminisces about his past life in the house before taking
his leave. After Mr Hudd goes out, his wife encounters a strange young couple on
the staircase looking around the house and invites them in. They say they'd heard
there was a room to let and hoped to find the landlord on the premises. She tells
them the house is full, though they claim a voice in the basement told them the
room occupied by the Hudds was free. They leave, and Mr Kidd turns up again and
tells Mrs Hudd she has to see a man in the basement. After Mr Kidd leaves, Mrs
Hudd receives a visit from the man she has been told about, who is blind. He says
he has a message for her from her father, who wants her to go home. Mr Hudd
returns, talking about his journey, and then strikes the visitor with a bottle. Mrs
Hudd locks up their front door.

Production Company: Secret Castle Productions/ABC
Producer: Robert Altman
Screenplay: Harold Pinter, from his own play
Cinematography: Pierre Mignot
Sound: Serge Beauchemin
Editor: Jennifer Auge
Music: Judith Gruber-Stitzer
Production Design: Violette Daneau
Cast: Linda Hunt (Rose Hudd), Annie Lennox (Clarissa Sands), Julian Sands
(Toddy Sands), David Hemblem (Mr Hudd), Abbott Anderson (Riley), Donald
Pleasence (Mr Kidd)
49 mins
(*The Dumb Waiter* and *The Room* were also combined as a double-bill called
Basements)

1988

Tanner '88

The series follows fictional Michigan congressman Jack Tanner, a very liberal
Democrat, as he goes on the presidential campaign trail with his enthusiastic
daughter Alex, his aides and a camera crew. While his campaign manager T. J.
Cavanaugh works on his image and makes a promotional tape with the tagline 'For
Real', Tanner encounters the real politicians busy canvassing and survives an

apparent knife attack. His journey takes him from New England down to Nashville, then on to Washington, where, drawn in by Alex, he is arrested for joining in a 'Free South Africa' protest. After an encouraging conversation with Bruce Babbitt, Tanner goes on to court musicians and actors in Hollywood and takes part in a television debate with Jesse Jackson in which he pushes for the legalization of drugs. Trouble ensues when it is discovered the divorced Tanner is in a secret relationship with Joanna Buckley, who works for his rival Michael Dukakis. Deciding to be open about it and proposing a quick marriage, he goes to Detroit and visits a deprived part of the city, and then returns to Washington, where the media frenzy leads him to call the wedding off. At the 1988 Democratic National Convention in Atlanta, Tanner is criticized for being too liberal, and in spite of the support of Kitty Dukakis, fails to garner enough votes. In his pillow talk with Joanna, he appears to withdraw from the race . . .

Episode 1: 'The Dark Horse'; Episode 2: 'For Real'; Episode 3: 'The Night of the Twinkies'; Episode 4: 'Bagels with Bruce'; Episode 5: 'Child's Play'; Episode 6: 'The Great Escape'; Episode 7: 'Something Borrowed, Something New (The Girlfriend Factor)'; Episode 8: 'The Boiler Room'; Episode 9: 'The Reality Check'

Production Company: Zenith and Darkhorse Productions/Home Box Office
Producer: Scott Bushnell
Screenplay: Garry Trudeau
Cinematography (video): Jean Lepine
Sound: Steve Ning
Editors: Alison Ellwood, Ruth Foster, Mark Fish, Sean-Michael Connor
Music: Allan Nicholls
Production Design: Stephen Altman, Jerry Fleming
Cast: Michael Murphy (*Jack Tanner*), Pamela Reed (*T. J. Cavanaugh*), Cynthia Nixon (*Alex Tanner*), Kevin J. O'Connor (*Hayes Taggerty*), Daniel Jenkins (*Stringer Kincaid*), Jim Fyfe (*Emile Berkoff*), Matt Malloy (*Deke Connors*), Ilana Levine (*Andea Spinelli*), Veronica Cartwright (*Molly Hark*), Wendy Crewson (*Joanna Buckley*), Greg Pocaccino (*Barney Kittman*), Sandra Bowie (*Stevie Chevalier*), Frank Barhydt (*Frank Gatling*), E. G. Marshall (*General John Tanner*), Harry Anderson (*Billy Ridenhour*)
Special appearances as themselves: Bruce Babbitt, Art Buchwald, Rebecca DeMornay, Bob Dole, Kitty Dukakis, Linda Ellerbee, Gary Hart, Jesse Jackson, Waylon Jennings, Ralph Nader, Pat Robertson, Dorothy Sarnoff, Gloria Steinem, Studs Turkel, etc.
300 mins
(Episode 1: 60 mins; Episodes 2–9: 30 mins each)

The Caine Mutiny Court-Martial
Stephen Maryk is on trial for taking over command of a minesweeper from Captain Queeg during a typhoon in December 1944. Much of the trial focuses on whether

Queeg has a disturbed personality and was therefore unfit to make proper decisions, and while the evidence against him is very strong, he fails to help his case by displaying a delusional fear of persecution. Maryk is acquitted, but his defence attorney Barney Greenwald has from the beginning suspected Maryk's friend and fellow officer Keefer, a cynical intellectual, as really being behind the mutiny. At a celebration party, Greenwald abuses Keefer by throwing a drink over him and storming out.

Production Company: The Maltese Companies Inc in association with Wouk/Ware Productions, Sandcastle 5 Productions
Producers: Robert Altman, John Flaxman
Screenplay: Herman Wouk, based on his own novel and play
Cinematography: Jacek Laskus
Sound: Mark Ulano
Editor: Dorian Harris
Music: Dan Edelstein
Production Design: Stephen Altman
Cast: Eric Bogosian (*Lt Barney Greenwald*), Jeff Daniels (*Lt Stephen Maryk*), Brad Davis (*Lt Commander Philip Francis Queeg*), Peter Gallagher (*Lt Commander John Challee*), Michael Murphy (*Captain Blakely*), Kevin J. O'Connor (*Lt Thomas Keefer*), Daniel Jenkins (*Lt [Junior Grade] Willis Seward Keith*), Danny Darst (*Captain Randolph Southard*), Ken Michaels (*Dr Alan Winston Bird*), David Miller (*Stenographer*), Matt Malloy, David Barnett, Ken Jones (*Legal Assistants*), Brian Haley, Matt Smith, L.W. Wyman (*Party Guests*)
100 mins

1992

The Real McTeague – A Synthesis of Forms
(Concept and Creative Supervision only)
A condensed television version of Robert Altman's production of the opera *McTeague*, composed by William Bolcom with a libretto by Arnold Weinstein and Robert Altman based on the novel by Frank Norris, as premièred at the Lyric Opera of Chicago. Extracts from Erich Von Stroheim's 1927 silent film *Greed*, also based on *McTeague*, appear throughout.

Production Company: A production of WTTW/Chicago in association with Thirteen/WNET and Lyric Opera of Chicago
Producer: Geoffrey Baer
Co-ordinating Producer: Frank Barhydt
Opera segments directed for television: Kirk Browning
Screenplay: James Arntz, Geoffrey Baer
Editor: Paul Thornton
Cast: Ben Heppner (*McTeague*), Catherine Malfitano (*Trina*), Timothy Nolen

(*Marcus*), Emily Golden (*Maria*), Wilber Pauley (*Lottery Agent/Inspector*)
Narrator: Studs Terkel
60 mins

1993
Black and Blue

A television record of Claudio Segovia and Donald K. Donald's Broadway musical revue, a sequence of performances by an all-black cast of hoofers and singers staged at the Minskoff Theatre, New York. With choreography by Cholly Atkins, Henry LeTang, Frankie Manning and Fayard Nicholas, and musical supervision and arrangements by Sy Johnson and Luther Anderson.

Production Company: The Black and Blue Company in association with Thirteen/ WNET, Japan Satellite Broadcasting and Reiss Media Productions Inc
Producer: David Horn
Co-ordinating Producer: John Walker
Supervising Producer: Scott Bushnell
Editor: Brent Carpenter
Conductor: Leonard Oxley
The Singers: Ruth Brown, Linda Hopkins, Carrie Smith
The Hoofers: Bunny Briggs, Lon Chaney, George Hillman, Bernard Manners, Jimmy Slyde, Dianne Walker
115 mins (US version)

1997
Jazz '34

Kansas City during the Depression, as depicted in the film *Kansas City*. At the Hey Hey Club in Kansas City, a group of top black jazz musicians play through the night in a non-stop jam session. As well as playing music by Count Basie and Duke Ellington, the performers recreate the legendary 'battle of the saxes' between Coleman Hawkins and Lester Young.

Production Company: Sandcastle 5/CiBy 2000
Producers: James McLindon, Matthew Seig, Brent Carpenter, Robert Altman
Screenplay: Robert Altman
Cinematography: Oliver Stapleton
Sound: Eric Liljestrand
Editors: Brent Carpenter, Dylan Tichenor
Music: Hall Willner, Susan Jacobs, Steven Bernstein
Songs: 'Tickle Toe', 'Indiana', 'Solitude', 'Blues in the Dark', 'Prince of Wails', 'Froggy Bottom', 'Harvard Blues', 'King Porter Stomp', 'Lafayette', 'Lullaby of the Leaves', 'Piano Boogie', 'Pagin' the Devil', 'Moten Swing', 'Queer Notions', 'Yeah Man'

Filmography

Production Design: Stephen Altman
The Hey Hey Club musicians: James Carter, Craig Handy, David Murray, Joshua Redman (tenor saxophones), Jesse Davis, David 'Fathead' Newman Jr (alto saxophones), Don Byron (clarinet/baritone saxophone), Olu Dara, Nicholas Payton, James Zollar (trumpet), Curtis Fowlkes, Clark Gayton (trombone), Victor Lewis (drums), Geri Allen, Cyrus Chestnut (piano), Ron Carter, Tyrone Clark, Christian McBride (bass), Russell Malone, Mark Whitfield (guitar), Kevin Mahogany (vocalist)
Narrator: Harry Belafonte
75 mins

Gun
A series created by James Sadwith, comprising six single dramas with a gun figuring strongly in the narrative. Other titles: 'Columbus Day', directed by James Sadwith; 'The Hole', directed by Ted Demme; 'The Shot', directed by James Foley; 'Father John', directed by Jeremiah Chechik; 'Ricochet', directed by Peter Horton.

All the President's Women
When the president of a Texas country club dies attempting to shoot a rattlesnake with his handgun, the path looks clear for Bill Johnson to take up the position. While he is employing handcuffs to spice up sex with his mistress, Phyllis, the former president's daughter, a package mysteriously turns up containing her father's gun. Back home with his wife Jill for dinner, Bill discovers another package has arrived addressed to her, containing the empty clip of the gun. Then, his lawyer – and ex-lover – Paula turns up at his office carrying another package, this time containing the bullets. All the women club together to help with Bill's campaign. Bill pays a visit on Phyllis but finds her mother Francis there and makes the excuse of checking out the gun. Phyllis comes in and her secret relationship with Bill is revealed. At his party at the club, Bill receives an unsigned note inviting him for an assignation on the course. Paula tells Phyllis that she now has a rival for Bill's affections, his new secretary Genny. On the course, Bill encounters a jealous Francis, who holds him at gunpoint, makes him strip and handcuffs him to a sprinkler. Eventually he is found by Jill, who throws his clothes into a nearby pond. Back at the club, Jill dumps the gun, but it is found by the maid Sally, who reveals she was responsible for sending the packages. But she is then confronted by her father, who says her mother found a pair of handcuffs chained to her daughter's bedpost and that he intends to kill the man responsible.

Production Company: Kusher-Locke Company/Sadwith Productions/Sandcastle 5 Productions
Producers: James Sadwith, Robert Altman, Rob Dwek, Donald Kuchner, Peter Locke
Screenplay: Anne Rapp
Cinematography: Roy H. Wagner

Sound: Lee Archer
Editor: Dorian Harris
Music: Roy Hay, Mike Burns
Production Design: Bernt Capra
Cast: Darryl Hannah (*Jill Johnson*), Sally Kellerman (*Francis Tyler*), Tina Lifford (*Sally*), Randy Quaid (*Bill Johnson*), Jennifer Tilly (*Phyllis Tyler*), Sean Young (*Paula*), Robert Andre (*Julio*), Dirk Blocker (*Clifford Sutton*), John Considine (*Harlan*), Nicolas Coster (*Parker Stanley Tyler*), Robert Do'Qui (*Jefferson*), Dina Spybey (*Genny*), Troy D. Bryant (*J.W.*), Kathryn Tucker (*Marcy*)
45 mins

2004
Tanner on Tanner
A sequel to *Tanner '88*, taking the characters sixteen years on from the first series. Jack Tanner is now a successful academic and is participating in his daughter Alex's retrospective documentary project about him called 'My Candidate'. But when her work-in-progress has a rough reception at New York's Rough Cut Film Festival, Alex follows Robert Redford's advice to seek out the participants in the 1988 campaign for their viewpoints by taking her crew and father to the 2004 Democratic National Convention in Boston. After a series of bungles she fails to get an interview with presidential candidate John Kerry, while her father is invited by T. J. Cavanaugh to get back into politics, killing off her best footage of him. Back teaching her film class, Alex shows the work of a student who followed her with his camera, which unsparingly reveals her pretensions and failure.
Episode 1: 'Dinner at Elaine's'; Episode 2: 'Boston or Bust'; Episode 3: 'Alex in Wonderland'; Episode 4: 'The Awful Truth'

Production Company: The Sundance Channel presents a Sandcastle 5 production
Producers: Matthew Seig, Wren Arthur
Cinematography (video): Tom Richmond, Robert Reed Altman
Sound: Antonio L. Arroyo
Editor: Jacob Craycroft
Music: House of Diablo, Allan Nicholls
Production Design: Dina Goldman
Cast: Cynthia Nixon (*Alex Tanner*), Michael Murphy (*Jack Tanner*), Pamela Reed (*T. J. Cavanaugh*), Matt Malloy (*Deke Connors*), Ilana Levine (*Andrea Spinelli*), Luke McFarlane (*Stuart DeBarge*), Aasif Mandvi (Salim)
Special appearances as themselves: Secretary Madeleine Albright, Steve Buscemi, Governor Mario Cuomo, Governor Howard Dean, Harry Belafonte, Al Franken, Janeane Garofalo, Alexandra Kerry, Chris Matthews, John Podesta, Ron Reagan Jr, Robert Redford, Martin Scorsese, Tom Brokaw, Dee Dee Myers, The Reverend Al Sharpton, Congressman Richard Gephardt, Governor Grey Davis, US Senator

Filmography

Joe Biden, Governor Michael Dukakis, US Senator Joe Lieberman, Charlie Rose
120 mins (4 × 30 mins)

*Television credits mainly drawn from research by Tise Vahimagi and Richard
Dacre, compiled for their forthcoming book on Altman's television career.*

Awards

1970 *M*A*S*H* – Cannes Film Festival, Palme d'Or; National Society of Film Critics Award, Best Picture; Academy Award, Best Adapted Screenplay

1972 *Images* – Cannes Film Festival, Best Actress: Susannah York

1975 *Nashville* – New York Film Critics Circle Award, Best Picture, Best Director; National Society of Film Critics Award, Best Picture, Best Director; National Board of Review Award, Best Picture, Best Director (both awards shared with Stanley Kubrick for *Barry Lyndon*); Academy Award, Best Song: 'I'm Easy'; David di Donatello Award, Italy; AFI Award, Australia, Best Foreign Film; Cartegna Film Festival, Golden Indian Catalina for Best Director

1976 *Buffalo Bill and the Indians* – Berlin Film Festival, Golden Bear

1977 *3 Women* – Cannes Film Festival, Best Actress: Shelley Duvall; New York Film Festival, Best Supporting Actress: Sissy Spacek

1978 *A Wedding* – San Sebastian Film Festival, Best Actress Award: Carol Burnett

1982 *Come Back to the Five and Dime, Jimmy Dean, Jimmy Dean* – Chicago Film Festival, Grand Prix

1983 *Streamers* – Venice Film Festival, Grand Prix: Acting

1985 *The Laundromat* – ACE Award

1985 *Fool for Love* – Festroia – Troia International Film Festival, Golden Dolphin

1988 *Tanner '88* – Emmy Awards, Outstanding Directing in a Drama Series; BAFTA Award, Britain, Best Foreign Television Series; FIPA Award, France, Best Foreign Series

1988 *The Caine Mutiny Court-Martial* – Monte Carlo Festival, Best Director

1991 Cinema Audio Society, Lifetime Achievement Award

1992 John Cassavetes Award (presented by Independent Feature Project)

1992 USA Film Festival, Great Director Award

1992 *The Player* – Cannes Film Festival, Best Director Award, Best Actor: Tim Robbins; New York Film Critics Circle Award, Best Film, Best Director; Boston Society of Film Critics Award, Best Director; Chicago Film Critics Association Award, Best Director; Golden Globe, Best Film (Musical or Comedy), Best Actor: Tim Robbins; Bodil Award, Denmark, Best American Film; National Syndicate of Italian Film Journalists Award, Best Director, Foreign Film; BAFTA Award, Britain, Best Director; Directors Guild of America Award, Outstanding Directorial Achievement; Southeastern Film Critics Association Award, Best Director

1993 *Short Cuts* – IFP Independent Spirit Award, Best Screenplay, Best Director;

Awards

Venice Film Festival, Grand Prix, Best Film (shared with *Three Colours: Blue*), Best Acting Award to Ensemble; Bodil Award, Denmark, Best American Film; Boston Society of Film Critics Award, USA, Best Screenplay; Swedish Film Critics Award, Best Film

1993 Joseph Plateau Life Achievement Award

1994 *Prêt-à-Porter* – The National Board of Review, Acting Award for Ensemble Cast

1994 Directors Guild of America, D. W. Griffith Award, Lifetime Achievement

1994 Cinema Arts Centre Award, Unique Achievement in Advancing the Art of Independent Film

1994 Film Society of Lincoln Center, New York, Gala Tribute

1995 American Cinema Editors, USA, Golden Eddie Award

1996 *Kansas City* – New York Film Critics Circle Award, Best Supporting Actor: Harry Belafonte; Los Angeles Film Critics Association Award, Best Score

1996 Venice Film Festival Golden Lion Award, Lifetime Achievement

1996 American Film Institute, Honorary Doctorate of Fine Arts

1996 University of Michigan, Honorary Doctorate of Fine Arts

1998 Classically Independent Film Festival, San Francisco, California, Independent Director Honoree

1999 American Society of Cinematographers, USA, Board of Governors Award

1999 *Robert Altman's Jazz '34* – 21st São Paulo International Film Festival, Audience Award, Best Documentary

1999 *Cookie's Fortune* – Guild of German Art House Cinemas Prize; Dallas-Fort Worth Film Critics Association, Award for Best Supporting Actress: Julianne Moore

2000 Gotham Awards, Life Achievement

2001 British Film Institute, Fellowship

2001 Women in Film, Mentor Award

2002 *Gosford Park* – Golden Globe, Best Director; Academy Award, Best Original Screenplay; American Film Institute Film Award, Director of the Year; BAFTA, Britain, Alexander Korda Award for Best British Film, Best Costume Design: Jenny Beavan; Evening Standard British Film Award, Britain, Best Film; Broadcast Film Critics Association, Award for Best Acting Ensemble; Florida Film Critics Circle Award, Best Ensemble Cast; Golden Satellite Award, Best Performance in a Supporting Role (comedy or musical): Maggie Smith, Outstanding Motion Picture Ensemble, Special Achievement Award; Italian National Syndicate of Film Journalists, Silver Ribbon for Best Director, Foreign Film; Kansas City Film Critics Circle Award, Best Supporting Actress: Maggie Smith (shared with Jennifer Connelly for *A Beautiful Mind*); London Critics Circle Film Award, British Film of the Year, Best Supporting Actress of the Year: Helen Mirren; National Society of Film Critics Award, USA, Best Director, Best Screenplay: Julian Fellowes, Best Supporting Actress: Helen Mirren; Online Film Critics Society Award, Best

277

Ensemble; Robert Festival, Best American Film; Screen Actors Guild Award, Outstanding Performance by a Female Actor in a Supporting Role: Helen Mirren, Outstanding Performance by the Cast of a Theatrical Motion Picture; Southeastern Film Critics Association Award, Best Supporting Actress: Maggie Smith (shared with Jennifer Connelly for *A Beautiful Mind* and Marisa Tomei for *In the Bedroom*); Writers Guild of America Award, USA, Best Screenplay Written Directly for the Screen, Julian Fellowes

2002 Berlin International Film Festival, Honorary Golden Bear

2003 San Francisco International Film Festival, Film Society Award for Lifetime Achievement in Directing

2004 Los Angeles Film Critics Association Award, Career Achievement Award

Appendix

Quintet – The Game

Following the creation of the deadly board game for the film *Quintet*, a version was prepared for marketing. The instructions below are based on the proposed rules and subsequent adjustments requested by Lion's Gate.

Object of game
To be the last player left on the board after all your opponent's tokens have been captured.

Equipment
Gameboard, 2 dice and 15 playing tokens, 3 × 5 kinds.

REDSTONE – GRIGOR – CHRISTOPHER – AMBROSIA – DEUCA

Background of the game
Quintet is a game of survival. The five sectors of the Quintet board reflect the five sectors of inhabitants in a futuristic civilization portrayed in the film *Quintet*. The film is set in a time of advanced technology within a city founded entirely upon the concept of five: five sectors, five levels in each sector, a population of five million.

As in the film, each player participates with a distinctive token: Redstone (Paul Newman), the mushroom-shaped token; Grigor (Fernando Rey), the starfish; Christopher (Vittorio Gassman), the scalloped cross; Ambrosia (Bibi Andersson), the red amulet; and Deuca (Nina van Pallandt), the ice crystal.

Because the Quintet players in the film exist at a time in the future when the earth and its inhabitants are near total devastation from a new ice age, they live in constant presence of death. People all around them are freezing to death every day, and it is just a matter of time before death will strike each one of them. So why wait passively for death to strike? The Quintet player lives to challenge and taunt death.

In the film *Quintet*, the most daring of the players expand their board game rivalry to compete with each other at a level of reality: the game's capturing order becomes a real-life killing order. The game becomes so real that in order to win the players must kill or be killed.

In the film, successful Quintet players are forced to look out solely for themselves. They form alliances which are broken when they are no longer self-serving. As the capturing order changes, friendships and loyalties change. All of life, particularly mankind's feelings and motivations for survival, is contained in the game of Quintet. For the true Quintet player, life becomes a game, and the game is all there is to life.

The Quintet game described here is, of course, a non-lethal version of the one in the film. Nevertheless, the ingredients of intrigue, plotting and deceit remain to make it a thrilling contest for every player. But remember, when you play to cheat death, be prepared for death to cheat you!

Appendix

Get Ready
Each player sits in front of one of the five sides of the Gameboard and chooses three matching playing Tokens. Each player rolls the dice, and the one who achieves the highest number plays first and decides the Capturing Order. In case of a tie, the first one to roll the highest number plays first.

Capturing Order
The first player sets up the Capturing Order by placing one of each player's Tokens in the middle of the Gameboard. These Tokens in the killing circle remain untouched until the matching Tokens are captured and are out of the game. They serve only as visual reminders of the Capturing Order.

The Capturing Order follows the arrows. The player can capture the piece ahead but in turn can be captured by the piece behind.

Strategy Points
ALLIANCE: Alliances happen when two neutral Tokens occupy the same space. Neutral Tokens cannot capture each other, and hence do not immediately precede or follow each other in the Capturing Order. Alliances protect both players since no other tokens can land on that space and must pass it.

BARRICADE: A Barricade is formed when both of a player's Tokens occupy the same space. No other Token can land on that space or pass it.

SAFETY SPACE: The spaces numbered VI (6) are Safety Spaces. If you roll a six on one dice, you may either move six spaces or enter the nearest Safety Space. If you roll double sixes, you may move both Tokens into Safety Spaces, if you still have both Tokens. If you roll six and another number, and you have only one Token left and you wish to move into safety, you must take the other number first.

You can remain in SAFETY as long as you roll a six or you can use the numbers you roll with your other Token.

Let's Play Quintet
1. ROLLING ON. The high roller rolls again and puts his two remaining Tokens in the correct spaces on his side of the board.

   Example: If a player rolls a four on one dice and a three on another, he places one Token on space three (III) directly in front and the other Token on space four (IV). If a player rolls double numbers, he places both Tokens in the same room, setting up a barricade.

   This is 'rolling on'. Play continues until all players have 'rolled on'.
2. To continue, the first player rolls again. He may move either piece the total number shown on the dice. Or he may split up his move and move

281

one Token the number shown on one dice and the other Token the number shown on the other dice. MOVES MAY BE TAKEN IN EITHER DIRECTION. When a player rolls double fives, they complete the moves and get an additional turn.

Example: If a player rolls a five and a four, they may move one Token five spaces in one direction and then move the same Token four spaces in the opposite direction, if they wish.

3. There can never be more than two Tokens on any space at any time.

4. During each other player's turn, he tries to capture one or both Tokens of the player directly after him in the capturing circle. NOT NECESSARILY IN THE ORDER IN WHICH PLAYERS ARE SEATED AROUND THE BOARD. You capture a Token by landing on that Token's place at the end of the move.

5. Each time a player's Token is captured, the captured piece is removed from the board. After a player loses both pieces, he is out of the game and his Token is removed from the Capturing Circle. IMPORTANT: At this time there is a new capturing order.

6. If a player has only one piece remaining, he must move according to the numbers of both dice with the one piece (see rule 2).

7. If a correct move lands a player on a space occupied by the Token that is trying to capture you, you are captured and your piece is removed from the board.

8. ALLIANCES can turn into captures! If a new Capturing Order happens and an old neutral piece that is sharing a space with you can now capture you, you are captured.

9. If a player is trapped between two BARRICADES and cannot move the full amount shown on the dice, he must forfeit that move.

10. If a player has a BARRICADE on one side and moving the other direction would make him land on someone who wants to capture him, he is captured!

Getting Out of Safety

11. Whenever a player has a piece in SAFETY and he wants to move out of SAFETY, he must move out according to the numbers on the dice.

Example: A player has one piece left which is in SAFETY and he rolls five and four. The player must move out of SAFETY to space five or four nearest that SAFETY. He may then take the other number in either direction.

12. Example: A player has a space in SAFETY and he must move out. If the only correct moves causes him to end his turn on a space occupied by a Token that wants to capture him, he is captured!

13. Example: A player has only one Token left and it is in SAFETY. If that player rolls a six and a four, he must go to space four on that side before returning to SAFETY. If space four (IV) is occupied by a Token that wants to capture him, he is not captured since he did not end his turn on that space.

14. IN THE CASE OF ROLLING DOUBLE SIXES: When a player has two Tokens and one Token is in SAFETY, one six may be used for that Token to remain in SAFETY. Then the second six is used by the second Token to move six spaces or to go into SAFETY.

   When a player has only one remaining Token or both Tokens in SAFETY, it/they must remain in SAFETY.

Bibliography

This is a list of the important books to have appeared in the English language relating to Altman and his films to date. Some are of a distinctly academic nature and therefore have a limited readership. The behind-the-scenes accounts are particularly rewarding, especially *The Nashville Chronicles*, and if you can track down a copy, C. Kirk McClelland's diary of the making of *Brewster McCloud* is refreshingly impartial and includes both the original screenplay and the final continuity script, offering a rare opportunity to judge how Altman changes his scripts. Only one biography exists to date: Patrick McGilligan's, published in 1989, much disliked by its subject but especially valuable for the chronicle of the Kansas City period and the television work. The recent compendium of interviews edited by David Sterrit make for stimulating reading, and one of the very best interviews with Altman I have read – not so much for information but for vividly conveying the man on a roll as he was mixing *The Player* – is to be found in David Breskin's excellent compendium.

Altman, R. and Barhydt, F., *Short Cuts: The Screenplay*. Capra, Santa Barbara, California, 1993.

Altman, R. and Rudolph, A., *Buffalo Bill and the Indians, or Sitting Bull's History Lesson*. Bantam, New York, 1976.

Altman, R., Schulgassar, B. and Leitch, B. D., *Robert Altman's Prêt-à-Porter*. Hyperion/Boxtree Ltd, New York/London, 1995.

Anobile, R. (Ed.), *Popeye: The Movie Novel*. Avon, New York, 1980.

AuWerter, R., *Robert Altman*, from *Directors in Action*, Bob Thomas (Ed.). Bobbs Merrill, Indianapolis and New York, 1973.

Biskind, P., *Easy Riders, Raging Bulls: How the Sex-Drugs-and-Rock'n'Roll Generation Saved Hollywood*. Simon & Schuster, New York, 1998.

Breskin, D., *Inner Views: Filmmakers in Conversation*. Da Capo Press, Inc., New York, 1997.

Carver, R., *Short Cuts: Selected Stories*, Robert Altman (Ed.). Vintage, New York, 1993.

Feineman, N., *Persistence of Vision: The Films of Robert Altman*. Arno Press (University of Florida), 1976.

Fellowes, J., *Gosford Park: The Shooting Script*. Nick Hern Books, London, 2002.

Fuller, G., *Altman on Altman*, from *Projections 2*, John Boorman and Walter Donohue (Eds). Faber and Faber Ltd, London, 1993.

Bibliography

Gilbey, R., *It Don't Worry Me: Nashville, Jaws, Star Wars and Beyond*. Faber and Faber Ltd, London, 2003.

Grant, R. E., *With Nails*. Picador, London, 1996.

Jacobs, D., *Hollywood Renaissance*. A. S. Barnes/Tantivy Press, New Jersey/London, England, 1977.

Kael, P., *Reeling*. Little, Brown and Company, New York, 1976; Marion Boyars Publishers Ltd, London, 1977.

Kagan, N., *American Skeptic: Robert Altman's Genre-Commentary Films*. Pierian Press, Ann Arbor, 1982.

Karp, A., *The Films of Robert Altman*. Scarecrow Press, Metuchen, New Jersey, 1981.

Kass, J. M., *Robert Altman, American Innovator*. Popular Library, New York, 1978.

Keyssar, H., *Robert Altman's America*. Oxford University Press, New York, 1991.

Kolker, R. P., *A Cinema of Loneliness: Penn, Kubrick, Scorsese, Spielberg, Altman*. Oxford University Press, New York, 1988.

McCarthy, T. and Flynn, C. (Eds), *Kings of the Bs*. E. P. Dutton and Co. Inc., New York, 1975.

McClelland, C. K., *On Making a Movie: Brewster McCloud*. New American Library, New York, 1971.

McGilligan, P., *Robert Altman: Jumping Off the Cliff*. St Martin's Press, New York, 1989.

Monaco, J., *American Film Now*. New York Zoetrope, 1984.

O'Brien, D., *Robert Altman, Hollywood Survivor*, B. T. Batsford Ltd, London, 1995.

Plecki, G., *Robert Altman*. Twayne Publishers, Boston, 1985.

Self, R. T., *Robert Altman's Subliminal Reality*, University of Minnesota Press, Minneapolis, 2002.

Sterrit, D. (Ed.), *Robert Altman, Interviews*. University Press of Mississippi, Jackson, 2000.

Stuart, J., *The Nashville Chronicles: The Making of Robert Altman's Masterpiece*. Simon & Schuster, New York, 2000.

Terry, B., *The Popeye Story*. Dell, New York, 1980.

Tewkesbury, J., *Nashville*. Bantam, New York, 1976.

Thomson, D., *A New Biographical Dictionary of Film*. Alfred A. Knopf/Little, Brown, USA/Great Britain, 2002.

Waxman, V. W. and Bisplinghoft, G., *Robert Altman: A Guide to References and Resources*. G. K. Hall, Boston, 1984.

Wilson, D., *Robert Altman*, from *Close-Up: The Contemporary Director*, Jon Tuska (Ed.). Scarecrow Press, Inc, Metuchen, New Jersey, 1981.

York, S., *In Search of Unicorns*. Hodder & Stoughton, London, 1971.

Selected Interviews/Articles

1971

Films and Filming, November: interview by John Cutts, mainly on *M*A*S*H*, *Brewster McCloud* and *McCabe & Mrs Miller*

1974

Film Comment, March/April, vol. 10, no. 2: interview by Jan Dawson, mainly on *The Long Goodbye*
Film Comment, September/October, vol. 10, no. 5: article by Michael Dempsey

1975

Sight and Sound, Spring, vol. 44, no. 2: article by Jonathan Rosenbaum
Rolling Stone, 17 July: article by Chris Hodenfield on the making of *Nashville*
Film Quarterly 29, Winter: interview by Connie Byrne and William O. Lopez, mainly on *Nashville*

1976

Playboy, August: interview by Bruce Williamson
Film Heritage, Winter, vol. 12, no. 2: interview by F. Anthony Macklin

1977

Film Comment, January/February, vol. 13 no. 1: article by Robert Levine, mainly on Lion's Gate
American Film, December, vol. 3, no. 3: article by Bruce Cook on the relationship between Altman and Pauline Kael

1978

Film Comment, September/October, vol. 14, no. 5: article by Jonathan Rosenbaum, interview by Charles Michener, mainly on *A Wedding*
Monthly Film Bulletin, December, vol. 45, no. 539: comments made by Altman at Berklee Performance Center in Boston, US

1979

Sight and Sound, Summer, vol. 48, no. 3: article by Richard Combs, mainly on *Quintet*

1980

American Film, December, vol. 6, no. 3: article (unsigned) on the making of *Popeye*

1981

Post Script, Autumn, vol. 1, no. 1: two-part interview by Leo Braudy and Robert P. Kolker
Sight and Sound, Summer, vol. 50, no. 3: article on *Health* by Richard Combs and article on *Popeye* by Tom Milne, with interview by Milne and Combs
Cinema Papers, July/August, no. 33: interview by Dennis Altman

1982

American Cinematographer, September, vol. 63, no. 9: article and interview by Herb Lightman and Michael Duvall on making *Come Back to the Five and Dime, Jimmy Dean, Jimmy Dean* in Super 16

1983

Film Comment, January/February, vol. 19, no. 1: article by Richard Corliss on cable-television productions, including *Two by South* and *Come Back to the Five and Dime, Jimmy Dean, Jimmy Dean*
Film Criticism 7, no. 3: interview by Harry Kloman and Lloyd Michaels

1984

Monthly Film Bulletin, September, vol. 50, no. 596: interview by Richard Combs on *Secret Honor*

1985

Film Comment, July/August, vol. 21, no. 4: article by Stephen Farber about five American directors, including Altman
Cineaste, vol. 14, no. 2: interview by Patricia Aufderheide with Altman and Donald Freed, mainly on *Secret Honor*

1986

Monthly Film Bulletin, July, vol. 53, no. 630: article on Altman and Woody Allen by Richard Combs

1988

Film Comment, May/June, vol. 24, no. 3: article by Richard T. Jameson on *Tanner '88*

1990

Sight and Sound, Spring, vol. 59, no. 2: article by Patrick McGilligan, mainly on the Calvin films

Monthly Film Bulletin, July, vol. 57, no. 678: interview by Richard Combs, mainly on *Vincent & Theo*

1991

Film Comment, January/February, vol. 27, no. 1: article and interview by Beverly Walker, mainly on *Vincent & Theo*

1992

Film Comment, May/June, vol. 28, no. 3: article and interview by Richard T. Jameson and Gavin Smith, mainly on *The Player*
Sight and Sound, June, vol. 2, no. 2 (ns): article by Michael Wilmington and interview by Peter Koogh, mainly on *The Player*

1994

Sight and Sound, March, vol. 4, no. 3: article by Jonathan Romney, mainly on *Short Cuts*
Film Comment, March/April, vol. 30, no. 2: article by Beverly Walker
Empire, April, no. 58: article and interview by Andy Gill, mainly on *Short Cuts*
Premiere, December, vol. 8, no. 4: extensive report with interviews by Nancy Griffin on the making of *Prêt-à-Porter*

1997

Film Comment, March/April, vol. 33, no. 2: article by Richard Combs on *Kansas City*
Premiere (UK edition), November, vol. 5, no. 10: article by Peter Biskind in which Altman and eleven other directors talk about contemporary American cinema
Creative Screenwriting, Fall, vol. 4, no. 3: article by Mike Golden; article by Charles Deemer, mainly on *Short Cuts*; article by Ira Nayman; article by Gregg Bachman, mainly on *McCabe & Mrs Miller*

1999

Premiere, May, vol. 12, no. 9: article by Nisha Gopalan, mainly on *Cookie's Fortune*

2000

Premiere, July, vol. 13, no. 11: retrospective interviews by Alex Lewin with participants in *Nashville*

2001

Empire, September, no. 147: article and interview by Angie Errigo

Variety, 10–16 December: spotlight section on Altman, 'Legends and Ground-breakers'

2002

American Cinematographer, January, vol. 83, no. 1: article by Eric Rudolph on the filming of *Gosford Park*

2003

Premiere, December, vol. 17, no. 4: article by Jill Bernstein on the making of *The Company*

2004

Village Voice, 28 September: article by Joy Press on *Tanner on Tanner*

2005

Time Out (UK), 12–19 January, no. 1795: interview by Geoff Andrew, plus eightieth birthday tribute to Altman

Note on the Editor

After graduating from Cambridge University, David Thompson worked in film distribution and exhibition before joining BBC Television as a film programmer. Following the 'Film Club' series, he went on to produce and direct numerous documentaries on the arts, including the artists Mark Rothko and Henri Matisse, the writer Anthony Burgess, the composers Aaron Copland and Karlheinz Stockhausen, and such film directors as Jean Renoir, Quentin Tarantino, Milos Forman, Paul Verhoeven and Robert Altman. Recently, he has made a film for the *Arena* series on Alec Guinness, *Musicals Great Musicals*, a survey of the Arthur Freed unit at MGM, a behind-the-scenes look at Bernardo Bertolucci's *The Dreamers* and an exploration of the Palace of Westminster with Dan Cruickshank. He has also programmed film seasons at the National Film Theatre, worked as a freelance journalist and was the co-editor of *Scorsese on Scorsese* and the author of the BFI Modern Classic on *Last Tango in Paris*.

Index

This index is compiled on a Word-by-Word basis so that for example La Scala precedes Ladd, Alan

Illustrations are in **bold** type

All films with which Robert Altman has been associated are indexed under Altman, Robert, as director, producer, scriptwriter or actor. His television and stage work are also indexed under Altman, Robert.

Printed in the USA
CPSIA information can be obtained
www.ICGtesting.com
W09080315072 4
11LV00004B/356

9 780571 220892